Transforming HR

Second Edition

HR Series preface

The HR Series is edited by **Julie Beardwell**, Associate Dean, Leeds Business School, and **Linda Holbeche**, Director of Research and Policy at CIPD, and is designed to plug the gap between theory and implementation. The books draw on real-life examples of strategic HR in practice and offer practical insights into how HR can add value to the business through transforming individual and functional delivery. Intended for serious HR professionals who aspire to make a real difference within their organisation, **The HR Series** provides resources to inform, empower and inspire the HR leaders of the future.

Transforming HR

Creating Value through People

Second Edition

Mark Withers, Mark Williamson
and Martin Reddington

AMSTERDAM • BOSTON • HEIDELBERG • LONDON • NEW YORK • OXFORD
PARIS • SAN DIEGO • SAN FRANCISCO • SINGAPORE • SYDNEY • TOKYO
Butterworth-Heinemann is an imprint of Elsevier

Butterworth-Heinemann is an imprint of Elsevier
Linacre House, Jordan Hill, Oxford OX2 8DP
30 Corporate Drive, Burlington, MA 01803

First Edition 2005
Second Edition 2010

British Library Cataloguing in Publication Data
A catalogue record for this book is available from the British Library

Library of Congress Cataloguing in Publication Data
A catalogue record for this book is available from the Library of Congress

ISBN 978-1-85617-546-3

Printed and bound in Great Britain

Attributions

To Anna, Mireille and Amelia

To Cathy, Tom and Emma

To Colin, James and Edward

Contents

Contents

Foreword

It is hard to imagine a more important time for the HR function to be able to make a strategic contribution to business. Today's volatile competitive context is driving the need for organisational change and innovation. Underlying shifts towards more knowledge and service-intensive economies place people centre stage as the principal source of competitive advantage and wealth creation.

Yet people are no passive source of economic activity. The 'right' people can be in short supply, they require the 'right' kinds of management and leadership and the right kinds of HRM practice if they are to perform at their best and to 'engage' with the organisation. If not, they go elsewhere. And if HR's primary responsibility is to devise and implement strategies to secure for organisations the talent they need to succeed, HR teams are likely to find that recruiting, motivating and retaining the right people are likely to be ongoing challenges in the years ahead.

But just having the 'right people on the bus' as Jim Collins would say, is of little use unless those people are able and willing to effectively deploy their talents in the interests of the organisation, even as their organisations change. Because even if today's challenging context makes transparent the need for organisational agility, many organisations have cultures which are not conducive to change or high performance. Building corporate agility and its underlying cultural capabilities makes special demands of both HR and line managers, and requires HR practitioners to develop new skills even as they deliver an organisational transformation agenda. So, HR transformation is far from being an end in itself: it is a means to the end of competitive success and organisational effectiveness.

In the first edition of this book, authors Martin Reddington, Mark Williamson and Mark Withers explored and illustrated the process of HR process transformation. They argued that by improving the way operational and transactional HR was delivered, HR professionals could free themselves up to make a more strategic contribution. And while the authors focused on the 'how' of HR transformation, they also raised the question of what a transformed HR service could deliver.

This new edition takes the logic of HR transformation to the next level. The authors focus not only on the 'how' but also on the 'what' and the 'why' of HR transformation. The authors show us what a strategic contribution by HR can look like. Success is about 'creating organisations that compete effectively in their chosen markets, delivering value to customers, superior performance and opportunity to employees'. But to be able to deliver that agenda, HR needs to develop its own delivery model and capabilities. The authors argue against a 'one size fits all' formula for HR delivery and instead provide helpful step-by-step approaches to guide the reader through the choices facing HR practitioners who want to transform their functions to produce higher value contributions.

The authors' combined expertise in HR transformation, based on their backgrounds in HR, research, management and consultancy, provides a powerful platform for their thinking and recommendations. And as the authors point out, unless HR can transform itself to the next level, the function's value becomes questionable. At this point of inflexion for the HR function I commend the authors for this helpful, inspirational and strategic yet practical book. Any HR practitioners aiming to move their function up the value chain will benefit from the wisdom, insight and sensible recommendations it contains.

Linda Holbeche
Director of Research and Policy
Chartered Institute of Personnel and Development
May 2009

Preface

The first edition of this book was written in response to the considerable demand by HR practitioners for robust practical advice in changing the way HR management is undertaken in organisations – HR transformation. Our conversations with HR practitioners identified four substantive needs:

1. To walk through the transformational process from 'starting out', right through to 'evaluating the outcomes';
2. To suggest ways to ensure HR transformation is joined up – that technology and process change are fully integrated with change around HR capabilities, culture and structure;
3. To address the critical questions which are reflected in our chapter headings;
4. To incorporate the latest research and practice on HR transformation and issues.

Although much progress has been made over the years since 2005 to transform HR's contribution in organisations, the needs that led us to write the first edition remain. Since 2005 there is evidence that many organisations have restructured their HR functions and have invested in better HR information systems. Yet, as these building blocks are put in place, new issues emerge and transformation looks less like a destination and more like a journey.

What is the same about this second edition is that we continue to draw on our experiences and the experiences of leading HR practitioners across a wide range of organisations in transforming HR's contribution in organisations. The material we present is still based on what we find has worked, underpinned by academic argument but not stifled by it. The contents are tried and tested and have proven to have been helpful at the cutting edge of change.

So what is different about this second edition?

1. We have greatly enhanced the content. There are new chapters on HR's value proposition, people and technology and benefits realisation. We have evaluated progress in HR transformation since our first edition. We have created specific chapters on stakeholder engagement and programme management.

2. We have been able to introduce new research on the experience of HR transformation in general as well as specific research we have been involved in on the experience of line managers and HR transformation and the use of Web 2.0/social media technology by HR. We have been able to reflect 4 years of new experience.

3. Our senior practitioners are drawn from a broader organisational base than those in the first edition – reflecting an excellent cross section of sectors and strengthening contributions from the public sector and medium-sized private sector businesses.

4. We have structured the book to more closely reflect the change cycle.

5. A new Part 4 takes a look at the challenges the HR function will need to address in the coming years to realise the promise of HR transformation.

6. We have tackled head-on value creation through people.

Our sincere thanks go to Linda Holbeche, Director of Research and Policy at the Chartered Institute of Personnel and Development. Linda has been a great sponsor, encourager and mentor to us throughout the writing of both editions. She commissioned the initial masterclass on HR transformation, when Director of Research at Roffey Park, which provided the catalyst for us to capture our experiences about HR transformation and to articulate them more coherently. We are grateful for the subsequent opportunity to publish our masterclass as one of Roffey Park's guides.

We would also like to thank our clients, without whom there would be no book. We are particularly indebted to all of the senior practitioners who have allowed us to interview them on their experiences of HR transformation, and who have shared with us in such a candid way the highs and lows of their transformation journey. We give full and proper acknowledgement to their contribution in the section 'Contributing Senior Practitioners'.

We would also like to thank all those who have been kind enough to review drafts and help us make our points more clearly. In particular, we would like to thank Hayley Salter, Sarah Long, Stalin Viswanathan and the team at Elsevier, Phil Lewis of KPMG, Professor Graeme Martin of Glasgow University, Jerry Arnott of the Department for Work and Pensions and Martin Moore of Sprint HR.

Finally, we would like to thank our respective families, who have been great supporters and encouragers through two editions of this book.

Mark Withers
Mark Williamson
Martin Reddington

The Authors

Mark Withers, Chartered Fellow, CIPD; MSc, BSc (Econ)

Mark is Managing Director of Mightywaters Consulting Limited, a strategic HR and organisational development consultancy. Mark is passionate about the need to create working environments which enable people to excel, in teams and individually. He is equally passionate about the contribution HR professionals can make in creating these high-performance cultures and in ensuring that the people agenda delivers real value to organisations.

Mark brings a 'whole system' way of thinking to HR transformation and works closely with HR leadership teams and senior executives to create a shared vision for the new HR delivery model, identify HR's value proposition, deliver the benefits of HR transformation and identify and build HR and line capability. He is a highly skilled facilitator and is able to use these skills to engage stakeholders and sustain commitment to change throughout the transformation journey. He enables organisations to identify the contribution they require from HR in order to deliver value through people.

His early career was spent with Shell and a Whitbread/Allied Domecq joint venture. Before founding Mightywaters Consulting in 1998 he worked with Price Waterhouse Management Consultants (PwC) in the areas of HR consulting and strategic change. Mark's clients include National Grid, National Express, BBC, AXA, Rackspace Hosting, London Midland Railway, BT, Cable & Wireless, ESAB and Mitsubishi UFJ Securities.

Mark holds an undergraduate degree in economics from the London School of Economics and a Master's, in Organisational Behaviour from London University (Birkbeck College). He is a Chartered Fellow of the CIPD and has written and spoken on organisational change internationally.

Mark Williamson, MBA, BEng (Hons)

Mark is a Partner at KPMG in the UK and leads their HR Transformation Practice, having joined the firm in 2008. Mark led the consulting team that supported Martin Reddington and the HR transformation programme team at Cable & Wireless – a project for which Mark and his team were recognised and honoured with a Management Consultancies Association Best Management Practice Award.

Mark has been at the forefront of HR transformation for over 10 years. He is a frequent commentator on trends in industry and has spearheaded work in business and HR strategy alignment, HR transformation business case development, HR operating model definition and implementation change management within HR and across the line functions. He is especially interested and adept in building the linkages between the technology elements of HR transformation programmes, the operating models and business processes, and the benefits that ensue.

During his career, Mark has undertaken assignments in a wide variety of industries and geographies, giving him a very broad base of project and programme experience. Mark's experience includes government, financial services, pharmaceuticals, utilities and telecommunications.

Before joining KPMG in the UK, Mark spent 14 years with a number of other leading companies, and 6 years prior to that, with Rolls Royce in a variety of line roles in the UK, mainland Europe and the USA. Following his first degree in Engineering from the University of Sheffield in 1987, Mark was awarded his MBA from Warwick Business School in 2000.

Dr. Martin Reddington, DBA, MBA, BSc (Hons), MCMI, MCIPR, MIEE

Martin runs his own consultancy, Martin Reddington Associates, and is Visiting Research Fellow at Roffey Park, the University of Glasgow and Edinburgh Napier University.

He performed the role of Programme Director, HR Transformation, at Cable & Wireless: a global programme which received acclaim at the National Business Awards and Human Resources Excellence Awards in 2002.

Since leaving Cable & Wireless, Martin blends academic research with consultancy. His doctoral thesis examined the perceptions of managers towards Web-based HR and how these perceptions can affect future HR-led investment decisions.

He is a member of the CIPD's national advisory group on technology and HR, and an expert adviser on HR transformation to the Public Sector Personnel Managers' Association (PPMA). He recently co-authored a CIPD Research Report which examines the impact of Web 2.0 in organisations and offers guidance to the HR profession on how best to utilise these new technologies.

Introduction

The past decade has seen an explosion of HR transformation activity. This has been in response to organisational pressures for HR functions to deliver greater value. Despite much progress in restructuring HR functions and implementing better HR information systems, recent research in the United Kingdom – *The Changing HR Function*, 2008 (led by Peter Reilly of the Institute of Employment Studies on behalf of the CIPD) and the United States – *Achieving Strategic Excellence*, 2007 (by Edward Lawler III, John Boudreau and Susan Albers Mohrman) makes some interesting observations.

The *Changing HR Function* shows:

That many HR functions have been striving to position themselves as strategic contributors to the business. To achieve this some of the larger organisations have consolidated dispersed administrative activities and standardised processes and automated where possible. But problems with managing the fragmentation inherent in the 'three-legged' model and with self-service technology have combined to limit success. Failure to devolve activities to the line or to deploy sufficiently skilled individuals in business partner roles presents further challenges.

Achieving Strategic Excellence concludes:

The future of the HR function in organisation is uncertain. On the one hand, if current trends continue it could end up being largely an administrative function that manages an information technology-based HR system and vendors who do most of the administrative work. On the other, it could become a driver of organisational effectiveness and business strategy. The unanswered question at this point is whether HR organisations will rise to the occasion.

These research findings suggest that whilst the HR function has made considerable progress along the road of transformation, considerable challenges remain if it is to deliver the promise of HR transformation.

One of the key themes of this book is that the advances in HR information systems provide organisations with great opportunities to re-think the way HR management is undertaken in organisations. Yet technology-driven change, often supported by structure change, is often disconnected from capability and culture changes needed to truly transform HR. Before any technology can be effectively deployed, the fundamental approaches to people management must be transformed. In most cases, this involves transforming the way HR management is done in organisations and the repositioning of the HR function: its ways of working, as well as the ways in which the HR function interacts with the wider organisation and external providers.

Why read this book?

Businesses do not have time to waste. The speed and complexity of change are increasing and organisations need to find new ways to compete effectively. These realities require new organisational capabilities to ensure that customer, investor and employee expectations are understood and addressed.

As we write, the global economy is in meltdown. Credit lines are tight, confidence low, job loss on the increase and the prospect of high public sector debt hanging over us for a generation. With every threat brings an opportunity. Arguably, there has never been a greater need, nor has there been a bigger opportunity, for those engaged in the field of people and organisational development to shape organisational performance.

This book will help HR professionals to address how best they can drive high performance in their organisation. Effective HR will enable organisations to adapt quickly and build new organisational capabilities – creating organisations that compete effectively in their chosen markets, delivering value to customers, superior performance and opportunity to employees.

As John Philpott, Chief Economist at the CIPD, commented on the first edition:

As Reddington, Williamson and Withers demonstrate in this stimulating book, the HR function must transform itself in order to guarantee that it provides what organisations are looking for. The authors pull no punches about what is at stake – unless HR is clear about the way it can add value, the threat is that the business will turn elsewhere for that contribution and the in-house HR function will become insignificant and impotent.... This practical guide to transforming HR thus amounts to a kind of managerial Viagra to help perk up the profession's resolve to face up to change.

We maintain that there is no guarantee of a place for HR professionals in future organisations. HR management will be undertaken for sure. But whether there is an HR function, as such, will depend on whether HR functions can transform sufficiently to demonstrate that they are creating value through people. Our view is that HR transformation needs to integrate technology, work processes, structure, HR capability and cultural aspects of change to put HR functions in a position to achieve this. We also argue that there is no 'one size fits all' concerning the way HR functions should be organised – it depends on your organisation, its market and what your organisation needs from HR. This book is not about following the herd, but in giving you the tools to apply your intelligence.

So why should you invest a few hours in reading this book? We offer you five other good reasons:

1. *It is a 'how to' book.* We do not claim to have a magic wand. But we offer approaches that we have seen work and that will help you to make decisions that are right for your business. In essence, we will give you the tools for you to work out what kind of HR contribution your organisation needs.
2. *It will help you accelerate transformation.* We present the content of this book because we are assured of its effective application across a wide variety of organisations.
3. *It builds your HR toolkit.* The approaches we present in this book to help you transform HR can also be deployed by HR professionals to change their businesses.
4. *It is current.* We have incorporated the latest research on HR transformation and new technologies such as Web 2.0/social networking, as well as up-to-date case studies.
5. *It presents a range of organisational experiences.* We include practitioner perspectives from a number of leading HR professionals who are on the transformation journey and are able to 'tell it as it is'.

The book is in four parts:

■ *Part 1* addresses the context for transforming HR.

Chapter 1: A Transformational Mindset presents the key change management tools that underpin the HR transformation journey. These tools and frameworks are practical and form an important backdrop to the remaining content. It is recommended that you take time to familiarise yourself with this material.

Chapter 2: How Are We Doing? reviews the key challenges identified for successful HR transformation set out in the final chapter of our first edition and examines what has actually happened since 2005.

Chapter 3: What Is HR's Value Proposition? is a new chapter and addresses how HR functions help organisations to create value through people.

■ *Part 2* focuses on the case for change.

Chapter 4: People and Technology is a new chapter and reflects largely on recent CIPD research and practitioner experience on the actual and potential use of Web 2.0 and social media technology by HR functions.

Chapter 5: Envisioning the New World of HR sets out a process and practical tools that will help you to get stakeholder agreement on how HR is currently being delivered in your business and the future HR delivery model you want to create. This is a critical phase of the transformation journey and frames how HR will deliver value in the future. The chapter presents envisioning tools that are helpful irrespective of whether you are just starting out or are already on a transformation journey and want to re-energise for the next phase.

Chapter 6: The Business Rationale naturally follows envisioning and explores the key considerations in developing the business case for HR transformation and, in particular, the case for capital investment in HR information systems. In addition to defining benefits and costs (the so-called 'hard' elements of the case), the approaches to building business commitment are also explored (the so-called 'softer' elements of the case). Taken together, these hard and soft elements build commitment and credibility and establish the foundations for transformation.

Chapter 7: Stakeholder Engagement and Communication provides practical tools that enable you to understand who your key stakeholders are and their likely reactions to your HR transformation proposals. We also present ways to move stakeholder opinion away from resistance to commitment.

■ *Part 3* deals with planning and implementation.

Chapter 8: Service Delivery Approaches reviews different approaches to HR organisation and some of the organisational interface issues that are being experienced. The chapter also addresses outsourcing and provides guidance to help organisations navigate through outsourcing decisions.

Chapter 9: Programme Management considers how programme management approaches can be used to engage purposefully with stakeholders through ongoing communication and the use of governance structures. We also explore issues and risks around technology-led HR transformation.

Chapter 10: Implementation: Capability and Culture focuses on the roles and capabilities in the newly transformed HR function. In particular, we explore the capabilities needed in shared services and strategic partner (generalist and specialist) roles and the ways to build these capabilities. We also consider the impact of HR transformation on the role of line manager.

Chapter 11: Implementation: Process and Technology sets out the main considerations in delivering the process and technology aspects of HR transformation, including the impact of HR information systems on employees and managers.

Chapter 12: Benefits Realisation looks at ways to track delivery of the business benefits of HR transformation, building on the content of Chapter 6.

■ *Part 4* looks to the future and realising the promise of HR transformation.

Chapter 13: The Business of HR considers the current economic situation and identifies six themes that HR functions will need to address over the coming years to support the creation of high-performing organisations.

The content of this book is aimed at organisations that may be at different stages of the HR transformation journey. Why not check for yourself? If you can relate to any of the statements below, then we confidently predict that this book is going to be of value to you and your organisation:

■ We are considering how the HR function can add greater value to our organisation.
■ We know we need to transform HR but have not yet developed a clear vision and/or business case.
■ We have different stakeholder views about the contribution we expect from HR and need to create a single vision.
■ We have not really thought about the impact of technology on the way HR is delivered in the organisation.
■ We need to think about the benefits of outsourcing parts of HR.
■ We have not really defined the benefits of HR transformation.
■ We need to have an effective way of delivering HR transformation.
■ We are unclear about the capabilities HR professionals need to enhance their contribution.
■ We are in the process of transforming HR, but are stuck.
■ We have recently restructured the HR function, but believe that there are still improvements that can be made.
■ We believe we have delivered a significant amount of HR transformation and are beginning to consider what is next.
■ We are on the verge of extinction and need help.

This book will help you to define and deliver the benefits of a transformed HR function, whether you have started along this road already or not.

Part 1

Context

Part 1 addresses the context for HR transformation.

Chapter 1: A Transformational Mindset presents the key change management tools that underpin the HR transformation journey. These tools and frameworks are practical and form an important backdrop to the remaining content. It is recommended that you take time to familiarise yourself with this material.

Chapter 2: How Are We Doing reviews the key challenges identified for successful HR transformation set out in the final chapter of our first edition and examines what has actually happened since 2005.

Chapter 3: What Is HR's Value Proposition examines current thinking addressing how HR functions help organisations to create value through people.

1

A Transformational Mindset

We cannot talk about transforming HR unless we adopt a transformational mindset. This transformational mindset underpins any business transformation and has four significant characteristics:

1. Transformation must be relevant to your organisation. We may draw lessons from other organisations, but there is no one size fits all and no best practice. We will stress the importance of *contingent thinking* and *leading* (rather than best) *practice*.
2. Transformation must bring about significant change in the whole organisational system and therefore a *systems mindset* is needed.
3. Systemic change can only be achieved through active involvement and co-creation of solutions with key stakeholders and therefore a *process consulting mindset* is needed.
4. The organisational benefits of transformation will best be realised if change is managed in a structured way with clear governance and benefits tracking, which requires a *project management mindset*.

This chapter explores the characteristics of a transformational mindset and sets out our definition of the scope of HR and its relationship with organisational development (OD). We recommend that you take time to read this chapter as the key concepts are referenced throughout the book.

Key themes

- Effective business change benefits from the application of tried and tested OD tools and approaches.

- HR professionals often fail to influence effectively because they are unfamiliar with OD tools and approaches.
- To be more effective in shaping transformational change HR professionals need to focus on the development of a 'systems mindset', 'process consulting mindset' and 'project mindset'.
- Systems thinking places HR transformation within the context of the wider organisational (and extra-organisational) system and challenges us to integrate the different facets of HR transformation.
- Process consulting is about being client-centred and focuses on the steps needed to effect change in ways that bring key stakeholders with you step by step. It also ensures that at each stage of the transformation journey there is learning and engagement with what is really happening in the organisation.
- A project mindset uses programme and project management principles to ensure HR transformation is delivered in a coherent and timely way.

Context

This book is not a theoretical text. It is intended to be practical: a book that HR practitioners will actually find useful.

However, for this to happen, we want to start by making a case for theory. We know that HR folk are essentially 'pragmatists' and 'doers'. They want to know about what works, and what they can use.

We agree with this bias for action, but only up to a point. We believe that to be an effective doer – to make interventions that work – you need to know *why* things done this way or that way work better. That is where theory comes in. Theory helps to explain why things happen. Good theory is the product of observable and generalised patterns. It is the product of shared knowledge and shared experience. Without theory, HR practices and interventions are little more than isolated acts. It is our contention that one of the reasons that HR has not been as influential in businesses as it should have been is the result of a real and lasting lack of engagement with our theoretical base.

It is not as if the theoretical base does not exist. HR professionals can draw from a strong theoretical hinterland: psychology, sociology, economics, business management, political science, law, statistics and so on. Each of these areas enables us to observe and analyse the role of people in organisations from different perspectives and make powerful contributions to complex business issues.

In this chapter, we will present a small number of theoretical models, frameworks and tools that will bring about more effective change and transformation. The remainder of the book focuses strongly on practical application. Having made a case for theory, this book does not attempt to give an exhaustive overview of prevailing theoretical models, but rather dwells on a few of the practices that have worked for us in supporting business change. We point you to other useful sources on change management tools and techniques in the 'Further Reading' section.

The change management approaches referenced in this chapter have been chosen because:

- They are actually *helpful* – enabling us to shape HR transformation in a way that accelerates the pace of change, maximises buy-in and delivers anticipated benefits.
- They are *tried and tested* – enabling us not only to learn from other organisations but to deploy these models and frameworks in a way that gives structure and focus to workshops and other interventions.
- They form *part of the HR professional's tool kit* – enabling HR professionals to take into their organisations a theoretical body of knowledge that will support their clients in bringing about effective organisational change.

HR and OD

What does the term 'organisational development', or OD, mean for you?

Although OD is a concept that has been around for more than 50 years it is a term that may mean nothing to you. Alternatively, it is currently used in many different ways – sometimes in its traditional sense, sometimes re-sprayed as OE (organisational effectiveness) or similar, and often used interchangeably with organisational design or talent management/leadership development – which can cause great confusion. As there is confusion (and even ignorance) amongst the HR profession concerning what is meant by OD, even basic OD principles and practices that could make a difference to organisational performance are not being deployed to best effect.

A CIPD briefing on OD (October 2007) sets out the history and typology of OD and an excellent article authored by Linda Holbeche and Mee-Yan Cheung-Judge in the CIPD's IMPACT publication (issue 26) explains the importance of OD in sustaining high-performing organisations. We suggest you look up both these sources online. In this book, we use the term 'OD' in a very specific way. For us, OD is about *the effective management of change* – intervening in the organisational system in ways that will help it to adapt and thrive in response to changes in the external environment.

For HR there are some profound implications. Clearly, senior line management have a key role in executing business change, including the people and organisational aspects of change. However, if we accept that HR has a strong theoretical base in the domains of people and organisational capability, then HR professionals must bring a strong functional/professional contribution to the area of business change.

This means not only operating within the traditional HR skill areas – managing headcount reductions, appointing to new structures, skilling people to perform new roles, managing employee relations, etc. – but also being able to deploy broader OD skills with clients. What this means in practice is being able to:

- understand your business and shape the business change agenda in the first place;
- consider the specific circumstances faced by the organisation in order to develop relevant solutions (not blindly copy 'best' practices applied elsewhere);
- construct and work through a change process;
- facilitate workshops;
- involve and engage people;
- help members of the organisation innovate and solve their problems;
- deploy change management tools and techniques throughout;
- support individuals as they adjust psychologically to change;
- work on organisational design;
- design and deliver learning and development interventions;
- improve the people management capability of line managers;
- analyse and improve the overall health of the organisation.

OD is about making change happen effectively and if we are to have any illusions about making a strategic contribution in our organisations, we must be at the heart of shaping and delivering business change.

This book is about HR seizing the opportunities it now has and, enabled by technology, using OD to execute its own transformation. In Chapter 10, we discuss in more detail the role of the HR professional in a transformed function and the capabilities they need to acquire. At the heart of this transformed role is the contribution HR professionals must make to the creation and sustainability of healthy, high-performing organisations.

About a transformational mindset

Transformation suggests change that is intended to bring about a distinguishably different outcome from the current situation. It is more than tinkering with the current operating model – changing job titles, restructuring or implementing a new HRIS. It is broader in scope and more ambitious in outcomes. To be transformational means adopting a mindset with three distinct characteristics:

- *Systems mindset.* All organisations are 'open systems'. They are *systems* in that they function through the interaction of different parts: change in one part of the organisational system will have an impact on other parts. So, for instance, we cannot deliver technology change without also addressing work processes, structure, people and culture. We discuss these parts in more detail in the 'System mindset' section. Organisations are *'open systems'* in that they can influence and be influenced by the external environment.

■ *Process consulting mindset.* Change is not linear and involves working through a set of dilemmas. An example of a dilemma might be where responsibilities lie for people management between line managers and HR professionals. To make change stick we need to work with our internal clients – step by step – so that we continually confront reality, understand emerging information and define ways forward that our clients will own. This does not mean abandoning our expertise, but it does mean that we need to deploy our expertise in a way that enables our clients to own solutions. We explore the process consulting mindset in more detail in the 'Process consulting mindset' section.

■ *Project mindset.* Using the principles and approaches of project management will enable you to organise and shape change more effectively. In this way, activity and effort are focused on the work that will add most value, work-streams are better integrated, benefits are tracked and proper governance is put in place. We discuss the project mindset in the 'Project mindset' section and explore the practical issues around programme management in Chapter 9.

A number of key models and frameworks that shape a transformational mindset are presented below. These are not only helpful in securing the effective transformation of the HR function but critical to HR's transformed role of strategic partner.

As Figure 1.1 illustrates, at the heart of a transformational mindset sits contingent thinking. Contingent thinking is about finding solutions that are relevant to each organisation's situation – we take account of the particular circumstances

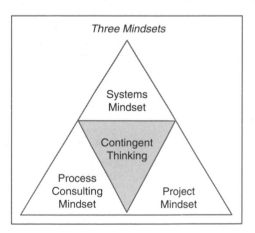

Figure 1.1 A transformational mindset.

and context within which we are working. Contingent thinking moves us away from attempts to adopt 'best' practices used in other organisations, without first adapting them to our situation. Of course we must learn from other organisations. But, we must work out for ourselves the solutions that will best serve our organisation and which will help us sustain competitive advantage.

System mindset

Human beings are natural systems developers. We do not just mean information systems, but systems in the broadest sense – families, nations and organisations. In an organisational context, a systems mindset is about working within the whole organisational system. This is not easy, but transformational change requires integration and coordination of change-related activity across all levers within the system – technology, work processes, structure, people and culture – if it is to be effective. In this section, we present three models that have helped us to approach transformational change from a systems mindset. These models are:

- Organisational levers
- Change cycle
- Change equation

Organisational levers

The organisational levers model is shown in Figure 1.2.

The expression 'levers' is used to represent the different parts in an organisational system. A systems approach seeks to respond to external influences

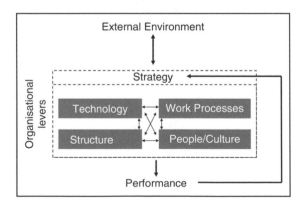

Figure 1.2 Organisational levers.

on the organisation and to integrate change across each of the organisational levers. Change in one lever will impact each other lever one way or another. Let us explore the model further. The main elements of the model are the following:

External environment: In the context of HR transformation, the external environment can be seen in two ways:

First, as the broader socio-economic and political environment within which the organisation as a whole operates. This external environment includes forces for change that come from government, regulation, societal changes, legislative change, competition, customer requirements, shareholder expectations, technological changes, products and service provision, etc. These are the forces we need to understand and interpret in order to develop strategy.

Second, in the case of HR transformation, the external environment can be the above plus those other business functions "external" to the HR function. So, in this instance, customers will be primarily internal clients; services will be the things that the HR function actually delivers to internal clients; technological changes could be the IS strategy, etc.

Taking a multi-layered approach to the external environment is important. As we will explore in Chapter 7, there is a major stakeholder engagement piece that is often overlooked when transforming HR. This then results in confused and dissatisfied internal business colleagues who feel HR transformation is being done to them rather than with them. In making the business case for change, it is also critical that we not only factor in external drivers but are clear about the internal benefits and impacts on business colleagues.

Internal organisational levers: In this framework there are four internal organisational levers. You might have come across other similar models that may use different terminology. It really does not matter what terminology is used or how many organisational levers are defined. The important point is the principle that the organisation is a system comprised of different parts that interact. For the purpose of this book, we will use the following internal organisational levers:

- *Structure* – which includes consideration of areas such as reporting structure (formal and virtual), job and work group design, role expectations/measures, facilities/offices and organisational integrating mechanisms (those things that help people to work together more effectively).
- *Technology* – the technological infrastructure of the organisation.
- *Work processes* – the key work processes, reflecting both the services that are delivered and the channels through which they are delivered.
- *People and culture* – the skills and knowledge, core capabilities, values, style and behaviours along with people policies and practices.

Performance: Performance is the final lever. Although changes in performance are often driven by the external environment (e.g., shareholder expectations or the realisation that new benchmarks have been set), it is important to recognise performance as a separate driver for change, not least because it has such a high focus in organisational life. We need to know whether we are achieving key performance indicators, being cost efficient, delivering value for money, achieving return on investment, delivering to customer expectations, being competitive against external benchmarks, setting and delivering to agreed service levels. Also, decisions around capital investment should be linked to anticipated benefits. Therefore, in making the case for investment in technology we need to be clear about the performance gains which we expect to bring to the organisation.

Strategy is also part of the organisational levers model. Strategy is about direction setting and is the product of considering what we need to do inside the organisation in response to actual or anticipated change in the external environment. As such it provides our context for change.

Change may be initiated in any of these organisational levers, and a systems mindset will recognise that there will be an impact on the other levers.

Okay, so that is the theory. But how do we apply this model in practice? Let us take the example of technology-driven change in HR: moving transactional and operational HR activities to an Web-based HR. As we consider the above model, we may easily make the link between *technology* and *work processes*, as many HR processes will become embedded in the new Web-based HR. But do the other organisational levers come into play?

The external environment: There may be a number of changes in the external environment that are influencing the use of technology in HR, for example: new Web-based software solutions; younger people expecting Web-based interaction with their employers/prospective employers; more affordable technology; convergence of technology and telecommunications; organisations that are adopting Web-based HR setting new benchmarks; new outsourcing/off-shoring possibilities being offered by suppliers, etc. There may also be drivers for change inside the organisation but external to HR, such as higher client expectations about the services that HR will provide; the desire of managers to have information about their people on demand; and so on.

Whatever the external drivers, this model will help you capture these and think through their impact on the HR delivery model. But in this example, how might the other organisational levers be affected?

Structure may be impacted in a number of ways through technology-led HR transformation. The types of roles needed in HR may change along with the number of people involved in transactional work/handling enquiries. Transactional and enquiry work may be outsourced (resulting in a different organisational sourcing model) or brought into a shared service centre (perhaps even outside the direct reporting lines of the HR function or in multiple geographies). What remains inside the HR function may be a different type of professional role. The need to integrate the work of HR management may increase as HR delivery channels become broader and outside the HR function's direct reporting lines. What line managers and employees are expected to do in terms of information management, may change.

When organisational structures change, *work processes* will also change. This means that organisational boundaries (whether between different roles or between different teams or groups) must be addressed in order to ensure that work is properly integrated. This means considering aspects of organisation that integrate work activity, such as communication processes, cross-organisational teams/committees and other forms of reporting and governance.

Performance requirements from HR are certain to be affected as a result of technological change. There may be fresh challenges around HR costs or ratios, expectations around service levels, delivery of a different kind of professional HR agenda. The way performance is monitored may also change, with clearer metrics and more transparent data.

As a consequence of the above, *people and culture* are impacted. New roles require new capabilities. Line managers will need to learn new skills. The relationship between HR professionals and the line managers needs to be recast. A new HR culture needs to emerge and expectations around HR's contribution re-set.

Hopefully, this illustration brings the organisational levers model to life and shows how change in one organisational lever impacts the others. What this model also illustrates is that if change initiatives are kept narrow in focus and not joined up, then the risk of conflict and dissonance between competing changes becomes very high.

In this book, we will show how this model has been used practically to support the HR transformation process: to undertake a gap analysis, to support the envisioning of the new HR, to shape the transformation programme and work streams and to monitor/mark progress.

Change cycle

The change cycle model is shown in Figure 1.3. The change cycle recognises that intentional change is a cyclical process. Like any model, it simplifies in order to draw out general principles. The change cycle shows that any change tends to go through four main stages:

- making a compelling case for change,
- planning the change,
- implementing the change,
- reviewing and sustaining the change.

17

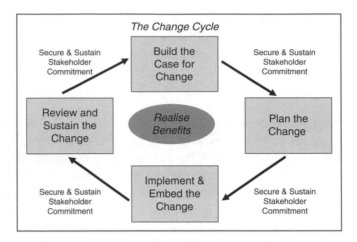

Figure 1.3 Change cycle.

Throughout the process there is a need to secure and sustain commitment to the change so that benefits are realised.

In reality, change is not quite as logical and symmetrical as the model suggests. There are often overlaps between the stages and there is a need to rework the content of earlier stages. The next level of detail (Figure 1.4) shows the main activities that are undertaken in each of the four phases and the most important change tools that support that phase of work.

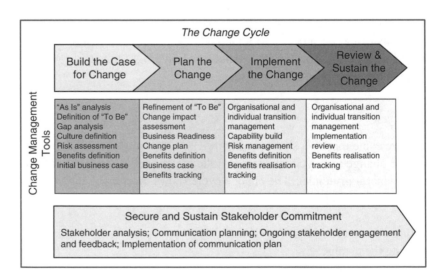

Figure 1.4 Change cycle – key activities and tools.

In applying this model, we have found that each phase represents a 'gateway' that, if properly signed off, will enable you to proceed with a high degree of confidence to the next phase of work. If key stakeholders are not committed, or if circumstances change, the chances are that you will need to remake the case for change at some point further down the change process. However painful it might be and however slow it might appear to be, there is little to be gained in trying to shortcut these phases.

Case study – Global telecommunications business

During one of the HR transformation projects we have supported, a great deal of effort was invested in making a compelling business case for change in HR to the various stakeholder groups. However, due to significant deterioration in the external business environment, what was thought to have been a clear mandate to proceed to the next phase proved not to be the case. The HR transformation team had to remake the case for change on a number of subsequent occasions to prove that the benefits justified the investment and for new stakeholders to satisfy themselves that there was a clear business case for change.

Change equation model

This change tool is extremely helpful in ensuring that both the rational and emotional aspects of change have been properly considered. Developed by Beckhard and Harris (1987), the change equation has been repackaged in a number of different ways over the years, and you may well have come across one of its various incarnations. This is version in Figure 1.5 we most favour.

The Change Equation

$$c \; f \; (a.b.d.e) > x$$

Adapted from R Beckhard and R Harris: *Organisational Transitions* (1987)

Figure 1.5 The change equation new.

The change equation proposes that change is most likely to be successful when four conditions exist:

a. dissatisfaction with the way things are;
b. a shared vision of how things should be in the future;
d. agreement and clarity around the appropriate next steps (note *not* the whole journey) to take to get from where you are now to where you want to be;
e. sufficient will among key stakeholders to make the change happen.

These conditions need to outweigh the perceived costs of change (x) money, time, resources, emotional, political, etc.

This is an extremely versatile model, which can be used to support a wide range of interventions: at the early stages of change when there is a need to test commitment; as a means of reviewing progress; as an aid to shape stakeholder communication; as a way to get people talking about change and as a framework for workshop design.

Case study – Large voluntary sector organisation

Key stakeholders were asked individually to rate out of 10, each of the dimensions in the equation. So if someone thought there were high levels of dissatisfaction with the way things are they gave a high rating. If they thought there was not a shared vision of how things should be, they gave a low rating and so on. At this stage, no consensus in ratings was sought. After each individual rating was logged, the group explored the spread in different scores so that a truer sense of what was happening in the organisation emerged. As a result we were able to identify those areas where further interventions needed to be made: in this instance, there was a need to be clearer about the next practical steps that needed to be taken.

If you only use these three models to develop your transformation effort, we can safely say that their application will significantly increase the probability of your integrating change and delivering target outcomes. Throughout this book we will refer to these models and give further illustrations of their use in practice to help you make better interventions.

Process consulting mindset

Before describing in more detail what a process consulting mindset is, it is perhaps fitting to start with a statement of what it is not. The word 'process' has been popularised in management literature in the past decade, and has become mainly associated with business process re-engineering/work process redesign. Re-engineering of HR processes is certainly going to feature as one of the HR transformation work streams. But this is not what we mean by 'process consulting' or the development of a 'process consulting mindset'.

'Process consulting' is a term first coined by Edgar Schein (see the sections on 'References' and 'Further reading' to learn more) and is about *the way* we bring about change. A process is a sequence of steps that leads to an outcome. Process consulting is about working with clients step by step through a change process. This involves taking account of new realities/information at each step and adjusting tactics accordingly.

The change tools/frameworks mentioned in the 'System mindset' section can help to shape this process. For example, the change equation is a good tool to use with stakeholders to develop a shared view of 'where we are now' and to identify the next practical steps that will best ensure progress. This means that those involved in the work of HR transformation (both internal and external consultants) must engage purposefully with their critical stakeholders. HR transformation is a collaborative effort, and when there are questions, concerns or resistance these must be properly dealt with rather than swept under the carpet. There is no place for those involved in leading work streams *doing* change to people.

Looking specifically at HR transformation, the relationship that the HR transformation programme team must establish with its internal clients should have the following goals in mind:

- engage in actions (with individuals or groups) that are most likely to promote successful change;
- establish a collaborative relationship;
- work to solve problems in a way that they stay solved;
- ensure that attention is given to both technical and relationship issues;
- develop internal client commitment;
- think constantly about how you can best deliver value.

To achieve this, it is necessary to work with clients through a change process. The HR transformation programme team brings tools, models, frameworks, and technical know-how to the table. But the ownership must remain with the clients.

How is this achieved?

First, by bringing our knowledge and expertise to the table in ways that enable our clients to make decisions, rather than presenting them with a *fait accompli*.

Second, by not remaining bound by the original plan. Regardless of how much time we may have invested in agreeing on the future vision for HR and developing an implementation plan with our key client stakeholders, the reality of change is that the unexpected happens and we need to make adjustments to reflect whatever new reality we now face. Change is not achieved through a business version equivalent of 'painting by numbers'.

Third, by focusing on the next practical step within the context of the overall programme goals (building on the change equation, 'in the light of what we now know, what is our most purposeful next step to get us from where we are now to where we want to be?').

A process consulting mindset also accepts that resistance to change is natural and seeks to surface it and work with it, even if embracing resistance appears to slow down the programme. A process consulting mindset also recognises that there will be multiple interests and that it is necessary to invest in building a strong coalition (but not absolute consensus) around a change vision.

Features of the process consulting mindset that we will refer to in this book, and which help us to achieve the above, include the following tools:

- The use of a *straw man* to engage people in decision-making. This means making a proposal that is robust enough to stand with credibility, but not so robust that it cannot be tested and potentially pulled apart and reconstructed. One of the main benefits of using a straw man is to surface opinion and issues so that areas of agreement are identified and disagreements resolved. We have found that the use of the straw man is a very effective way to accelerate decision-making.
- The use of *workshops* to engage people in key discussions and decisions. Often preceded by one-to-one meetings, workshops nevertheless have great value (and are time efficient if well structured) in bringing key stakeholders together to work through issues and make decisions. (Although a convenient way of getting time in diaries, one-to-one meetings alone will not lead to purposeful dialogue and collaborative working.)
- Adopting a *facilitation* role with key stakeholders: working with groups; being able to present information in ways that will engage key stakeholders; surface issues/resistance and areas of agreement; and mobilise to take the next step.

Let us look at an example of a process consulting approach in practice. There are often very different stakeholder perspectives on what HR transformation means. Even within the HR function, there can be considerable distance between people on how technology will be used; the contribution HR professionals should make; which HR activities should be in-house or outsourced; how to develop new skills and capabilities in HR professionals, etc. The approaches we will describe in this book show that investing in a process that engages people in conversations about critical questions about HR transformation early on (and throughout) is fruitful, productive and necessary. So a process consulting approach recognises a situation of multiple perspectives and co-creates a process with stakeholders to work through these perspectives. This approach builds checks and balances into the way change is implemented, allowing those leading the transformation to accelerate or slow down in ways that ensure stakeholders remain committed.

Project mindset

HR transformation must be run as a programme (i.e., a collection of projects) if it is to be in any way effective. This is not an area of strength for many HR functions but the structure and disciplines of programme management will enable the complexities of HR transformation to be managed within a proper governance structure. We deal with the specifics about programme management in Chapter 9.

Why the focus on developing a project mindset?

If an organisation is serious about HR transformation, it will form a HR transformation programme team. Within this team there will need to be some people with high levels of project management/programme management skills and the team as a whole will need to adopt programme management practices. We hope that we do not need to try too hard to make this particular case.

However, the point about the development of a project management mindset is that it needs to extend beyond those people responsible for effecting change in HR. It needs to be embedded as a way of working and thinking across the whole HR function, not least because of the need for strong input from users throughout the transformation process.

Additionally, we have already made it clear that the tools and models we use to support HR transformation are not just right for HR transformation, but are also right for the way HR professionals will need to work with their clients in the transformed HR function; we are role-modelling practices that the HR function needs to embed as working practices. As a generalisation, we have found that the HR community is not particularly strong in the area of project management.

So, although there is no ambition to turn HR professionals into certified PRINCE 2 programme managers, there is an ambition to develop a way of thinking akin to external consultants, who package work using the principles of project management. We will explore this theme in more detail in Chapter 10 when we discuss capabilities for HR professionals.

Figure 1.6 presents a very simple framework which we have used to help HR professionals focus on the key principles of project management without overwhelming them with procedures, paperwork and plans.

When we present this framework to clients, there is typically quick intellectual buy-in: it is not difficult to understand! However, the challenge is to actually use the framework so that there is a clear focus on deliverables and what it will take to achieve these.

Within HR functions, we have often met with some initial resistance to a project approach. There is an argument that you cannot do the 'day job' using project management principles, as the work of an HR professional is unpredictable and reactive. There is an element of truth in this, and it is not our belief that all HR work can be managed this way. However, we know that a high percentage of HR work can be managed more effectively through the development of a project mindset (just think about recruitment, L&D, case management, reward cycles, talent management processes, communication cycles, etc.).

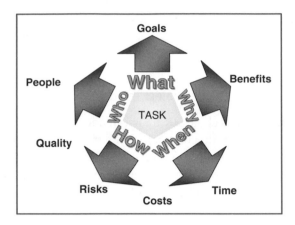

Figure 1.6 A project management mindset – key questions.

Our observation of the HR community is that some of the reasons why this way of working is often resisted are due to:

- reluctance to be pinned down about deliverables;
- inability to articulate concrete business benefits;
- unwillingness to identify and be held to deadlines (projects have to fit around the day job);
- lack of process consulting skills;
- unwillingness to share resources across HR's organisational silos.

These are generalisations, and we are not saying that this list in its entirety is true of all HR organisations we have worked with. Nor are we saying that all points will be true of your organisation. However, as you reflect on this list, you may find that some of the points resonate with you. As a slightly provocative parting shot on this point, you may want to consider how you would respond if an external consultant made a proposal to you that lacked any project management element – no clear deliverables, no timeline, no milestones, no resource estimates, no project scope, no budget, no sign off/change control, etc. You may also want to think about the impression HR makes with internal clients when there is an absence of these elements in proposed work.

The important points that we hope you take away are that:

1. developing a project mindset is a key to effective delivery of HR transformation and the ongoing work of HR;
2. developing a project mindset will not come easily for most HR communities because people are not used to working this way.

Summary

In this chapter, we have discussed the importance of OD in a transformed HR function and how this OD role is expressed through the development of a transformational mindset which embraces a system, process consulting and project mindsets. We have also presented a small number of key models and frameworks that underpin our approaches to HR transformation. It is important for HR professionals to engage with these models and frameworks, as they are relevant to all types of business change and not just to HR transformation.

2

HR Transformation – How Are We Doing?

In the first edition of this book, we presented our thoughts on the future direction of HR and addressed what HR leaders should be considering post-transformation. In doing so, our intention was to identify trends and pose questions which we hoped would guide you to your own conclusions and actions. In this chapter, we review these earlier themes in order to identify how far HR has travelled on its transformation journey.

Key themes

- Recent research presents a fixed view on the progress of HR transformation.
- HR's proximity to, and interaction with, other business functions is a key indicator of the success of transformation. The ubiquitous 'seat at the table'; HR as change leaders; what HR generalists and specialists actually do and the reputation of HR within the organisation are all relevant indicators of progress.
- The seven issues we identified and key questions we posed in our earlier edition remain valid.

Context

It is over a decade since Dave Ulrich wrote *Human Resource Champions*. During this period much has been written and spoken about the need for HR to transform. The first edition of this book sought to address a gap, which was not why or whether HR should transform but how. It is therefore appropriate that in opening a second edition of this book we review recent research on HR transformation and revisit the seven issues we set out at the end of our first edition to test whether they remain valid.

Recent research findings

In the introduction we pointed to recent research studies in the UK – *The Changing HR Function* (led by Peter Reilly of the Institute of Employment Studies on behalf of the CIPD) and USA – *Achieving Strategic Excellence* (led by Edward Lawler III, John Boudreau and Susan Albers Mohrman). We will explore these comprehensive studies in more detail along with research from KPMG, the Economist Intelligence Unit/Deloitte, McKinsey, and another research report from the Institute of Employment Studies.

So, what does the research tell us about the extent of HR transformation?

Achieving Strategic Excellence is the fourth report in a longitudinal study of HR transformation and offers significant insights into the perceptions and realities of HR transformation. Looking at the percentage of time spent on various HR roles, the research found that 'there has been little change in the last nine years in terms of how HR executives report the HR function spends its time when they report current activities … and raises serious questions about the validity of the reports by our respondents about how things were five to seven years ago'. A summary of the research findings is shown in Figure 2.1.

Lawler et al. observe that the results can be explained as follows:

- HR executives have a better idea of what they do currently than what they did 5–7 years ago – and therefore the 'current' assessment of time spent may be the more accurate reflection;
- HR executives overstate the amount of change that has been made as they want to see themselves more as a strategic partner now than in the past.

A conclusion made by Lawler et al. irrespective of the actual split in time spent is that 'although the world of business has changed a lot since 1995, how HR spends its time has not. HR continues to believe it has changed, even though it has not!'

Achieving Strategic Excellence also examined HR's role in business strategy and found that managers not in the HR function report lower levels of strategic involvement on the part of the HR function than are reported by their counterparts in HR. In the most recent study, 40% of HR executives reported that they are fully involved in developing and implementing business strategy compared with 21% of managers who saw HR playing this full role. The report concludes that 'overall, it seems that managers simply do not see HR as

	1995		1998		2001		2004	
ROLE	5-7 years ago	Now	5-7 years ago	Now	5-7 years ago	Now	5-7 years ago	Now
Maintaining Records Collect, track and maintain data on employees	22.9	15.4	25.6	16.1	26.8	14.9	25.9	13.2
Auditing/Controlling Ensure compliance to internal operations, regulations and legal and union requirements	19.5	12.2	16.4	11.2	17.1	11.4	14.8	13.3
Human Resource Services Provider Assist with implementation and administration of HR practices	34.3	31.3	36.4	35.0	33.1	31.3	36.4	32.0
Development of Human Resources Systems and Practices Develop new HR systems and practices	14.3	18.6	14.2	19.2	13.9	19.3	12.6	18.1
Strategic Business Partner As a member of the management team, involved with strategic HR planning, organisational design and strategic change.	10.3	21.9	9.4	20.3	9.1	23.2	9.6	23.5

Figure 2.1 Percentage of time spent on various HR roles (from *Achieving Strategic Excellence*).

involved in business strategy as do HR executives, even when it comes to such specifics as recruiting and developing talent'.

This finding is backed up in the Economic Intelligence Unit/Deloitte study – *Aligned at the Top*. They note that 'HR leaders and senior business executives agree that people issues are strategic to their companies' – more than 85%. However, the survey showed a clear gap between business needs and HR's perceived focus and capabilities: 'when senior business executives talk about HR they focus on administrative activities such as rewards and benefits, performance evaluation and HR operating efficiency. When those same executives talk about people issues, they focus on talent management, workforce productivity and leadership development and, in many cases, the HR function isn't even mentioned'. The report goes on to state that 'the strategic people agenda is not being addressed by HR, presenting a common challenge to HR leaders and senior business executives alike'.

The same report found that:

- 60% of senior business executives consider people issues 'very significant' or 'highly significant' to strategic decision making now – and this figure rises to 90% when looking at the next 5 years.
- 4% of senior business executives describe their company as world class in people management and HR, with 46% stating their people capabilities as adequate. This means a half thought their people management is less than adequate.

■ Two-thirds of senior business executives reported that they rarely or never consult their senior HR team on mergers and acquisitions.

The ability of HR executives to contribute strategically is also highlighted in a KPMG paper – *HR: Architect or Artisan?* (2008) and a McKinsey study – *A Dearth of HR Talent* (2005). The KPMG paper quotes the CEO of a major high street retailer as follows: '*When the marketing director comes to the executive board data is presented on our consumers and we are given enormous insight about their buying habits, their aspirations, their concerns and their hopes. We have clear demographic data and we can predict with real accuracy how patterns will evolve. But when HR presents information about our employees it is less precise, less concise, less insightful and less predictive*'.

The McKinsey study reports that 'European companies appear to be struggling to find human resources professionals with the right mix of skills to support business unit managers ... the troubling gulf between the needs of the business and the ability of HR to respond will force many companies to rethink their approach to the recruitment, training and development of HR employees'. The report concludes that 'to deliver what the business needs, HR must put its own house in order, starting with the skills and capabilities of its staff'.

The Changing HR Function reports that 'the primary driver for structural transformation is the desire for the HR function to be a more strategic contributor'. This driver was above the need to improve service, increase business focus or even to reduce costs. Those completing the survey suggest that the HR function has doubled the proportion of time it spent on strategic inputs over the past 3 years at the expense of administrative activities. In the light of the Lawler et al. findings, we may need to handle this finding with some caution. This report found that the support for line managers and HR administration were still the most time consuming tasks for HR functions, 'suggesting that further progress in rebalancing the workload is needed'.

The final and most recent report, led by Wendy Hirsh of the Institute of Employment Studies – *What Customers Want from HR*, gives us an additional and, arguably more powerful, perspective on the state of HR as her research team interviewed more than 100 'customers' of HR along with 840 survey responses. The questions posed by the research were: 'what do line managers, senior managers and employees really want from the HR function?' and 'what do they think of what they get?' Reassuringly the answers are not a torrent of abuse, reporting that the HR function is seen to be making a vital potential contribution to business and to working life. The report also suggests that HR could do better, especially if it learns to 'listen to its customers more carefully and gaze at its own navel a bit less'. This point is underlined with the statement that 'HR has been busy transforming itself in recent years, but mostly in line with its own models of what it wants to be'. A summary of this report's findings and *What Customers Want from HR* are shown in Figure 2.2.

We will give more flavour on these important reports in the 'Key issues for HR' section. What they suggest is that whilst a lot of restructuring has happened in HR, the promise of transformation has not yet been fully realised. Progress has been made but there is still a gap to close if HR is to contribute as effectively as it might.

In focusing on these key reports we are mindful that they inevitably generalise. You may be thinking that in your organisation HR has made greater progress along the transformation journey than these reports suggest. In dealing with

---

- 31% of managers and 24% of non-managers were satisfied or very satisfied with HR services
- 34% of managers felt HR was improving, but 36% felt it had got worse over the past couple of years
- 50% of non-managers could see no change in the quality of HR services, although 23% thought it had improved
- What people say they value in HR is not always the same as the factors that correlate with their overall satisfaction with HR.

The factors that correlated most strongly with line managers' and employees' satisfaction with HR were:

- Being well supported in times of change (although only 27% of managers and 15% of non-managers felt well supported in times of change)
- HR giving good advice to employees (although only 38% of managers and 23% of non-managers felt that HR gave good advice to employees)
- Being well supported when dealing with difficult people or situations (41% of managers but only 14% of employees felt well supported in dealing with difficult people or situations)
- HR getting the basics right (although only 31% of managers and 37% of non-managers thought HR got the basics right).

The key things internal 'customers' wanted from HR were:
- HR needs to find out what its customers need and what their experiences of current HR services are
- HR needs to be responsive—clear about what it is there for and what services it offers, easy to contact, and able to respond quickly, efficiently and effectively
- An independent minded HR function that understands the workforce and can help management balance employee and business needs
- An HR function with strategic business impact—but this is about solving problems that are strategically important for the business not about writing HR strategies
- A proactive HR function that spots issues ahead of time and works closely with managers to address them
- Professional support from real 'people partners'.

Figure 2.2 Main findings from the report: *What Customers Want from HR*: Institute of Employment Studies.

our clients and in hearing the experiences of our senior practitioners, we are also mindful that there is some excellent work being performed by HR functions out there and that where HR has shifted its contribution this has been highly valued by colleagues in their organisations. Throughout this book we hope we can represent some of these successes so that we learn what HR functions are doing and how they have made the contribution shift.

Key issues for HR

So, how have we done as authors? At the end of the first edition we addressed where we thought the HR function as a whole was on its transformation journey and posed a number of questions and seven issues that we believed still needed to be addressed. We believe it is important to revisit these statements to test whether they still hold.

The situation in 2005

In 2005, we summed up HR's journey in the following terms: 'HR has moved from a broadly administrative and transaction function to one that adds more tangible value to the wider business'. We gave the following reasons for making this statement:

The HR function is actively addressing the transactional aspects of its work. If the quality of HR information had been world-class in the past, then the case for change would have been difficult to argue. However, this has not been the case. HR administration is often deficient and HR information unreliable. Whilst not the glamour end of HR, good HR administration consistently features highly on manager lists of their expectations of HR. Transactional HR needs to be done well – but it is not the be-all and end-all of HR management. Fortunately, transactional HR is standardising and alternative options to the old, fragmented, labour-intensive, expensive in-house model now exist. Shared service centres (whether in-house or outsourced) are now present in many organisations, and there is increasing uptake of Web-based HR. The challenges for HR remain justifying organisational capex on Web-based HR and then delivering the full benefits of that capital investment. Ultimately, these solutions must deliver better service to managers so that HR professionals are truly freed to contribute to higher value issues.

There is greater appetite amongst HR professionals to move into the value-adding space. Whilst the horizons of many HR professionals are still focused on 'case work' around sickness management, grievance and disciplinary handling, the role of the HR professional as a 'business partner' has really caught the imagination of the profession. Although there have always been high value-adding HR professionals closely aligned to their line management colleagues, the years since the publication of Ulrich's *HR Champions* (1997) have given people a vocabulary and focus for the HR role. The challenges remain those of building the capability of HR professionals to move onto the ground of strategic business partnership, and changing the attitudes of line managers who still see HR as an administrative/ advisory function.

The business drivers that are pulling a stronger contribution from HR are still present and arguably stronger now than ever before. People costs remain one of the largest elements (if not the largest element) of organisational fixed costs, and we are hearing much more in recent years about the need to 'value' and 'leverage' human capital. There is now a high level of interest in finding ways of measuring the contribution of people other than as costs. Work undertaken by Lev (2001) and others around the measurement of intangibles is enabling HR to engage with the business more purposefully. Additionally, a growing body of research linking progressive HR to superior business performance is slowly beginning to register on the minds of senior business leaders.

Key issues and questions

We then turned to the future and presented a small number of 'big ticket' questions for organisations to address and seven key issues currently faced by the function. We emphasised and reiterated our belief that there is no one single organisational solution for HR as each organisation needed to work out what kind of HR contribution was needed for that organisation in its business context.

But are all questions and issues still valid?

We posed a couple of big ticket questions we believed were key to bringing about successful HR transformation. These questions were:

- What role does the business need the HR function to play when moving beyond the current phase of HR transformation?
- What will HR professionals do that will bring most value to the wider organisation beyond the current phase of HR transformation?

We believe that these questions are still valid. The research cited earlier suggests that HR functions are still not effective at engaging with internal customers and providing a delivery model the business needs as opposed to the one HR wants. We also believe that there is still a gap to be bridged in identifying how HR professionals can add the most value in organisations. We did not explore the issue of HR value sufficiently in the first edition and have written a new chapter (Chapter 3) to stimulate thinking in this area.

We also identified seven issues we believed still needed to be faced up to build a clearer picture of future priorities in taking HR transformation to its next step. It is worth revisiting these issues to test their continued relevance.

Issue 1: HR professionals and line managers

What we wrote in the first edition   A common mantra in recent years is that line managers should manage and HR professionals should support them. Yet effective HR management depends on a strong partnership between HR professionals and line managers, where there is mutual recognition and respect and where both sides are working towards a common goal. This kind of relationship does not come easily and will not happen through wishful thinking. An honest review of current relationships needs to be held and the expectations of both sides aired. Some issues that we encounter are the following:

- lack of manager time to build sufficient expertise in HR policies;
- the HR business partners being a one-stop shop – up to a point;
- lack of accountability concerning the way managers manage people.

These points are interrelated. Managers are under enormous pressure to deliver the technical/business aspects of their role, and they feel that they do not have the time to navigate the Intranet and/or attend training to build sufficient expertise to deal with people issues that a good HR professional should be able to help them with. Similarly, there is frustration when managers hear a great deal about the HR generalist being able to support managers on the full range of HR issues, but when they need advice are told to contact a service centre or look things up on the Intranet. At that point in time, they do not feel that HR is adding value. Finally, organisations often pay lip service to the people management aspects of a manager's role – how many line managers are rated as poorer performers if they deliver on the technical aspects of their job but are not good people managers? There are too few, in our experience. Organisations need to face up to these issues in an honest way if an effective HR delivery model is to be implemented.

Comment   *The Changing HR Function* reports that 'the division of people management responsibilities between HR and the line was largely unchanged since 2003, despite HR's wish to have more work transferred to line managers. HR still takes the lead on remuneration and implementing redundancies; the line has prime responsibility for work organisation; whereas recruitment, employee relations and training and development activity is more shared. Overall, the principal reasons for HR's lack of success in achieving greater transfer of tasks to the line appear to be line manager priorities, their skills, the time available to them for people management tasks and poor manager self service'.

We believe that this issue of both defining the people management responsibilities of managers and then equipping them with the skills to deliver these responsibilities remains an issue that needs to be addressed.

Issue 2: The role of shared service centres

What we wrote in the first edition   Service centres are now a part of all our lives. We deal with them when we contact our bank, utility and insurance companies and even when we order office supplies. We are used to using them and they can be relatively inexpensive – which is a major factor in support of their existence. The first organisations to use them had an advantage over their competitors, but now they are more 'business as usual' with many companies. Costs per transaction can be so low that in some cases they are approaching the cost benefits of fully e-enabled systems, with their attendant development and operating costs. But e-HR costs should, in theory, continue to fall in the future. So, where should organisations be making their investments?

Some larger organisations will develop 'global' service centres, handling all the transactional needs of many divisions and even corporations. Finance, procurement and information technology can all be handled remotely, with information provided on top as all transactions are performed within them.

Consider taking this to the logical extreme. Why not scrap the fancy e-HR system and go down the service centre route? e-HR then simply becomes a message-bearing conduit and storage/enquiry system.

If you believe that this is the future (e.g., you are one of those reading this book in a bookshop and have flicked to the last chapter, but have a lot of people writing a business case back at the ranch), then consider this possibility. There will still be costs and a need for a business case, but why invest in technology, if economies of scale barely work? Why not invest instead in a service centre, outsourcing tasks and people to those who can provide those services to managers?

Another development could be that e-HR systems become more intelligent, with the result that there are no service centres. What are the implications? You do not incur the costs or have the complexity of outsourcing and/or setting up service centres. But it means that your systems need to be excellent and that they must be used. There is no backup. What happens in a shared-service-centre-free world is that managers and employees have no choice but to do all HR transactions online. In working online, for less frequent and more complex tasks, people will need an expert systems approach that is business scenario based and that will lead people through to the solution. Also, there is an underlying presumption that it is worth managers spending their time completing these more complex transactions, even if the system is well-designed and even infrequent transactions are made easy to undertake.

Some considerations are:

■ How realistic is a predominantly e-HR world without the need for a shared service centre(s)?

■ If you need a shared service centre(s), where can you get efficiencies of scale, either within the boundaries of HR or through merging back office activities?

■ How do you maintain/improve service levels, creating a better customer experience?

■ How do you get that balance right between technology and person interfaces with line customers?

■ How far do you want to manage transactional activity through relationships or by contracts/service level agreements?

Whether provided in-house or outsourced, there are clearly opportunities to re-alise efficiencies and improve service levels by merging the activities of HR, IT finance, procurement – all the so-called 'support' functions. Although superficially attractive, some organisations that have tried this route have found that the lack of functional control has resulted in a significant dip in service and quality levels, leading to the shared service centres being returned to functional control and functional specialisation. This experience underlines the need to think through carefully what kind of service you need as a business and the trade-offs you need to make in working through the issues above.

Comment *The Changing HR Function* reports that 'shared services is a phenomenon for large – rather than small – organisations. Overall, the structure of shared services varies by organisation, especially in a global context. Only 4% of our survey respondents said that they wholly outsourced their HR shared services operation and around 25% outsourced part. We came across other examples where HR shared services had been transferred out of the function but not out of the organisation and we found cross-functional as well as single HR service centres. Outsourcing remains a tactical rather than a strategic matter for most organisations … the exception being where outsourcing was considered to fund technological investment'.

The debate we set out in our first edition still holds. Shared services are not as prevalent as we may have anticipated and the rush to outsource is at best a trickle with much scepticism remaining over the promises of outsourcing. Perhaps the area we overstated in our first edition was the extent to which Web-based HR would develop to a point where it would replace the need for a shared services centre. We see little evidence of this and, whilst technology continues to create new possibilities for HR (e.g., Web 2.0 which we explore in Chapter 5) there is still a need for organisations to think through the various options surrounding shared services and how HR administration and advisory services are delivered efficiently and effectively in the absence of a shared services centre.

Issue 3: The role of the HR generalist
What we wrote in the first edition   Organisations need to settle on the place of the HR generalist in the HR delivery model. Should the role be assumed by line managers, shared service centres, expert systems, external vendors or in-house strategic business partners?

If there is an in-house generalist presence, there is also a secondary issue to address concerning the level at which the generalist operates. Linked to some of the debate set out earlier there is, in our view, an emerging need for an HR role that sits between strategic business partner and the HR administrator – dare we say it but akin to the old 'personnel officer' role. Driven by manager demand (and a preparedness to pay for this support), organisations need to consider whether there is a role for a cheaper and more effective local partner who does 'HR stuff' one level above the routine transaction processing that individuals and line managers do. In these instances, what organisations may need is access to someone to provide a sounding board 'on the ground' – where managers are based. What we have already noted is a relatively low-level (compared to the potential) exploitation and use of the wealth of information that is gathered and stored by e-HR systems. Some of this, of course, is relatively easy to report on and use. But there is other information, particularly around forecasting, planning and trends, that managers will look at infrequently or not at all. So, the new role is potentially about making the most of the information that is present. It is about proactively looking at the information and taking the analysis of that information to line managers and suggesting ways to deal with it, or asking them what they want to do with it.

This is subtly different from the role of a strategic change agent. What we are suggesting here is that there is someone within the business (not placed in a service centre or down a phone line) available to work with middle management to help them to get far more out of their people. What we are also suggesting is that while a modern manager should be competent at looking after and managing their people, there is a debate to be had concerning whether they should in fact concentrate on their core strengths and what they can do to enhance the health and success of that business.

Taking this suggestion forward, this is explicitly *not* about trying to bring everyone up to the same standard, trying to iron out weaknesses in management and therefore potentially harming the core business activity. This is about concentrating on strengths. This model recognises that managers are not necessarily appointed as a result of their people management abilities, but more for other attributes and capabilities, such as thought leadership in their fields. The role of this junior HR generalist should be to proactively mine the e-HR system for relevant data, equipped with a mandate to reach line managers and be the credible, value-adding face of HR.

This, we suggest, is a 'grey area' between strategic level work (senior business partners within the organisation who look after people strategy and overall change) and the transactional level, which makes the employee champion role very real and works with the business to get the best out of teams at a lower level. Another added benefit from the line manager's point of view is that there is now a credible face of HR that middle managers can relate to, rather than a faceless service centre or outsourced function that may seem remote from the business.

Similarly, organisations need to explore how a strategic business partner approach should work in practice. In particular, there is the issue of proximity to the business that needs to be resolved: is the HR strategic business partner an integral part of the management team, or is the role played out as a partnership along the same lines as a strategic alliance with an external vendor might be?

If HR evolves to a position where the HR function focuses on strategic change, working primarily on significant projects (addressing the implications of new software and legislation and providing support on specific organisational changes), this indicates a move to a professional services type role – that of an internal consultant. Internal consultancy services may not be new, but having HR play a leading role as an internal consultant is. Taking this a step further, how beneficial would it be for similar-minded experts from other functions to join together to offer a combined set of services to bring solutions that cut *across* those functions – where relationship managers would work with the business to bring those solutions to the customers in an effective and focused way? This is a model that is very similar to professional service firms.

There may be benefits in this approach, particularly linked to clarifying the value proposition of internal support functions and being able to make better like-for-like comparisons with external providers. There are also significant downsides, not least the inefficiencies of internal charging and the different dynamic between internal and external support. Having said that, in exploring the generalist role of HR and in particular HR's value proposition, it is worthwhile presenting an internal consultancy model so that the organisation can work out the value it gains through day-to-day contact and involvement in the life of the business, and how much it is prepared to pay for this less tangible value.

Comment *The Changing HR Function* points to gaps in service provision and one of the options to fill some of the cracks was 'to provide operational support for line managers'. This reinforces the need for the discussion we believe is still absent concerning how to fill the gap between strategic business partner and manager.

We see little evidence of organisations moving to an internal professional services/consulting model in HR – not in terms of resource management and costing at least. *Achieving Strategic Excellence* suggests that centres of excellence should provide services in a consulting capacity to the business, but this remains aspirational rather than reality. What is clear is that there is an expectation that HR generalists (and specialists) will apply consulting skills if they are to perform effectively in their roles. It is also clear that (as the report *Achieving Strategic Excellence* suggests) 'HR suffers from a skills deficit' and we highlighted this as our seventh issue below.

What the HR generalist does, how this role adds value and how people are equipped to perform in this role remains an issue as does the gap that exists between the more strategic HR generalist and manager.

Issue 4: The reputation of HR

What we wrote in the first edition   When considering the evolving reputation of HR, one of the things to bear in mind is the question around transactional versus strategic roles: whether the organisation should only see HR in a strategic role and not in the transactional space at all. The question of what creates positive reputation builds on, and complements, some of the arguments discussed earlier. If users/customers/clients experience poor transactional execution, the reputation of HR will be tarnished.

An argument suggests that transactional activities should be separated from strategic HR roles. This would mean that HR functions build reputation solely from their strategic contribution. But if you think about how HR actually gains respect in organisations, it generally starts with doing the transactional stuff which then opens the door for HR to address more strategic issues. If transactional HR is delivered poorly, then developing a role that is more strategic will not get a look-in. Also, if HR is divorced from knowledge and data, then the link between more strategic roles and information will be diminished.

So you need to identify which areas are building and destroying HR's reputation; the activities managers put a value on and how effectively these are delivered. There are implications for HR measurement (see below) and for HR's ability to market itself and its capabilities to the business.

Comment   *What Customers Want from HR* gives good insight into the issues around HR's reputation. We do not intend to repeat the findings of the research set out in Figure 2.2 as it is clear that whilst HR's reputation has generally risen in recent years, there is still some way to go before the overwhelming view of HR is favourable. This report highlights the need to engage more seriously in finding out what internal customers need and this willingness to engage with the plurality of HR stakeholders is probably a critical challenge if HR is to build a strong and positive reputation in organisations.

Issue 5: HR performance

What we wrote in the first edition   The use of benchmarking in HR has improved greatly in recent years, and it is now commonplace in most HR functions. Benchmarking, though, has its limitations: ensuring that there is like-for-like comparison and focusing on lag performance indicators being two of them. But, we recognise that there is an important place for benchmarking metrics, and expect them to be used into the future.

A bigger challenge for the HR function is to measure more clearly the value it contributes to each respective business. This involves talking to line managers more about the performance expectations of HR, and taking more time to link work to these expectations.

So, in considering your next steps in HR transformation, you need to address:

- how HR currently measures its performance;
- how managers measure HR's contribution (whether formally or informally);
- what set of measures is appropriate as a framework for the future.

Linked to issue 4 – the reputation of HR – there is also a fruitful debate to be had concerning how managers want to engage with HR's performance. Annual reports on HR, surveys of HR value delivery, regular management reporting and HR operating plans can all be effective ways of building partnership between the line and HR.

Comment   *The Changing HR Function* reports that 'on measurement, it was noteworthy that HR appeared not just to be assessing its process performance but also considering its broader effectiveness. Thus, virtually all organisations measured HR's efficiency and over half examined HR effectiveness through people management practice and its effect on outcomes such as absence. The main indicators used were business performance, surveys of managers/employees and customer satisfaction metrics. System or policy evaluation still did not appear to be common which is problematic when considering the success of HR transformation'.

Achieving Strategic Excellence concludes that 'the growing attention to HR metrics and analytics seems well placed, considering the potential for improvement and value. It is also important to note that all measurement elements are not equally valuable . . . Measures often thought to be related to HR effectiveness and strategic influence (such as benchmarking) are actually not related to it . . . Intermediate measures (such as scorecards and HR programme effects) appear to offer opportunities to enhance HR strategic influence. There also appears to be an emerging measurement emphasis on impact, which is not yet well understood'.

This suggests that some progress has been made in improving the way HR measures its performance and contribution, but there is still a way to go. The limits of benchmarking are becoming more clearly understood and, as HR functions continue to explore the questions we posed earlier, we anticipate that a broader range of measures addressing efficiency, effectiveness and impact emerge.

Issue 6: Organisational boundaries

What we wrote in the first edition Organising to deliver HR is becoming more complex, involving the HR function (which is likely to include generalists, specialists and possibly shared service centres), line managers, employees and external vendors of various types. Where you land organisationally should be driven by the requirements of your business. Some of the broader issues to be addressed will concern the following:

- balance of resources between HR generalist roles and in-house specialist roles;
- types of generalist needed (see above debate on the HR generalist) and their skill levels;
- role of the line manager in managing people and their skill levels;
- need for a shared service centre (transactional) or not and where it is located (in HR, in-house but external to HR, or outsourced);
- level of involvement of external vendors/suppliers/consultants.

Wherever the organisational lines are drawn, the challenges will be in managing the interfaces between the different organisational areas. The more complex the organisation, the greater will be the effort invested in managing these interfaces. As you develop the next step in your organisational model, you should think through these boundary issues: how you integrate the different elements of HR delivery and the investment you will need to make in ensuring a coherent and seamless service delivery.

Comment *The Changing HR Function* reports that 'the three-legged stool model (shared services, centres of expertise and business partners) attributed to Dave Ulrich was the most common HR structure, although fewer than 30% of the organisations surveyed said that they had implemented the model in full. Where such a model had not been introduced, the most common type of structure was a single HR team incorporating generalists, specialists and administration.... Looking at the components of the three-legged stool model we found a great deal of variation in the formats used'. This was particularly true of the role of business partners/generalists. The report goes on to say, and to align with the Lawler et al. report, that 'the quality of relationships within HR and between it and customers were the key to success not the organisational structure of HR. . . . Structural reform may not be sufficient to reposition HR. . . . If HR fails to become more strategic, the cause of the problem may lie elsewhere – the quality of HR staff, a lack of process reform or the people management capability of line managers'.

We contend that all structural change replaces one set of organisational boundary management challenges with a new set. How people work together will contribute to the success of structural change. We remain convinced that in many HR functions there are huge disconnects between generalists, specialists and those delivering HR administration whether they sit in the three-legged stool model or in a single HR team. The other determinants of successful HR transformation – such as HR and Manager capability and process improvement – are addressed elsewhere in this book.

Issue 7: HR capabilities

What we wrote in the first edition   We address this issue extensively throughout this book and we recommend that you draw on the content in these chapters to take the debate forward in your organisation. It remains our contention that HR professionals need to build new capabilities above and beyond the traditional areas of HR. Specifically, they need to build a sound theoretical basis in the areas of organisational behaviour, business finance and economics, and psychology in order to support organisational development and change. Above all else, HR professionals must be recognised first and foremost for their contribution as business people – they must know their business and appreciate the drivers of value in their business. It is from this position that HR professionals will become influencers in their business.

The issues you may need to confront in thinking about your next steps in HR transformation are likely to include:

- what kind of capabilities you need to develop in your HR professionals;
- how your current HR professionals benchmark against these new capabilities;
- what investment you are prepared to make to develop these capabilities;
- what alternatives you have if your current HR professionals cannot step up.

There is a larger issue about HR capability touched on in this book, which is this: if people are the greatest asset of a business, why is it so difficult to get the most able people into HR? This is not to say that there are no able people in HR – there are, and we have worked with and encountered many. But it is true to say that the profession has a talent deficit, and the demands that should be placed on HR in the future mean that we need to create an environment where people know that they will have an opportunity to work on some of the organisation's most difficult issues. Perhaps this too is an issue that might be explored in your business.

Comment This remains, arguably, the greatest challenge faced in transforming HR. The lack of capability to perform a business focused, more strategic people role is highlighted in just about all reports and is given prominence throughout this book. The KPMG report (2008) identifies 'HR practitioners with critical capability gaps' as the number 1 challenge facing the function. The questions posed in our first edition remain valid – arguably more so since we first wrote them. With notable exceptions, investment in HR professionals is generally low, but where we have seen organisations address this we have also seen HR's contribution shift markedly. Linda Holbeche, writing in the CIPD's Impact magazine (Issue 21) sums up the issue well: '*What also became apparent was that many new business partners were underprepared or underpowered for their roles, lacking the skills, confidence or the delivery capability as consultants to ensure that value was being added over what had existed before. Increasingly it was recognised that consultancy, relationship management and third-party management skills together with commercial acumen were prerequisites for effectiveness in business partner roles*'.

The issue of talent and career management is also valid. Lawler et al. raise on a number of occasions the need for cross-unit teams and for rotation of people between HR and line functions. The challenge for HR to be a 'must have' experience on the CV of high potentials still lies in the land of hope rather than reality.

Conclusion

We have used recent research in the UK and USA to present as up to date a picture of the HR function as possible. We accept that this inevitably involves generalisation and that not all HR functions will look like the picture painted – some better and some worse!

The changing HR function notes that over 80% of HR functions have undergone some form of change in the past 5 years. It is clear that much of this change has been based on a strong desire by HR professionals to achieve greater alignment between business and HR strategy and to drive more cost-effective and improved delivery. However, it is also clear that structural change and re-labelling job titles is insufficient. The issues we set out in our first edition remain valid and all the research published in recent years points to further improvements HR functions need to make.

In this respect the HR transformation journey is not over, but has only really just begun.

3

What Is HR's Value Proposition?

The subtitle to this book is 'Creating Value through People'. Value creation is at the heart of any organisation – whether in the private, public or voluntary sector. If no value is delivered, there is no point to your organisation. In this chapter, we will therefore address the following questions:

- What do we mean by value creation?
- What do we mean by value adding HR?
- How are HR professionals adding value?
- How did they make this shift?
- What challenges remain for HR to create value through people?

Key themes

- There is little academic consensus on what value creation is and how it can be achieved.
- Value creation needs to be understood from a contingency perspective – value is in the eye of the beholder.
- HR value add is delivered through four key sources: transactional value, process value, strategic value and reputational value.
- HR professionals need to get much better at analysing data and understanding financial management.
- Challenges remain for HR functions to deliver value in organisations.

Context

Terms such as 'value adding' and 'value creating' are much used in organisations and have become by-words that articulate what HR transformation is seeking to achieve. 'We want to move from transactional to "value adding" HR' is a typical, and justifiable, aspiration for HR transformation. It suggests that even though HR professionals are currently delivering worthwhile work in organisations there is still something missing: a contribution to key business challenges that is not being made currently; contributions that will make colleagues sit up, pay attention and find valuable.

Ask a line manager or business leader what they value from HR and you are likely to get a divergence of opinion. Paying people on time is valued; accurate employee information is valued; support to managers who are handling difficult disciplinary, sickness or grievance cases is valued; slick people processes are valued; efficient restructuring is valued. We should not delude ourselves that these activities are somehow worthless. They are not. HR adds value through these activities.

But there is still something missing. What about the people issues we are not engaged in, but could be? What about working the data so that we bring real insights to business colleagues?

This kind of 'value add' is what an Economist Intelligence Unit/Deloitte report in 2007 (*Aligned at the Top*) called 'the big challenge' and their research drew an interesting distinction: *'When senior business executives talk about HR, they focus on administrative activities such as rewards and benefits, performance evaluation and HR operating efficiency. When those same executives talk about people issues (our emphasis), they focus on talent management, workforce productivity and leadership development and, in many cases the HR function isn't even mentioned'.*

A KPMG report – *HR: Architect or Artisan?* (2008) reported the following insight from the CEO of a major high street retailer: *'When the marketing director comes to the executive board meetings he presents data on our consumers, and we are given enormous insight about their buying habits, their aspirations, their concerns and their hopes. We have clear demographic data, and we can predict with real accuracy how patterns will evolve. But when HR presents information about our employees it is less precise, less concise, less insightful and less predictive'.*

These CEO insights cannot be dismissed and they set out challenges of relevance and data insight the function must respond to.

In this chapter, we propose to unpick what is meant by value creation referring to recent research and then examine HR practitioner perspectives. We will outline how some HR functions are responding to this desire to extend the range of value adding contributions and finally highlight a number of challenges that remain if HR is to create value through people.

Value creation – what it means and how it is created

In their earlier book, *'The HR Value Proposition'* (2005), Dave Ulrich and Wayne Brockbank stated that 'now more than ever, business success comes from HR. And the "DNA" for HR success is the HR Value Proposition'. The framework proposed by Ulrich and Brockbank is presented in Figure 3.1.

The two shaded boxes in the framework reflect the need for HR to understand the realities faced by your organisation – contingent thinking – and to address value from a multi-stakeholder perspective. Both these drivers of value are underlined by the findings of research undertaken by David Lepak, Ken Smith and Susan Taylor which is expanded upon later in this section. The rest of the framework concerns how HR should organise in order to deliver value and the value delivered through relevant people practices. These latter three elements are a key focus of HR transformation and the contents of this book.

Ulrich and Brockbank went on to identify 14 criteria which you can rate (1–5) to establish whether you have a clear value proposition. These 14 criteria are shown in the box below:

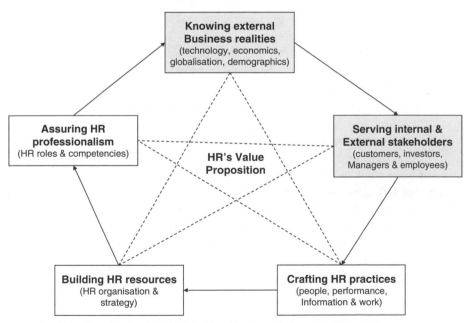

Source: Dave Ulrich, Wayne Brockbank, The HR Value Proposition Havard Business School Press 2005

Figure 3.1 The HR value proposition.

HR value proposition criteria

From Dave Ulrich and Wayne Brockbank, *The HR Value Proposition* (2005)

Knowing external business realities

1. To what extent do the HR professionals in my department understand how the external realities of technology, economics and demographics in the global context affect our organisation?

Serving external and internal stakeholders

2. To what extent does our HR work link to the intangibles that investors value?
3. To what extent do we use HR practices to build long-term connections with target customers?
4. To what extent do we audit and create organisation capabilities that will turn strategy into action?
5. To what extent do we have a clear employee value proposition that lays out what is expected of employees and what they get in return?

Crafting HR practices

6. To what extent do our HR practices that focus on people (staffing, training, development) add value?
7. To what extent do our HR practices that focus on performance (setting standards, allocating rewards, providing feedback) add value?
8. To what extent do our HR practices that focus on information (outside-in and inside-out) add value?
9. To what extent do our HR practices that focus on work flow (who does what work, how is the work done and where is the work done) add value?

Building HR resources

10. To what extent does our HR strategy process turn business goals into HR priorities?
11. To what extent is our HR organisation (e-HR, service centres, centres of expertise, embedded HR and outsourcing contracts) aligned with the business strategy?

Assuring HR professionalism

12. To what extent do our HR professionals play employee advocate, human capital developer, functional expert, strategic partner and leadership roles?
13. To what extent do our HR professionals demonstrate competence in strategic contribution, HR delivery, business knowledge, personal credibility and HR technology?
14. To what extent do we develop our HR professionals and our HR department?

Ulrich and Brockbank suggest that if you score 50+ then you are in good shape.

More recently, an excellent article published in the Academy of Management Review (2007, Vol. 32, No. 1, 180–194) by David Lepak, Ken Smith and Susan Taylor draws together a wide range of academic research on the subject of value creation and value capture. They state that 'value creation is a central concept in the management and organisation literature for both micro level (individual, group) and macro level (organisation theory, strategic management) research. Yet there is little consensus on what value creation is, or on how it can be achieved'. They consider this observation to be one of the most important conclusions from their research.

Two significant reasons cited for this lack of consensus are:

1. Management is a multi-disciplinary field and therefore people tend to see value creation through their particular lens. For example, those from a strategic management, marketing, strategic HRM or entrepreneurship background may emphasise value creation for business owners, stakeholders or customers, whereas those from an organisational behaviour/psychology background may emphasise value creation that targets individual employees, employee groups or teams. Those from a sociological or economic background may focus on value creation in terms of society or nations. None of these are right or wrong – they just place different emphasis on the targets for which value can be created.
2. Value creation is used with reference both to the content and process of new value creation and these are often confused with one another. Content addresses questions regarding what is value/valuable, who values what and where value resides. Process addresses the ways value is actually generated and the role, if any, of management in this process.

Having set out the points of divergence amongst those writing about value creation the article goes on to address the question 'what is value creation?'. This is not just academic philosophising. There is an important point here so stick with it for a little longer.

The article differentiates between use value and exchange value.

Definitions of value

Use value: The specific quality of a new job, task, product or service *as perceived by users* in relation to their needs.

Exchange value: What users are prepared to pay for the new task, good, service or product.

The article suggests that value creation depends on the relative amount of value that is subjectively realised by a target user who is the focus of value creation. In other words, 'value is in the eye of the beholder'.

So, acknowledging the reality of subjective, multiple stakeholder perceptions is the key to unlocking our understanding of value creation. Internal clients will value those things that address their needs and pay for those things they value.

This then leads us to the question *how is value created*?

The article dismisses the 'one size fits all' view of the world and rightly adopts a contingency perspective. This means that in answering the question of how value is created we need to define the source and targets of value creation and the level of analysis. We summarise the value creation from the perspective of the individual and organisation in the box below. (The article also examines value creation from the perspective of society but this is far less relevant to this book and if you are interested you can look up the article.)

Individuals create value through developing new, relevant tasks, services, jobs, products, processes and other contributions which stakeholders consider to meet their needs and which are financially more beneficial than using an alternative provider of that task, etc.

Organisational value is created when:

1. Firms develop/invent new ways of doing things using new methods, technologies and/or new forms of raw material (Porter, 1985) that benefit the target user.
2. Firms develop dynamic capabilities, which can include product and process development, organisational evolution and management capabilities. Much of the research in this area is focused on internal factors and emphasises knowledge creation, learning and entrepreneurship in creating advantage.
3. Processes enable new organisational knowledge to be generated. A focus of this research is on the extent of social networks (that extend outside the organisation) and their ability to combine and exchange information in a way that produces organisational knowledge.
4. There are high investment human resource management systems: practices that develop employee skills, enhance employee motivation, and engage and empower employees.

Lepak, Smith and Taylor conclude their paper by emphasising that understanding value creation is complex because it is subjective in nature, means different things to different organisations and is defined largely by target users/stakeholder perception.

So, what are the themes we can draw from the above? We have identified four:

1. We add value when we apply contingent thinking: we understand our organisation, its environment and what needs to be done from a people and organisational perspective to drive high performance.
2. We add value when we engage with multiple stakeholders (inside and outside the organisation) and understand what matters to them.
3. We add value when we organise HR (a whole systems perspective) so that it has the capability to deliver value through the people agenda.
4. We add value when we focus on deliverables (outcomes).

In this book, we address all four of these themes, majoring particularly on the third.

Value adding HR

Moving from the world of academic research to the experience of HR professionals, we have identified an interesting dilemma that needs to be faced: if we accept that 'value add' is essentially what stakeholders consider to be of value to them (PULL) – how do we also influence stakeholders so that their needs change (PUSH)? Put more simply – if managers consider value adding HR to be excellent HR administration, slick HR processes and timely and helpful case management support, how do we also help managers to understand that HR professionals can add value not only through delivering the basics, but also through delivering business projects more successfully, managing change, or shaping the strategic agenda? Returning to the Economist Intelligence Unit/Deloitte report quoted earlier – how do we influence senior executives so that they see HR and people issues as one in the same?

In conversation with Frances Allcock (BBC), we were able to articulate this dilemma as shown in Figure 3.2. This figure captures well the challenges faced by HR professionals – how do we shift the conversations we hold with our business colleagues so that we not only hold the conversations we need to hold with colleagues but also engage in those areas they don't expect us to? As an illustration, Allcock has observed that one of things managers value from HR is excellent and slick reorganisation – the implementation piece. If HR does this well they get to the table. Yet HR is often unable to get to talk about the really challenging aspects of change because managers either do not have the time or they do not see it as an area where HR can contribute (sometimes with justification).

Answering the question 'what do we actually talk to managers about?' will vary from organisation to organisation – you may want to reflect upon Figure 3.2 to

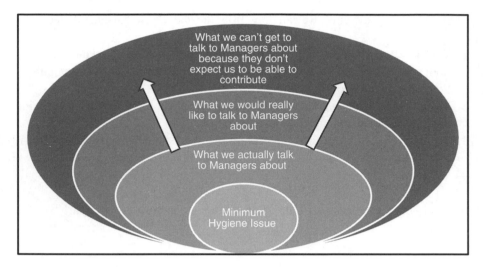

Figure 3.2 Shifting conversations.

review your own conversations with business colleagues. What is important is that we create value not just by meeting stakeholder needs, but in shaping their thinking and influencing their decisions. As Alison Grace (National Express Group) put it: 'it is about working in ways that make a positive difference to our businesses and that means bringing fresh thinking to the table, challenging assumptions and getting the business to grapple with tough issues from multiple perspectives'.

If changing the conversations we have with colleagues is one of the challenges we need to confront another is measurement. Many HR departments are involved in measuring their company's operational performance against key performance indicators (KPIs). Fewer have a role in measuring and providing hard evidence of the efficiency and value they are adding to delivery of their organisations' strategic objectives.

As Martin Moore (Royal Mail) put it: 'The problem with many HR measures is that we measure what is measurable not what we need to measure'. Sticking to traditional measures of HR effectiveness also induces a way of thinking and working leading to a heavy reliance on the latest fads and fashions of espoused 'best' practice and over-preoccupation with benchmarking.

One commentator, Gary Hamel, has suggested that this is the Achilles heel for HR. He has noted that 'unlike the Finance function, HR does not have an explicit and accepted theory about how it adds value to the business'.

The reason for this is addressed in the research led by Lepak et al. cited above: non-financial benefits of the sort offered by effective HR functions are very rarely based on a set configuration of cause-effect but rather, value is derived through a combination of connecting processes, information, strategy and service delivery

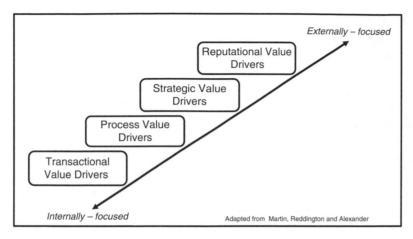

Figure 3.3 Value drivers.

aligned to the specific needs of each business. Whereas finance is largely based on a universal model of added value, HR is based on a situation-specific model of added value. In other words, we need to take excellence in people management practices and align these with the specific needs of our organisation.

But where to start?

In our conversations with senior practitioners there is a strong appetite for HR to develop ways of measuring the impact of core business issues. To frame this discussion, we have been able to identify four ways in which HR drives value (see Figure 3.3):

- *Transactional value* – running HR administration in ways that capture and provide accurate, timely and insightful information and advice. Measures of transactional value include: costs/value for money, data and information quality, reporting capability and flexibility, delivery against service levels, etc. A test of transactional value will be whether managers get high quality information and advice when they need it and whether this information tells them anything new.
- *Process value* – putting in place people processes that are efficient (speed, cost, quality), fit for purpose – relevant to the circumstances of your organisation, meaningful and engaging for users and aligned to organisational goals, etc. A test of process value is the *experience* people have of the process, for example, with regard to selection – does the selection process build commitment and engagement from the first point of contact through to decision?
- *Strategic value* – participating in shaping strategy so that people and organisational issues are surfaced from the outset and supporting the effective

53

execution of strategy. Tests of value in this context include challenging thinking, aligning people and business strategies, executing strategy in a way that makes change stick, delivering projects and securing stakeholder commitment to change. It also means adding value through shaping organisational design and being confident in manipulating data so that the organisation is able to gain insights concerning the workforce profile and cost structure.

■ *Reputational value* – doing things that help to deliver the strategy *and* which build a positive internal and external image of the organisation. Examples of this are ethical and sustainable practice, good governance and leadership, effective risk management, being seen as a good employer, etc. A test of reputational value may be that those people you need to attract really want to work for your organisation.

Clearly, all value drivers are 'strategic' but the sense we have used strategic above is to focus particularly on the delivery of the business change agenda. Each of these ways of value creation also requires a multiple stakeholder approach and a deep understanding of external and business realities. This emphasis on relevance to stakeholders and to your organisation aligns with Lepak et al.'s research in the 'Value creation – what it means and how it is created' section and with the contingency approach to organisational development.

What has HR done to add value?

The HR function has made good progress in trying to add value in organisations and in this section we provide some examples. We underline that each example given is a response to the situation that organisation found itself in. The examples are therefore provided as 'leading practice' and our intention is that these illustrate themes set out in previous sections.

Transactional value

Cost reduction and efficiency improvements are generally the main drivers for HR systems changes and the adoption of a shared services delivery model. Jerry Arnott (Department for Work and Pensions – DWP) emphasises the importance of efficiency improvements within the DWP's HR transformation programme and states that it is critical that HR adds value on essential administrative and support services. This scale of saving is mirrored in other organisations we have worked with.

HR's ability to deliver transactional value is the main litmus test for managers. As Maggie Hurt (Renolds) points out: 'Our clients judge us on getting the basics right, like pay and offer letters – what we might regard as mundane. We then get the attention of our clients and earn the right to contribute at a more strategic level'. HR services delivered at the transactional level are most immediately relevant to day-to-day management and therefore play strongly into tests of competence and relevance. It is essential therefore that HR works with the rest of the business to agree on expectations in the following areas:

- Target cost base (measured through various ratios)
- Service levels
- Quality
- Reporting

Underpinning these tangible measures will be less tangible (but arguably the real determinants of value) measures of responsiveness and experience (the personal touch).

All this is great, and if HR can get all the above right it will be adding transactional value. But we believe HR can deliver more in this area:

1. *Data modelling* – HR needs to turn information into insight. What is more likely to get the attention of the CEO/CFO, a turnover figure (say 15%) set alongside an industry turnover average (say 13%) or data showing the true costs of turnover: where we are experiencing it; the kind of people leaving, an impact analysis that shows what it costs to lose then replace someone? We believe the latter will, especially if the financial impact can be estimated.
2. *Reporting what is useful* – we need to report what managers will find useful. This means thinking more deeply about the kind of data we collect and how we present it. Ian Elms recalls that in his time at Kingfisher an annual 'census' was produced showing a breakdown in company demographics, compensation data, etc. This gave the executive team insights about the workforce.
3. *Assessing impact on performance* – getting under the skin of data so that we can better assess the impact on performance. Other functions do this really well (e.g., marketing, finance) and we have much to learn from these in order to build a compelling story using both narrative and data.

Process value

We often view HR processes solely through the lenses of efficiency and effectiveness. Efficiency and effectiveness measures are important, but value adding processes deliver more than this. As Maggie Hurt (Renolds) puts it: 'I am keen to get across to my team that the value that comes through good HR is not through ticking the box in a work process. It is about ensuring the output is right. We need to engage the brain – develop "thinking HR" at all levels of the function'. So processes need to deliver specific outcomes and these outcomes must drive engagement, commitment and performance.

Take the selection process as an example. How well this process works could be measured in terms of recruitment cycle time, quality of candidates, costs of recruitment, number of recruits, etc. – all standard activity, efficiency or effectiveness measures. The outcomes of recruitment though are, arguably to:

- find the best fit person (role and organisation) and for that person to have the potential to grow and develop further;
- ensure that that the unsuccessful candidates leave with a positive impression of their experience.

To secure the best candidate will be the result of many interactions that person has with the organisation or its agents – from the first point of contact through to the period before joining. One of our senior practitioners who has recently moved roles talked of a selection process that did not go smoothly and contrasted a poor impression given by the headhunter at the initial meeting (which nearly resulted in the person leaving the interview) to extremely favourable impressions of the organisation itself: even when the process did not run smoothly senior managers behaved in a way that not only recovered the situation but turned it into a positive experience. For this person, these are excellent examples of value adding moments during a process.

A different type of process value in selection is seen in the way KPMG UK recruits graduates. Graduates value straightforward, quick and transparent selection processes. In response, KPMG was the first large employer to go 100% online (back in 2000) and the first to have online reasoning tests. The KPMG process is one of the quickest in the marketplace with most decisions being taken within 1 month from initial application. Graduates are told in advance what they will be assessed against and KPMG gives feedback to candidates at each stage of the process regardless of outcome. When offers are made candidates are sent a link on the same day that takes them to their electronic offer. They can accept online and access all the relevant documentation online.

Rackspace, a global managed hosting business, demonstrates process value in their approach to on-boarding. This is presented in the case study below.

Case study – Rackspace

Rackspace has enjoyed considerable growth in recent years and differentiates itself from others in the market through a strong corporate culture. 'Fanatical Support' is its value proposition and therefore the successful on-boarding of new talent, so that they are not only productive quickly but assimilate into the Rackspace culture, is a critical success factor for the business.

The philosophy that underpins the Rackspace approach to Rackers (or 'employees' in more conventional language) is that if you get the Racker experience right, Rackers will get the customer experience right.

You probably get the drift already that Rackspace is no ordinary company. Fanatical Support is not just a front end proposition, it applies to all functions. So on-boarding is no conventional experience either. There are four parts to on-boarding:

- Rapid Induction Programme (RIP)
- Rookie Orientation (Rookie 'O')
- Team On-boarding
- Pathfinder

RIP is your day 1 experience. Led by Steve Pegler, a trainer in Rackspace University, the day involves the usual paperwork and briefings on health and safety. But it is informal, it is personal (people are walked around the whole office and they get to meet fellow Rackers), it is non-hierarchical (if the MD or other Directors are sat at their open-plan desk they are introduced to new Rackers), they are shown the many photo walls with pictures of fun days, charity events, parties and the hall of fame – fanatic of the month and they get to feel the culture.

Rookie O is a 4-day orientation run monthly. But this is no 'chalk and talk' orientation. There is no job-specific training. It is all about the culture. So, Rackers are given some of the Rackspace values to think about and during the 4 days they have to gather real life examples from around the organisation of these values being lived. So new Rackers need to get out and about and talk to people. They also get to understand the business. They visit a data centre and literally get under the floorboards to understand what the business is all about. Perhaps the most compelling part of Rookie O is that during the week every function gets to present to new Rackers. This could be very dry and lead to death by PowerPoint. Not at Rackspace. It is highly competitive and new Rackers get to rate each presentation against a set of customer engagement measures (NPS) on how much they have learnt and how engaging the presentation was. At the end of Rookie O week (Friday afternoon) all Rackers are invited to celebrate the arrival of new starters and awards are given – including which function presented best! Needless to say, this approach has resulted in some very creative presentations being developed around game shows and the like.

Team on-boarding has two distinct characteristics. First, a framework is given to managers for them to decide how best to on-board their new Racker. So, managers will be expected to set expectations/standards; discuss training needs; brief communication protocols, etc. but how they do this is up to them. This is to ensure consistency. Second, as with most Rackspace on-boarding, managers are encouraged to be creative. So, for example, instead of simply giving people a list of business contacts/resources, new Rackers are given direction and they then need to go and actually meet people/find resources for themselves.

Finally, Pathfinder focuses on job-specific training. What is interesting about this training is that it is assumed that new Rackers will know the technology. The focus is therefore on how this technology is used/how things are done at Rackspace.

Rackspace has been recognised in the Sunday Times Best Companies to Work and the Financial Times Great Place to Work and has won the most welcoming company award.

We present this case study as an excellent example of process value and how a people process is fully aligned to the business goals and value proposition.

An exercise we completed with the HR leadership team of a FTSE 20 company was to review people processes and consider whether each was having a positive, neutral or negative impact on employee engagement. This was an illuminating experience and revealed that most were either neutral or negative. As a result, we were then able to identify what could be done to shift the employee experience for each key people process.

Strategic value

Driving strategic value means helping the organisation perform in the short and long term. Alison Grace (National Express) summed up as follows: 'HR adds value when it delivers stuff that makes a positive difference to the business, which means addressing those areas that need to be addressed in each business and not by adopting a "this is good for you/everyone is doing it" approach. It is about being relevant, about identifying a change agenda and then helping the business deliver this agenda'. This means being clear about what really matters to the organisation. This was echoed by Martin Moore (Royal Mail) who also emphasised that strategic value was delivered when HR was at the heart of change. For Ian Muir (ESAB), delivering strategic value means building an engaged workforce so that a performance edge is created through people. Roger Cooper focused on HR's strategic role in working issues proactively, in creating healthy organisations and in identifying and managing risk.

An excellent example of strategic value-add can be seen in National Express Group when Alison Grace was their Group Leadership Development Director and which is presented in the case study below.

Case study – National express

When Alison Grace became Group Leadership Development Director, National Express Group had no previous experience of HR contributing at a group level. The business was devolved and operated as largely stand alone business units. As an organisation of 30,000 people operating in the UK, North America and Spain, there was a strategic need to develop future leaders. In rolling out a framework called DNA – Driving National Express Achievement – it could be argued that the HR team put in place the kinds of people processes you would expect to see in any large organisation: a leadership capability framework; a talent management process; new reward arrangements; common leadership development programmes, etc. However, DNA was more than this. As Alison Grace explains: 'DNA was a vehicle for the business to ask and answer some critical questions it needed to ask, for example, "how far should we be integrated as a group of businesses?" and "what drives high performance in our businesses?" Although led from HR, this work created a series of powerful conversations and debates at senior levels in the business. It meant HR challenged prevailing business thinking and helped shape the strategic direction of the organisation. Through this challenge, the business took the opportunity to put greater professionalism into core people processes such as performance management, reward and talent. It also gave people the opportunity to set expectations concerning the type of leadership the business needed. This work was the precursor that enabled discussion and decisions to be taken about a National Express Group brand and gave people an opportunity to get excited about being part of National Express Group rather than just their business unit'.

So in this example, the development of a leadership strategy provided a catalyst in helping the business engage in a conversation about the kind of organisation it needed to become to deliver high performance.

Reputational value

Reputational value has both an internal and external focus. Internally, it is about whether people think this is a great place to work, whether they would recommend people to work for the organisation, whether they speak highly of the organisation publicly. How this translates into value is whether people's regard for the organisation makes them want to go the 'extra mile' – whether they are prepared to give high levels of discretionary effort to get the job done – and whether organisations are able to hold on to those people, 'key talent', they need to. This is a key component of employee engagement and, we believe, an under-emphasised facet of the employer brand. Externally, it is about how multiple stakeholders (shareholders, customers, governments, potential employees, etc.) perceive the organisation and whether it is an organisation they want to do business with. In the 'war for talent' reputation differentiates employers. How differentiation is achieved is through the employer brand, good governance, corporate social responsibility, public reporting and leadership. In the public sector, public value can also be added to this list (Martin, Reddington, & Alexander, 2008).

John Kay, one of the UK's leading economists, has argued that reputation is one of only three bases on which companies in developed economies can compete (the others being brand and knowledge) – and that all three rest on an organisation's ability to develop strong trust relations with multiple stakeholders. We all know that good reputations take many years to develop but a very short time to destroy.

What does this mean for HR? This is probably the area where HR functions have the most work to do. Below we identify four implications.

First, the kind of employer you are matters – not just for current employees but to multiple stakeholders. How you communicate yourself to the public matters. Ethics, social responsibility and corporate stewardship count.

Second, there will undoubtedly be an increasing requirement for greater public reporting on the people aspects of organisation – whether mandatory or voluntary. Whether we call these people profit and loss accounts or human capital accounts is immaterial. Greater public scrutiny of the investment made in people will be a feature of greater regulation and an enhanced role for government in the economy. An example of this is the increasing requirement on firms tendering for government contracts to report on measures to ensure non-discrimination at work.

Third, corporate governance will receive stronger attention, particularly executive compensation. Organisations will need to be more accountable than ever before about the way people, especially senior executives, are rewarded.

Fourth, employer branding will become a key way for organisations to differentiate.

Robert Peston, the BBC's Economics Editor, expressed well the challenges faced by organisations in driving reputational value when he wrote (8 December

2008): 'Those running our biggest commercial businesses will have to be more visible. They'll have to manifest a genuine understanding not only of the anxieties of their employees but of all taxpayers. Those chief executives who succeed will be those who imbue in their businesses very simple, commonsense standards of decency. And they'll almost certainly be paid less for doing so'.

An example of how an organisation has taken deliberate steps internally to build reputation (to address both an internal and external audience) is at KPMG. We present this case study below.

Case study

KPMG in the UK has won the Sunday Times Best Big Company to Work for three times in the past 5 years, winning in consecutive years 2008 and 2009. These awards are based largely on the views of KPMG employees. This level of external recognition was not always the case. Back in 2004 KPMG UK faced significant obstacles to achieving its goal of becoming the best professional services firm experiencing significant retention, morale, people management and development issues. In response Managing for Excellence was introduced and stands at the heart of KPMG's people strategy. Its aims are straightforward – to professionalise the way people are managed: to embed effective line management. What it has achieved in practice marks a culture shift in the way that people are managed and developed: moving the focus from process compliance to a people centric. The results have been dramatic not least a halving of employee turnover and year on year increases in employee engagement. As Rachel Campbell, Head of KPMG's Global People, Performance and Culture and partner in the UK firm says 'Achieving sustainable competitive advantage is all about attracting, developing and retaining diverse talent and doing it better than our competitors. Our people strategy is not just about securing competitive advantage, it's also about defining what sort of firm we are, what we stand for. It's about doing the right thing by people even when it's difficult – especially when it's difficult. It's about being open, honest, fair, consistent, fulfilling promises, keeping confidences. All of these are important in their own right and they are all at the heart of Managing for Excellence'.

Challenges for HR

Challenges remain for HR to truly deliver value. Using the Ulrich and Brockbank criteria set out in the 'Value creation – what it means and how it is created' section would be a good starting point to frame a discussion on HR value add. Similarly, engaging colleagues in HR and other parts of your organisation in thinking through the four drivers of value presented in Figure 3.3 – identifying what HR does well/ could do better would also be an excellent starting point. Whichever you use, the important point is that you do something to understand what stakeholders in your organisation value about HR and to identify what HR can do to raise its contribution. So that is the first challenge: *Ask your stakeholders what they value about HR.*

In our discussions with senior practitioners we identified four other challenges:

Challenge 2: HR must understand the critical drivers of success in their organisation. How do HR professionals see their world? When we talk about our organisations do we see them through an HR lens or a business lens? An example given to us by one of our practitioners referred to a meeting they once attended when a senior group of HR business partners were each asked to present their business unit to their colleagues to build understanding of the whole business. Clearly this is a worthy objective! However, what was presented focused on headcount numbers, payroll costs, organisation charts, spans of control and turnover. There was no focus on strategic goals, critical business issues, change challenges, leadership capability/bench strength, etc. This is a good example of changing the way we think about what HR is and ensuring that we understand what makes our organisation successful.

Challenge 3: We need to change the way we engage with our stakeholders. So many HR professionals still struggle with the notion of peer or upward challenge. HR pulls its punches and this is not healthy nor will this approach help us add value. As Frances Allcock (BBC) put it: 'we need to bring a way of thinking and working that is future orientated, commercially focused and data driven so that we change the conversations we hold with business colleagues. We need to be prepared to challenge, bring fresh thinking to the table and be courageous. Rather than undermine relationships, this approach will build relationships as it is based on getting the best outcome for the business and we all want that'.

Challenge 4: HR needs to shape and not just implement the change agenda. As we enter a period of unprecedented economic change and uncertainty, the ability of organisations to change quickly and purposefully is even more critical. Knowledge sharing, collaboration, creativity/idea generation and capture are also significant challenges faced by many organisations. We know that most change efforts fail to deliver the anticipated benefits because organisations do not get the people side right. So there is much to play for. We also know from our review of recent research in Chapter 1 that equipping HR professionals so that they are skilled to play this role remains a challenge.

Challenge 5: We need to keep working at delivering transactional and process value. For those HR functions that have already delivered significant savings, the ongoing challenges are to:

- keep refining the cost base to realise further productivity gains;
- assure data integrity through quality controls;
- deliver information in a 'manager-friendly' way;

- provide timely and accurate advice – whether through on line or help desk support;
- deliver real data insights;
- produce stronger, data driven, business cases showing how proposals will impact organisational performance (including financial impact).

We believe that there is still much to be done in driving process value. As generation X becomes generation V (virtual) this personalisation of processes will become even more important. (We develop this theme further in Chapters 4 and 13.) Process value will not just be the domain of the HR function either, it will also challenge managers to create the climate (on-boarding, recognition, freedom to perform, releasing people's skills and talents, etc.) for people to succeed.

How might you respond to these challenges? Here are some suggestions:

- Think of your organisation, the context it finds itself in, its overall goals and some of the dilemmas you may need to work through, for example, you may be asked to reduce headcount and raise levels of employee engagement. Then use the four value drivers to identify what areas are most likely to drive value in the short and medium term.
- Consider who you are driving value for. As the Lepak research suggests there are likely to be multiple stakeholders and you need to think what matters to each. If you do not know, think about how you might find out, for example, if you do not normally get exposed to what investors want talk to investor relations or colleagues who may know.
- Think about relevant measures of value. This is not about 'measurement frenzy'. Identify a small number of lag (measuring the past, e.g., profit per employee) or lead (setting goals to be reached in the future, e.g., to be recognised as one of the top 50 best places to work within 3 years) measures.
- Engage with relevant people in order to identify how to move work forward in this area and how to put in place an appropriate range of measures.

Summary

In this chapter, we have set out our thinking on how HR adds value. We have highlighted the importance of contingent thinking and the engagement of multiple stakeholders with regard to value creation. We have identified four drivers of HR value: transactional value, process value, strategic value and reputational value. Many HR functions have already taken significant steps to ensure that HR is value adding. However, challenges remain and we have identified five key challenges for HR functions to address.

Part 2

The Case for Change

Part 2 focuses on making the case for HR transformation.

Chapter 4: People and Technology presents recent CIPD research and practitioner experience on the actual and potential use of Web 2.0 and social media technology by HR functions.

Chapter 5: Envisioning the New World of HR sets out a process and practical tools that will help you to engage stakeholders on how well HR is currently being delivered in your business and the future HR delivery model you want to create. This is a critical phase of the transformation journey and frames how HR will deliver value in the future. The chapter presents envisioning tools that are helpful irrespective of whether you are just starting out or are already on a transformation journey and want to re-energise for the next phase.

Chapter 6: The Business Rationale naturally follows envisioning and explores the key considerations in developing the business case for HR transformation and, in particular, the case for capital investment in HR information systems. In addition to defining benefits and costs (the so-called 'hard' elements of the case), the approaches to building business commitment are also explored (the so-called 'softer' elements of the case). Taken together, these hard and soft elements build commitment and credibility and establish the foundations for transformation.

Chapter 7: Stakeholder Engagement and Communication provides practical tools that enable you to understand who your key stakeholders are and their likely reactions to your HR transformation proposals. We also present ways to move stakeholder opinion away from resistance to commitment.

4

People and Technology

Technology is a powerful tool that can be used internally within HR to improve performance, reduce costs and improve access to services, as well as being used externally to change the way that people management is delivered by the line.

The range of available technologies can be bewildering. At one end of the spectrum there are professional packages which deliver HR databases and payroll systems, which can also be integrated with other back office services such as finance and procurement. Whilst at the other end of the spectrum there are interactive Web-based tools that enable organisations to engage with staff in virtual forums and blogs and issue courses and communications to iPods, mobile phones and hand-held devices. In the middle of this spectrum are self-service tools which automate and simplify core people management processes such as sickness absence, performance management and leave.

The challenge is to understand which technologies are most appropriate for your organisation and your objectives for HR transformation and how to identify and select these technologies. The right technology can be a powerful enabler in transforming the HR service and the way that people management is delivered in your business. The wrong technology can be an expensive mistake which undermines the credibility of HR and the services that are delivered.

Key themes

- The range of technologies that are available are many and varied. Packages exist which run payroll, deliver a HR database, deliver self-service and integrate HR with other back office services such as finance and procurement. Packages are also available which exploit Web technology to support online recruitment, online learning and development and to create virtual environments in which it is possible to engage in a two-way communication process with staff. Technology, including Web 2.0, is opening up new ways to deliver key people processes and engage with staff.

■ The key to choosing the right technology is to understand how you currently use technology, what you wish to change within HR and people management and to be clear on what you want from technology. This provides a clear scope and criteria against which to select a package or different packages.

■ Web 2.0 creates opportunities to add business value by improving employee engagement and collaborative knowledge sharing. A multiplicity of options is available and HR practitioners need to be aware of their uses and not left behind in the groundswell of interest which is driving these new social media technologies.

Context

This chapter will provide a brief overview of the key technologies that are currently available, how to determine what is right for you, how to select the right packages and what issues to consider when choosing how to deploy and deliver these technologies. A number of leading edge models are described with case illustrations.

Informing the people and technology debate

There is a rich seam of literature which addresses 'people and technology' and in broad terms the themes which arise are set out diagrammatically in Figure 4.1 based on the work of Martin (2005). The appearance or promise of liberation, empowerment and decentralisation is shown with its contrast of control, domination and centralisation.

Different forms of technology and technological change have been at the heart of many of the issues concerning the management of people and the work of human resource professionals for many years. In more recent times, however, these issues emanate from the role of newer technologies in transforming societies, transforming economic progress and in how we work in such societies. Excellent overviews on different aspects of the role of information and communication technologies (ICT), the 'new' economy and work can be found in the work of Castells (1996), Coyle and Quah (2004), Slevin (2000) and Taylor (2004). This has resulted in a renewed interest in the relationship between these new technologies and the management of people (see, e.g., Malone, 2004; Nathan et al., 2003).

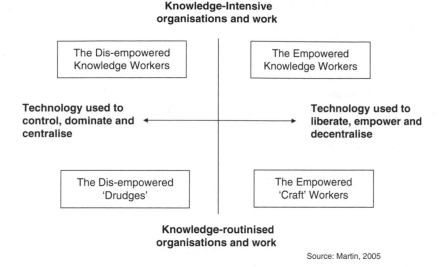

Figure 4.1 Contrasting impacts of technology.

These more macro and intellectual concerns have been accompanied by the actual influence of technologies on the practice of human resource management. For example, Sparrow, Brewster, and Harris (2004) singled out technology as a transforming force, especially in the e-enablement of HR and its impact on the creation and transfer of knowledge.

As we have explained in earlier chapters, signs have been mounting for some time that previously accepted concepts of organisation and strategy have come to an end. The fundamentally Newtonian paradigm of organisations as machines and strategy by numbers has given way to structural change that shifts the emphasis from physical inputs and outputs to intangible ones such as knowledge, learning, creativity and initiative. The old paradigm of top-down control and hierarchical organisation appears to have exhausted its capacity to generate innovative responses to turbulent business conditions and intensifying global competition – indeed, far from fostering innovation, many managers feel it is holding them back.

The preliminary analysis of the literature – old and new – helps to inform the debate about the impact of, and relationship between, new technologies and people management. It suggests that these technologies are a moving target, which is likely to pose new problems and new contexts for organisations, especially as they move into newer stages of technological development.

With the new knowledge-based technologies advancing at a rapid pace, people management becomes an important mechanism for challenging the 'forces of conservatism', whether found in management or the workforce, and hence enabling organisations to more rapidly translate investments into better performance. This implies that in a knowledge-based economy, organisations certainly need to invest more in research and development, technology and capital equipment and skills, but these are not sufficient in themselves to make a step change in performance. Therefore to work, they need to be knit together in a truly people-centred business model, working as a system to learn and improve the offering to customers.

In Chapter 3, we attempted to explain how the business models of organisations exert an array of competing pressures on HR functions, which create ambiguities and tensions in what it delivers, how it delivers, how effectively it delivers and to whom it delivers (Martin, Reddington, & Alexander, 2008).

To deliver HR strategy, organisations typically respond to the competing pressures with a mix of re-organisation of the HR function itself and new ICT approaches. The re-organisation of the HR function involves new HR service delivery approaches models, often based on a tri-partite model of shared services, centres of excellence and strategic or business partnering along the lines recommended by Ulrich and Brockbank (2005) with *outsourcing* and, in some cases, *off-shoring* of key services, especially shared service centres (see Chapter 8 for a more comprehensive explanation of these alternatives). The introduction of ICT, often in combination with new HR delivery models can then rationalise or transform HR's internal operations (Reddington, Williamson, & Withers, 2005).

It should be emphasised at the outset that these organisational, process re-engineering and ICT solutions are interdependent. Without progressively sophisticated ICT, new HR delivery models would not be as effective: indeed it is the increased reach and richness of technology-enabled information and organisational learning that have facilitated simultaneous centralisation and delegation of decision-making in HR, cited by academics, observers and practitioners as the single most important claimed distinctive capability of new HR delivery models. One of the logical consequences of these developments is the potential 'virtualisation' or, at least, significant 'leaning' of HR which results from simultaneously reducing the numbers of specialists required to deliver HR services internally while improving the quality of these same services and developing new HR business models.

The introduction of technology, therefore, offers the potential to transform HR's role. It promises to do this by:

- increasing the HR function's influence as consultants focused on the needs of managers and employees;
- enabling new flexible and responsive methods of delivering HR services, such as self-service via the Internet or Intranet;
- expanding HR's reach as the experts of the organisation's people processes and the developers of value propositions for different employee groups.

Thus, the 'bandwagon' of technology-enabled HR solutions seems to be growing at a rapid rate driven by some evidence of promising practices and positive evaluations of technology and outsourcing projects. However, this bandwagon in support of technology adoption is also fuelled by some 'dangerous half-truths' or 'total nonsense' (Pfeffer & Sutton, 2006).

To address the various challenges set out earlier, we now offer advice, supported by theoretical frameworks which are based on recent research and case study evidence. Our collective experience gained through working with a variety of companies to transform their HR functions through the design and implementation of technology shows that technology investments are frequently under-used and do not release the full benefit to the organisations concerned.

Technology choices and architectures

It is important to understand that any HR technology implementation requires a 'core' HR system. This is often referred to as the Human Resource Information System (HRIS) and is the primary transaction processor, editor, record keeper and functional application system that lies at the heart of all computerised HR work.

Figure 4.2 highlights the factors that influence the overall technical solution, which will comprise the core HR system and other functional elements. How each factor impacts on the various elements of the solution depends on the importance that an organisation applies to each. However, all these factors will have a significant impact on the overall cost (see Chapter 6). For example, legacy systems could be used 'as is', 'upgraded' or even 'replaced' by newer, more advanced systems. These decisions depend on factors such as the capabilities of the legacy systems, the nature and scope of existing contracts with third parties, and the expected functionality required in the long term. Each choice will have a cost and benefit which has to be weighed against the desired outcomes. Further elaboration of these considerations can be found in Table 4.1.

Essentially, there are four options:

- *Option 1* – HR core system with integral modules that can be 'switched on and configured' to create a 'single' HRIS.
- *Option 2* – HR core system with modules bought, configured and hosted separately (still on internal networks) and connected back to the core system.
- *Option 3* – HR core system with modules hosted and managed externally and connected back over the Web to a core system – also known as application service provision (ASP).
- *Option 4* – Outsource of all systems including the core HRIS.

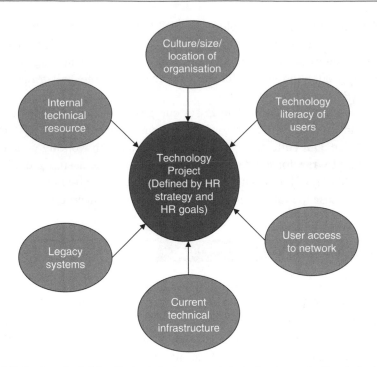

Figure 4.2 Factors that drive the technical approach to technology adoption (adapted from Field, 2008).

The benefits and disadvantages of these options are outlined in Table 4.1. The decision about which option to take is most important because it affects the complexity of the build, architecture and cost.

Note: it is possible to have a combination of options 2 and 3 where some modules are outsourced and others are hosted internally.

Planning the elements of the technology project

The timing and sequencing of the different elements of the technology project are key to successful implementation. To realise an integrated solution, it is important to understand the technical and data requirements for each stage of the development. Figure 4.3 highlights the underlying system architectural requirements within the context of a four-stage technology-enabled project road map. This sequencing of the development is equally important when considering the change and training requirements at the implementation stage of the project, for example, by introducing discreet levels of functionality into the organisation so as not to swamp the potential users with complex

Table 4.1 Benefits and disadvantages of each of the main technical options (Field, 2008)

	Benefits	*Disadvantages*
Option 1: company system	■ Predefined process ■ Low complexity of data connectivity between modules ■ Relatively low level of internal IT support for implementation and operation required ■ Ease of upgrades and regression testing over system ■ Similar user functionality across all modules ■ Ease of reporting across modules ■ Organisation management and workflow engines span all modules	■ High cost of implementation and licensing ■ Rigid process structure leads to system driving process re-engineering rather than system adopting best fit for organisation ■ Difficult to configure beyond basic look and feel ■ Some modules are not necessarily 'best in breed' ■ Can require constant external operational support if there are low levels of IT skills within the organisation
Option 2: separate internal modules and core HRIS	■ Allows 'best in breed' purchase of each HR module ■ Potentially allows for a 'cheaper' option than the core HR system ■ Ability to negotiate better prices for each module ■ Allows system configuration for each module to match company processes better	■ Complex connectivity issues between individual modules and core system ■ Higher levels of support required for each separate system ■ User interfaces have to be configured more heavily to ensure consistency in the user portal ■ Workflow and organisation management and reporting become more complex to manage across different systems
Option 3: internal core HRIS with ASP modules	■ Managed services require less internal HR and IT skills ■ Particularly good for complex HR modules that require a high degree of skill, for example, benefits management and pensions management ■ Less operational risk to HR. No requirements to keep on top of change, legislation and good practice ■ Reduced complexity in HR cost planning	■ More expensive for a managed service ■ HR has reduced control over delivery of services to the business ■ Complex connectivity issues with core internal HR systems ■ Increased configuration to ensure standard user interface ■ Increased complexity in managing workflow organisation management and reporting ■ Increased complexity in security across the net, encryption and single sign on for users

(Continued)

Table 4.1 Benefits and disadvantages of each of the main technical options (Field, 2008) — cont'd

	Benefits	Disadvantages
Option 4: outsource all systems	■ Reduces risk to the business ■ Reduces requirements for HR admin and IT skills in the business ■ Reduces complexity of cost planning and resourcing in HR ■ Fully managed and supported service ■ Contracts and SLAs to support required service levels ■ Economies of scale and ability to share good practice across all outsource clients	■ High cost ■ Could involve significant, detailed process mapping and long implementation time table if existing operational arrangements within client organisation differ markedly from those of the outsource provider ■ Complex contracts and services levels have to be agreed in advance ■ Rigid service delivery to the organisation ■ Ad hoc and unforeseen services create high cost for the business ■ Lack of control over service provision ■ Loss of administration skills internally

operations. Also, developing the technology-enabled HR service brand and not over-stretching HR's ability to support the systems will all become important criteria in the overall success of the project. These factors are discussed in more detail in Chapters 10 and 11 where we discuss the implications for the capabilities of the HR function and the wider organisation during technology implementation.

The timing and sequencing of the different elements allows the HR function to articulate its vision for the project and forms the basis of a more detailed business case with which to persuade the organisation to make the investment decisions – see Chapter 6 for more information about development of the business case.

At this stage, it becomes apparent which modules must be delivered first to create a 'foundation layer' for the services that follow. Importantly, it provides a graphical illustration of investment that must be made 'upfront' with the prospect of minimal benefit until other modules are added or integrated to provide progressively more advanced services.

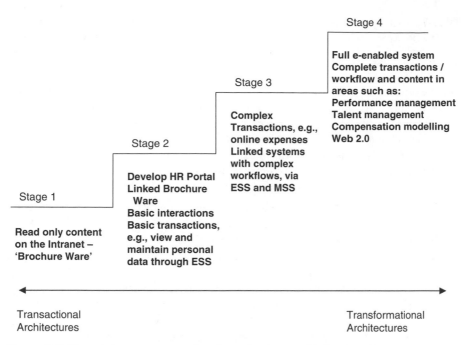

Figure 4.3 Phased steps to a comprehensive technology-enabled HR service.

To assist practitioners with these considerations, Table 4.2 sets out some key factors that shape the technology architecture and associated outcomes and refers to other chapters that deal more comprehensively with each factor.

Another way to inform the decision-making process is to undertake an analysis of where your organisation is positioned on the 'maturity scale' set out in Figure 4.4. Key questions to ask are:

- Where are we on this model?
- Where do you want to be?
- What needs to change in HR and the business and what do you need the technology to do?

The answers to these questions inform the 'starting' and envisioned 'future' positions, which in turn influence the approach to technology adoption. More relevant information about evaluating the current and envisioned future state of HR's delivery model can also be found in Chapter 3.

Table 4.2 Factors influencing the adoption, implementation and integration of technology-enabled HR (based on Martin et al., 2008; Reddington et al., 2005; Shrivastava & Shaw, 2004)

Factors	*Examples*	*Chapter*
(1) The drivers behind the implementation of the technology-enabled HR service model	■ Transactional – that is, cost reduction, automation, productivity? Improving the delivery of HR services and improving managers' ability to make informed decisions ■ Transformational – that is, about creating cultural or organisation change, releasing HR professionals to focus on value-added activities	Chapters 5, 6 & 8
(2) The approach to needs/requirements analysis	■ Time made available and the quality and experience of the analysts ■ The extent and variety of stakeholders included (e.g., senior management, IT professionals, employee reps., etc.) ■ The nature of analysis: whether the analysis was process-driven (i.e., buy technology that fits the existing processes) or technology-driven (i.e., adapt the processes to fit the chosen technology)	Chapters 7 & 11
(3) The approach adopted to technology and suppliers	■ The number of vendors approached and how they were assessed ■ Building technology in-house versus buying technology ■ Whether a single HR system is procured or different modules from different suppliers are sourced (the 'best of breed' approach) ■ The extent to which the organisation is willing to change or adapt its processes to accommodate the technology ■ The extent to which the internal IT department itself is willing and able to work with HR or place technology-related HR requirements as a priority within its IT strategy	Chapters 4, 8, 10 & 11
(4) Expectation setting	■ The degree to which expectations were accurately set by the technology supplier(s) to HR, and by HR to the wider business	Chapter 7
(5) The approach to implementation	■ If the decision is to buy off-the-shelf technology, the extent to which it is customised (changed) versus configured ('vanilla') ■ Whether deployment is phased/incremental or 'big bang'	Chapters 4, 8 & 11

(Continued)

Table 4.2 Factors influencing the adoption, implementation and integration of technology-enabled HR (based on Martin et al., 2008; Reddington et al., 2005; Shrivastava & Shaw, 2004)—cont'd

Factors	*Examples*	*Chapter*
(6) The management of change	■ Change within the HR department(s), including job losses, job changes, re-skilling ■ The need for and provision of training to both HR people and other users, for example, managers and employees ■ The use of senior and/or local champions to promote adoption ■ Whether or not a pilot system is deployed initially	Chapters 7, 10 & 11
(7) Outcomes	■ Whether broader cultural or organisational change is attempted as part of the implementation, or left until the technology is embedded in operational practice (Transformational Outcomes) ■ Whether cost cutting is achieved and employees and managers appreciate and use new self-service tools for transactional purposes (Transactional Outcomes)	Chapters 4, 8 & 12

The emergence of Web 2.0

The previous sections of this chapter have been predominantly concerned with technology systems that support interactions with a variety of user types such as HR experts, managers and employees, and modern systems allow these interactions to be performed through Web browser software. These systems, however, mostly operate pre-defined processes, controlled by the organisation. The most recent developments in Web-based technology represent a move away from prescriptive, organisation-centred systems to collaborative Web-based applications, collectively called social media technologies or Web 2.0.

This section, which draws heavily on a CIPD report by Martin, Reddington, and Kneafsey (2009), describes the key elements of these new technologies and how they are being used to support strategic HR initiatives.

The term Web 2.0 is now freely bandied around in the popular press and has been the subject of recent articles in HR professional publications such as people management. However, the available evidence on the use of these social media technologies in Human Resource Management (HRM) and people management (e.g., Birkinshaw & Pass, 2008) suggests that HR professionals have little understanding of the nature and potential of these technologies, though they are aware

*Scale of Maturity in People Management & Using
Technology*

Employees	Line Managers
• Happy to take responsibility for their own career path, benefits, motivation, work scheduling & leaving the business • Fully automated processes – no HR intervention • Intranet is the prime source of all HR policy and instruction	• Line managers design and deliver major people management events (e.g., workforce planning, grievance, disciplinary, identification of future career path requirements, recruitment campaigns, L & D programmes, CPR and performance reviews, salary review) • Shadow HR 'roles'/few if any additional resources within the line • Intranet is the prime source of information and manager self-service is used to record and manage people transactions
• Fully proficient at using self-service – available via phone, email, Internet/Intranet • Tend to have few direct dealings with local HR/happy to ring call centre if necessary • HR issues first researched using Intranet and then via the service centre only if complex • Document management/scanning/filing handled by HR data system	• Respected, capable managers of highly engaged teams – grievance, disciplinary supported by service centre and HR for highly complex issue • High levels of people management capability driven by healthy investment • Understanding of the value of people related activities to the bottom line • Most processes supported by technology and managers using self-service support most people management activities from absence management career management to development
• Becoming proficient at using self-service options before calling HR General acceptance that their line manager is responsible for people management with regional visible HR support • Sometimes use local HR team for queries • Some automated HR processes and forms	• Task & people focused; less reliance on HR support but still not taking of people management responsibility • Deliver people management tasks as a tick list rather than embedded when/? working with full ownership. • Increasing levels of people management capability with little involvement disciplinary, appeals and grievance • Use self-service tools for absence management, approving training and performance management
• Inclination is to rely on HR to deal with all people related issues – 1:1 (face/phone) consultation whenever requested • Tend to see store HR advisor as 1st point of call for people management issues e.g., wage queries, policy advice • Mainly 1:1 (face/phone) issue handling or referrals e.g., requests to change hours, vacancy information, advice • Use basic self-service functionality – update personal information, record holiday	• Primarily task focused; heavy reliance on local HR support rather than taking on full people management responsibility • Line managers integration with the HR function in this limited role • "I'm here to manage the job, not the people" • Use basic self-service tools, such as approving leave • Almost no involvement in disciplinary/grievance

Figure 4.4 Maturity model.

of the risks of allowing employees access to social networking sites at work and of employee 'misbehaviour' on blogs and social networking.

According to experts in the field, these media have enormous potential to change the way people collaborate, communicate, organise their work and give voice to their opinions and expectations, especially when they are physically dispersed across time and space. Equally important, they help organisations communicate with and learn from a new generation of employees which have grown up with such technologies – the so-called V(irtual) Generation. Because of these features, Web 2.0 offers HR professionals an opportunity to transform its 'business model' – new ways of adding value to internal stakeholders and a more contemporary organisational architecture – to make a greater contribution to their organisations' strategic and reputational aims (Martin & Hetrick, 2006; Martin et al., 2008).

What do we mean by Web 2.0?

Although at an early stage, a family of powerful Web-based technologies are being adopted by some organisations to:

- encourage greater collaboration among employees, customers, suppliers and partners;
- give customers, business partners and employees greater opportunity for more authentic forms of 'voice' on issues that matter to them;
- help organisations, employees and potential employees learn about each other, and share their knowledge and experiences to create organisational learning.

These 'social and sociable' media technologies have come to be known as Web 2.0, following the introduction of the term in 2004 by Tim O'Reilly, a media guru. The most highly publicised of these technologies among HR professionals are blogs, social networking sites such as Facebook, MySpace and LinkedIn and virtual worlds such as Second Life.

Martin, Reddington, and Kneafsey (2009) research showed that it is perhaps even more important than normal to be clear on our use of terms and our understanding of the key features of Web 2.0, why it is different from earlier, Web-based applications and what its potential is forecast to be. So, we begin by setting out a working definition in Box 4.1 below, culled from a number of sources (readers might also wish to go to the Glossary of Terms in Appendix 1).

The important points to take away from this definition are the differences with earlier non-interactive, Web-based technologies and the people-centred, rather than organisation-centred, nature of these new technologies. To elaborate a little, experts in the field have identified five characteristics of Web 2.0 that have enormous importance for HR. These are described in Box 4.2.

Box 4.1 Web 2.0, a working definition for HR professionals

Web 2.0 is different from the earlier Web 1.0, which focused on the one-way generation and publication of online content. Web 2.0 is a 'read–write' Web providing a democratic *architecture for participation*, encouraging people to *share ideas*, promoting *discussion* and fostering a greater *sense of community*. In this sense it is a 'people-focused' Web, embracing core elements of the philosophy and practice of modern human resource and people management – conversations, interpersonal networking, personalisation, authentic voice and individualism.

Box 4.2 The characteristics of Web 2.0

Participation and collaboration
Web 2.0 is driven by increased participation and collaboration among users, most obviously apparent in social networking, social bookmarking, blogging, wikis and multimedia online gaming. Indeed, it is these so-called 'network effects' that define Web 2.0 and make it so valuable – see case illustrations later.

Openness
Web 2.0 has come about because of a spirit of openness as developers and companies increasingly provide open access to their content and applications. Good examples include the emergence of open source course material, online encyclopaedias such as Wikipedia and Web browsers such as Firefox and Google's 'Chrome'. For some writers, it is this open source element that is the most important feature of Web 2.0, differentiating it from in-company attempts to deploy social media behind their firewalls – so-called Enterprise 2.0 (see Box 4.6).

User control
Web 2.0 users control the content they create, the data captured about their Web activities, and even their identities – they can choose to be anonymous, create virtual identities or present their real selves. In the case of the latter, Gordon Brown, the British Prime Minister and Barack Obama, the newly installed President of the United States of America, have done broadcasts on YouTube which have been viewed around the world.

Decentralisation and democratisation
Web 2.0 is also a decentralised 'architecture', relying on distributed content, applications and computers rather than a centralised system controlled by managers or IT departments. While decentralisation is necessary for

wider participation, openness and positive network effects, it is also the most worrying aspect of Web 2.0 among many HR professionals because of the potentially damaging effects of brands through the organisational misbehaviour of 'ranting' bloggers (Richards, 2007) and because they are not able to control corporate messaging.

Standards

Universal standards provide the basis for Web 2.0. Common interfaces and creating and accessing content are the things that allow the decentralised system to be created. This includes technologies such as XML, Java and media streaming to MP3 players and mobile phones to help create content available to everyone, as is the case with e-learning.

Modularity

Web 2.0 is built from many components from the bottom-up rather than top-down, which gives it greater flexibility. For example, traditional pro-grammes of learning through university degrees are built top-down, with a 'programme, course and module' structure designed in that hierarchical order. However, it is equally possible and desirable to build from the bottom-up, creating highly flexible e-learning courses from standard 'chunks' of learning (so-called learning objects) to create modules and then courses, according to the individual needs of learners. In the same way, different Web 2.0 applications and mechanisms can be aggregated and re-mixed to create flexible outcomes that suit user needs. Personalised Google home pages are good illustrations of this characteristic.

How does this affect HR?

There are undoubtedly challenges and degrees of risk associated with the adop-tion, diffusion and exploitation of Web 2.0. So, despite most of the evidence on Web 2.0 diffusion showing a rapid take-up among Internet users (Madden & Jones, 2008), recent reports have noted some dissatisfaction among existing users of Web 2.0 and conventional networking tools. And from the early survey evidence, it seems that HR professionals continue to be reluctant innovators and to be more worried about employee misbehaviour, their lack of control over these technologies and the uses to which they are sometimes put (see Box 4.3).

These cases provides an important, if negative, justification for HR profession-als to understand the challenges presented by Web 2.0 and to develop realistic HR policies and programmes of education to prevent problems like this re-occurring. While problems like this continue to dominate media headlines, our core argument is that HR professionals also need to take advantage of the genuine opportunities

---

Box 4.3 Employee misbehaviour on Facebook

The BBC Web site on 31 October 2008 reported that 13 cabin crew staff had been dismissed by a UK-based airline for gross misconduct in misusing a social networking Web site.

The misconduct related to claims by passengers that staff had used a Facebook site to criticise safety standards in the airline and to use disparaging language about its passengers.

The BBC reported the following statement from a senior airline representative:

It is impossible for these cabin crew members to uphold [our] high standards of customer service ... if they hold these views... .

[There] is a time and a place for Facebook.... There is no justification for it to be used as a sounding board for staff of any company to criticise the very passengers who ultimately pay their salaries... We have numerous internal channels for our staff to feed back legitimate and appropriate issues relating to the company.

A few days after this case appeared in the press, another UK- based airline began an investigation in Facebook postings by employees who described passengers as 'smelly' and 'annoying'.

The Economist article in which this appeared said that this 'public relations disaster' occurred despite the airline having a policy that 'forbids employees posting online information about the firm without specific authorisation' (Economist, *'Losing Face'* 8 November, 2008, p. 82).

---

created by Web 2.0 to enhance collaboration, learning, employer branding and employee voice; if they fail to do so, they are likely to be left behind in a 'groundswell' which is forecast to take root among new generations of employees (Li & Bernoff, 2008; Schuen, 2008).

Leaving aside for the moment the genuine problems posed by the cases set out in Box 4.3, support for our more optimistic and strategic view comes from evidence produced by academics, consultants and application providers. The weight of this evidence is that Web 2.0 is emerging as a major force in altering how organisations function and in the business models they employ. One such example comes from John Chambers, CEO of Cisco, who recently claimed that Web 2.0 is the 'future', causing him to change the direction of his company. As he pointed out, '... We are moving our company as fast as we can to collaboration and Web 2.0 because of its potential for significant impacts on productivity and product design'. Don Tapscott and Anthony Williams (2008), authors of the best-selling book *Wikinomics* made even more extravagant claims that Web 2.0 social media are '… the biggest change in the organisation of the corporation in a century …'.

So, if HR professionals are to be judged by these prophesies and the sheer volume of current articles, books, blogs and discussion in media and technology publications, they could be forgiven for thinking they are in danger of being left behind in the race to become virtually connected to everyone and anyone in their social and work-related networks.

Having sifted through a significant body of evidence which includes apparent 'hyperventilation' from technology gurus and the more sanguine evidence from various surveys, we are drawn to two drivers, identified in the Martin, Reddington, and Kneafsey report (2009), which offer significant valueadding opportunities to organisations and to the HR function. Our confidence is premised on two related arguments. The first of these is *the generational driver*, encapsulated by Adrian Sarner – see Box 4.4. This is evidenced by various claims made for a distinctive V-generation of 'digital natives' or 'networked employees' (Madden & Jones, 2008; Prensky, 2001; Sarner, 2008), which has grown up working, learning and communicating with social media, more prosaically illustrated by the rapid growth of social and professional networking sites such as Facebook, MySpace, Bebo and Xing (*Economist*, 27 September, 2008).

The second driver is the need for organisations to *collaborate* to add value in modern economies. Collaboration is essential for knowledge creation and innovation among organisations; however, collaboration costs money, especially in large-scale, geographically distributed organisations. One of the promises of

---

Box 4.4 The V(irtual) generation

Among the most recent attempts to set out a new group of online users is one by Gartner, a leading firm of technology consultants, which coined the term, Generation-V. This term encapsulates multiple age groups which make social connections online. As Adam Sarner, one of Gartner's principal consultants writes:

Unlike previous generations, Generation Virtual (also known as Generation V) is not defined by age – or gender, social demographic or geography – but is based on demonstrated achievement, accomplishments and an increasing preference for the use of digital media channels to discover information, build knowledge and share insights. Generation V is the recognition that general behaviour, attitudes and interests are starting to blend together in an online environment.

(Sarner, 2008)

Web 2.0, however, it that it can substantially reduce the costs of such collaboration, especially when these forms of virtual communication become standard in organisations. These so-called *economic networking effects* not only rely on cost reduction claims but also on better quality decision-making and knowledge creation. The 'wisdom of crowds' thesis, which underpins applications such as Wikipedia (Tapscott & Williams, 2008), states that collective intelligence by groups often results in better decision-making than could be made by any individual.

So, by using these social media technologies with customers, business partners and employees, they help organisations substantially improve their business performance in five important ways (Li & Bernoff, 2008):

- by more effective 'talking' to employees and other stakeholders;
- by more effective 'listening' to employees and other stakeholders by giving them more effective forms of voice;
- by 'energising' key employees and stakeholders to spread key messages;
- by 'helping' employees and stakeholders to support each other;
- by 'engaging' employees and other stakeholders as collaborators in value adding activities.

Getting the most from Web 2.0

These points are elaborated in the model shown in Figure 4.5, which links Web-based user inputs with HR outputs.

Some Web-based user inputs will be familiar to readers, such as online text, images, video and instant messaging; other inputs may be less familiar, for example, podcasting, video, online voting, social book-marking, tagging and subscribing to RSS feeds (see Appendix 1 for a full Glossary of Terms). The important point to understand about these user inputs is that collectively they create value for organisations through network effects. Network effects describe how early adopter individuals and organisations rely on other users to build up online 'traffic' and turn them into a standard form of communications. The more people are drawn into using these technologies, or are compelled to use them, the more viable the system becomes for all. This is how email and the Internet developed into a standard system of communicating among two-thirds of the total American workforce that have been labelled 'networked workers' (Madden & Jones, 2008). It is also what is behind the thinking in some of the case study examples shown in Box 4.5, which seek to build on the power of online discussion forums, wikis and blogs.

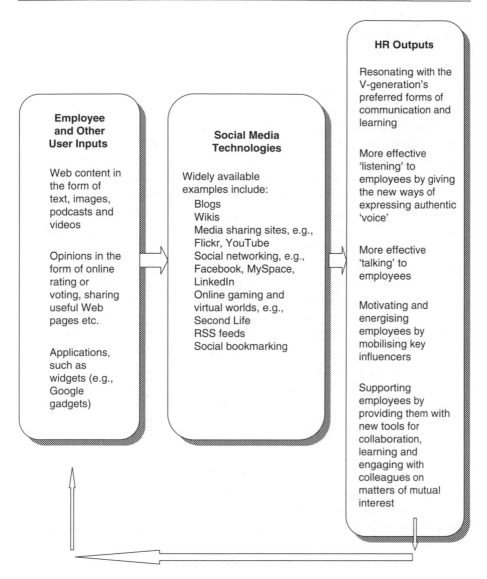

Figure 4.5 The Web 2.0 system and people management (Martin, Reddington, & Kneafsey, 2009).

The impact of engagement and control on HR policy

The cases and discussion so far highlight two related sets of questions for the future of Web 2.0 social media technologies concerning *engagement* and *control*. Engagement by employees with these technologies and control over their use are

---

Box 4.5 Case illustration: Discussions forums, online chat and message boards in three UK government departments

UK government departments have a number of Web 2.0 and Enterprise 2.0 applications, the most widely used of which are chat and message boards, online conversations, management blogs and podcasts. Given their relative success, other departments are planning to use these technologies. Three good examples are the Department of Communities and Local Government's Director General and Ministers Monthly Staff Webchat, the Department for Work and Pensions Online 'Staffroom' Forum and Display Space and HR Revenue and Customs (HRMC) Suggestions Scheme and Online Discussion Forum.

The Department of Communities and Local Government's Director General and Ministers Monthly Staff Webchat is chaired by a Director General. Staff can ask questions directly to Board Executive members in an asynchronous chatroom. The online chatroom has a formal agenda, and transcripts and action points are fed back to Board members. The Webchat is marketed internally through various channels of communication and usually attracts over a hundred discussion postings a month.

The Department for Work and Pensions Online 'Staffroom' Forum and Display Space is slightly different in providing feedback to senior civil servants on a range of issues in which employees can 'Have a Say' on any issue they wish to bring up. It also has a 'Hall of Fame' for celebrating success in the Department.

HMRC's online discussion forum is an important channel for employee contributions to the corporate suggestion scheme, 'Angels and Demons'. Suggestions are being sought on how to improve work organisation and processes, and on culture change, along the lines of the BBC's Dragon's Den. According to the Web site, more than 12,000 HRMC employees had registered by October 2007, 8000 had contributed to online discussions on specific themes and 500 innovative business ideas had been logged. The online discussion forum had not required propriety software but had been developed using open source tools.

---

critical issues for organisations, which will determine the speed of adoption of social media technologies and the value they create in enhancing communications, employee voice and collaboration.

Technologies and engagement
By engagement we mean whether employees:

- *Identify* with a particular technology (does it help employees express their personal and organisational identity?);

- *Internalise* the technology's built in values (does the technology embrace the values they hold?);
- Feel a degree of *psychological ownership* over it (to what extent is the technology 'theirs'?).

So, with respect to Web 2.0 social media technologies, the key question we have to answer is:

- How easy is it for employees to engage with a particular technology (or combination of technologies) to collaborate, share knowledge, communicate and express an authentic voice in their organisations?

By easy, we mean not just ease of use and access, but also these aspects of identification, internalisation and psychological ownership. Indeed, identification with technological change by employees has been shown to be one of the key factors in its acceptance. V-generation employees, as we have discussed and illustrated in some of the cases, are much more likely to identify and engage with these social media technologies than other generations.

Technologies and control
Control is another widely discussed and contested idea in management and employee relations, especially in relation to the distribution of power between employers and employees. In the context of Web 2.0, control seems to be expressed as the answer to an important question:

- How easy or difficult is it for organisations to cope with the power employees enjoy from easy access to decentralised and open forms of communication and collaboration?

Four scenarios of communication and collaboration in organisations

Bringing these two ideas together – engagement and control – we can envisage four scenarios that describe modes of communications and collaboration in organisations (see Figure 4.6). These scenarios might help us think about the challenges which HR faces and possible strategic choices over communications and collaboration.

Scenario 1 – Traditional face-to-face communications and collaboration
This scenario represents the typical, existing face-to-face system of collaboration and communications, the latter of which is typically conducted through the formal

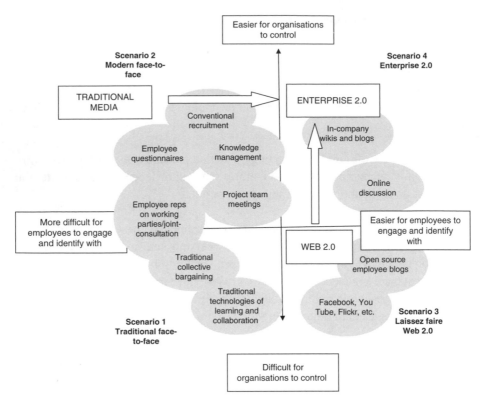

Figure 4.6 Scenarios for Web 2.0 (adapted from Martin, Reddington, and Kneafsey, 2009).

collective bargaining system. Union representation provides the main medium for employee voice, and knowledge management and collaboration continues to be viewed as a 'contested terrain'. Knowledge and skills are seen as issues to be bargained over since knowledge is power and not something to be readily given up by employees, who seek to capitalise on their often tacit knowledge and skills.

In this scenario, the challenges to both managers and union representatives are that:

■ New generations of employees begin to use Web 2.0 technologies as a means of expressing their own, often negative, voice, as unions are seen by an increasing number of workers to be less relevant in expressing their interests (Willman, Bryson, & Gomez, 2006), and
■ Employees do not engage in much formal or informal collaboration and knowledge sharing with one another since their tacit knowledge and skills are their main source of power to enhance their careers at work.

Managers view employees' use of these technologies in a largely negative light, often attempting to proscribe their use at work, or else ignore them as a means of finding out what employees think and want to discuss.

Such a scenario may be typical of many organisations in traditional manufacturing and service industries, and in certain parts of the public sector with high levels of manual and basic administrative grades.

Scenario 2 – Modern face-to-face communications and collaboration

This represents a modern, consultative system in which communications take place through working parties, joint consultation and regular attempts to tap into employee voice through attitude surveys and the like. Collaboration and knowledge management are typically based on face-to-face team working, project teams and traditional employer-centred knowledge management systems, which attempt to capture knowledge, store it and disseminate it in a top-down fashion.

Such a scenario is probably typical of most organisations in the UK in many of the knowledge-intensive and creative sectors of the economy, including 'professional bureaucracies' such as healthcare, education and professional services, in defence, the prison and police services, and in industries such as financial services (Birkinshaw & Pass, 2008). It is often the case that data protection in these organisations is a sensitive issue, as are concerns over protecting brand identities and the desire to exercise a duty of care.

HR's role in this scenario remains focused on policing, rather than encouraging, the innovative and experimental use of Web 2.0 social media. Thus, it is no surprise that Richards (2007) found the majority of his blogger respondents coming from these sectors.

Scenario 3 – Laissez faire Web 2.0

This represents a relatively anarchic situation in which some organisations may find themselves in the not-too-distant future. Organisations may begin in scenarios 1 and 2 but come to resemble a more decentralised system of informal bottom-up communications and knowledge sharing as more and more people, especially members of the V-generation, become employees. Much communication becomes virtual, in which knowledge sharing and employees voice their concerns *outside of formal employer-controlled media*, especially in locations geographically and functionally distant from head office among remote workers (CIPD, 2008) and among higher educated and paid networked workers (Li & Bernoff, 2008; Madden & Jones, 2008; Sarner, 2008).

It is this scenario that seems to worry a number of HR professionals in those organisations represented by scenario 2. As we have noted it is the lack of organisational control over Web 2.0 and the ease with which employees can engage with various applications which causes many organisations and HR professionals to worry about these social media, with some organisations placing outright bans on their use at work or substantially restricting the ability of employees to access them at work. Time-wasting at work and the potential for organisational misbehaviour by disenchanted employees has dominated the HR agenda over Web 2.0.

The Government Communications Network's (2007) review of social media is particularly relevant here. Drawing on questionnaires to government departments and interviews with specialists in the field, it found a number of barriers to a more widespread adoption of Web 2.0 among various departments, even though as we have noted, government ministers have begun using these techniques to communicate and engage users in dialogue. These barriers were:

- a lack of understanding and expertise among civil servants, especially higher level ones;
- following on from this lack of understanding, a lack of high level support for wider use;
- lack of data and uncertainties about the costs and benefits of various media;
- the risk of public exposure, damage to customer and employer brands and general loss of control;
- the limitations placed on Web 2.0 by IT departments that did not want to damage the integrity of their systems.

Underlying such concerns were the very features that make Web 2.0 attractive to organisations and employees. These were its openness, the ease of use for employees and users to engage with Web 2.0 technologies (spontaneity, conversational and democratic), its new rules of engagement and the different behaviours required by civil servants and its newness and experimental nature.

Scenario 4: Enterprise 2.0
Enterprise 2.0 is recognition that social media technologies are fast becoming a fact of life among the higher educated and paid networked workers and new generations of employees – see Box 4.6. This scenario is one where organisations are driven by the V-generation or by the need to secure the collaboration and voice of increasingly geographically dispersed workers, often in other countries, working from home or who rarely visit head office locations. Organisations attempt to regain control by developing the technologies of Web 2.0 inside of their firewalls and encouraging or facilitating employees to make use of these technologies.

Box 4.6 Defining enterprise 2.0

McAfee defines Enterprise 2.0 'as the use of emergent social software platforms *within* companies and their partners or customers'. He uses the term 'social software' to describe how 'people meet, connect and collaborate through computer mediated communication and form online communities'. Platforms are defined as 'digital environments in which contributions and interactions are widely visible and persistent over time'. Emergent means the software is freeform, in the sense that people can choose to use it or not, is egalitarian and can accept different forms of data. He rules out (a) open Web-based platforms, such as Wikipedia, YouTube, Flickr and MySpace, because they are widely available to individuals, (b) corporate Internets because they are not emergent and (c) traditional email and SMS because they are not persistent.

According to Andrew McAfee from Harvard University, who is usually credited with coining the term 'Enterprise 2.0' in 2006, this route is probably the most promising way forward for organisations seeking the benefits of Web 2.0 but wishing to minimise the downside.

Figure 4.6 shows a potential trend away from the very open Web 2.0 towards Enterprise 2.0. The diagram also hints at the potential trend away from traditional media used to give employees a say in decisions, such as face-to-face representation in consultative committees, focus groups and online surveys towards Enterprise 2.0 read–write media. Just as the Web has allowed the so-called power law to operate in firms such as Amazon by allowing them to cater to the long tail of profitable customers comprising only 20% of its total sales (Anderson, 2008), so organisations can now reach out to the long tail employees. These comprise previously marginalised or disengaged groups who were not economically possible to reach or who rejected the normal consultation process through union representation and organisationally determined (and often meaningless to them) questionnaires.

Summary

In this chapter, we have set out the main factors involved in deciding on the most appropriate technology applications and architectures, and their potential impacts on the user experience. These factors, elaborated by models which are intended to allow the HR practitioner to make informed decisions, draw on a variety of research, case illustrations and the collective experience of the authors.

Importantly, we have drawn attention to the latest developments in Web 2.0 and used a systems framework to help HR professionals think about how Web-based content in the form of text, images, videos, opinions and other applications can be transferred through new Web 2.0 social media technologies into important HR outputs. Perhaps most importantly, we have shown how these technologies can and might be used to add strategic value to organisations. If HR professionals are able to develop their thinking along these lines, they are likely to help their organisations achieve their strategic goals through more effective people management in a contemporary way that will connect with new and older generations of employees alike.

5

Envisioning the New World of HR

Irrespective of whether you are just starting out on your HR transformation journey or are initiating a new phase of HR transformation, it is essential that you spend time working out what a transformed HR function looks like. We call this 'envisioning' and in this section, we address a number of key questions critical to this phase:

- What is our starting point/current reality?
- What is the business imperative to do things differently?
- What would 'different' and 'better' look like?
- How do we start the process of moving from where we are to where we want to be?
- Is there sufficient organisational energy to deliver the proposed change?

Key themes

- Whilst there are many common factors influencing the direction of HR, there is no 'one size fits all' solution to HR transformation; that is, each organisation will need to develop its own unique vision for HR transformation.
- HR transformation needs to be aligned with the goals and needs of your business and the vision for HR needs to be one that encapsulates technology, process, structure, culture and capability.
- A shared vision for HR needs to be developed quickly amongst critical stakeholders.
- A range of envisioning tools can be employed effectively to stimulate discussion and conversation, and ensure the speedy development of a shared vision.
- Envisioning is the springboard to build an effective and robust business case for HR transformation.

Context

Five strategic opportunities

The proposition that HR needs to focus less effort on transactional/administrative tasks and become more strategic in focus is not new. Over the past couple of decades, much has been written about transition to a strategic HR function (and, to be fair, in some organisations a great deal of progress has been made). Yet in too many organisations, the identity of HR remains firmly in the transactional/operational/advisory zones – comfort zones that often suit HR practitioners and line managers alike.

Yet the opportunities for a more strategic and value-adding contribution from HR are probably greater now than ever before.

Here are five opportunities that explain why:

1. *Many critical organisational issues are about people/organisational development*

Some examples of these issues are as follows:

- developing organisational cultures that will adapt quickly to external change;
- performing despite economic downturn;
- raising organisational, team and individual performance year on year;
- improving customer service;
- delivering operational efficiency;
- securing business benefits from capital investment/strategic projects;
- attracting and retaining prized staff;
- reducing overall personnel-related costs/managing workforce costs more effectively;
- improving management 'bench strength';
- dealing with increased globalisation/scale/complexity in organisational life;
- increasing organisational flexibility;
- driving higher levels of employee engagement;
- improving the people management capability of line managers;
- encouraging and capturing innovations.

The list could go on. Hopefully, you will recognise the relevance of many of these issues to your business. The door of opportunity stands open for HR to be an active contributor in each of these areas.

2. Advances in technology

There are now many major players that offer enterprise-wide technology solutions. This has enabled the HR function to make its business case for technological investment alongside other support functions, such as finance and procurement. Although there is still likely to be debate in each organisation concerning the extent to which Web-based HR will be adopted, there is now sufficient critical mass to give organisations genuine cost-effective alternatives. Additionally, the core HR Information System (HRIS) backbone offers in-built 'leading practices' in HR processes and the ability to apply solutions globally. HR not only has the opportunity to utilise technology, but now the means to make a convincing business case for this investment as well.

The creation of Web 2.0 and social networking (addressed in Chapter 4) provides HR with even greater opportunity to use technology to engage with people more effectively.

3. New organisational alternatives

In the past two decades, the management consultancy sector has grown rapidly, offering genuine alternatives to the in-house HR function. At the strategic end, consultants are increasingly stepping into the HR strategy and organisational development spaces where the in-house HR function either has insufficient capacity, or lacks sufficient capability to make a full contribution. At the operational level, there are now many sourcing alternatives in the areas of recruitment, training and development, reward, HR policy development, etc. At the transactional/advisory end, there are now serious players offering HR outsourcing, not just from a technological infrastructure/transactional perspective, but increasingly pitching at a full service handling back office recruitment, learning and HR decision support/advisory functions. The different approaches to sourcing HR services are covered in more detail in Chapter 8.

4. Research linking developed people management practices and performance

There is now a growing body of research linking progressive people management practices to superior organisational performance. Research undertaken by Becker and Huselid (1998), for example, found that firms with the greatest intensity of HR practices that reinforce performance had the highest market value per employee. Their thesis is that improving HR practices can impact enterprise market value quite significantly. Their conclusions are hugely challenging for organisational leaders: that the best firms achieve strategic and operational excellence in HR.

5. Clearer functional view on what a strategic contribution means

The emergence of the HR management movement and the contributions made by academics (and especially Dave Ulrich) have helped HR find a greater sense of identity. The HR roles set out by Ulrich (see Figure 5.1) have found resonance within the HR community, and have become the starting point in exploring what business partnership means for HR.

Dave Ulrich: HR Champions (1997)

Figure 5.1 HR roles.

Whilst the above developments suggest that there are some clear opportunities for HR, the challenge for each HR function is to define for itself a way of making a value-adding contribution that is right for its organisation. In a nutshell, there are no 'off-the-shelf' solutions, and unless HR is clear about the way it can add value, the threat is that the business will turn elsewhere for that contribution and the in-house HR function will become insignificant and impotent.

It is also true that aspiring to be in the top two quadrants of the Ulrich model without delivering effectively in the transactional/administrative area will not give HR business partners sufficient credibility with line managers for there to be a serious conversation around strategy and change. HR functions must still deliver on the basics if value is to be added and credibility gained.

Seven irresistible forces

While thinking about the new world of HR, it is important to recognise that there are a number of external forces that will shape the future.

In the first edition of this book we listed, what we termed, seven irresistible forces. In 2005 this was a bold claim. Some years on now we have revisited this list to test whether they have, in fact, been irresistible. We can confidently state that they are as relevant now as they were then. In many ways these forces have been strengthened. So, as part of the envisioning process, these forces form an important part of the context within which the new world of HR is envisioned.

These seven irresistible forces are as follows:

1. Technology will play an increasing role in the way HR delivers value.
2. HR processes will continue to standardise around technology.
3. The HR administrative backbone will increasingly be delivered by centres of expertise (whether in-house shared service centres or outsourced service centres).
4. The shape of the in-house HR function will continue to change and HR staffing levels will continue to decline, with the headcount profile shifting from administrative/advisory roles to higher value decision support/specialist/strategic roles.
5. The delivery of HR management in organisations will continue to disperse across each of the delivery channels.
6. The need for HR professionals to bring a unique value proposition to internal clients will increase as line managers become more confident with self-service tools and seize opportunities for genuine choice in sourcing professional HR support.
7. The outsourcing and/or offshoring of transactional, administrative, advisory and specialist HR activity will continue to increase.

Using the above material

As this book has a strong bias towards application, we suggest that you engage people with these irresistible forces to stimulate debate within and outside the HR function. In this way you will be able to:

- set the context for discussion about the future HR function in your organisation, maybe through a discussion paper or presentation;
- present the consequences for your organisation of ignoring them/staying as you are;
- engender a common framework for thinking prior to an envisioning workshop, where you can follow up a discussion paper or presentation with one-to-one discussion and debate with key stakeholders;
- confirm the parameters for discussion at any envisioning workshop, so that key stakeholders are starting from the same contextual base.

You are unlikely to reach consensus on how to respond to these forces at the first attempt. For example, one organisation we have worked with found it hard to come to terms with the fact that the HR function would need to shrink significantly, losing most of its in-house training and recruitment teams. It took 9 months and some poor business results before the HR leadership team really confronted the headcount issue.

Our intention is that this section will give you material to engage people, start conversations and help shift thinking about how HR can and should contribute to the business.

Going about envisioning

Perhaps the most important thing we have learnt about this phase is the importance of actually doing it! Many HR functions embark on the HR transformation journey without really engaging business colleagues and the broader HR team in shaping a vision for HR.

Here are the three principles that should underpin your approach to envisioning:

1. *Adopt a systems mindset.* HR transformation is about change, and change cannot be effected in isolation; for example, technology-driven change inevitably impacts structure, processes, capability and culture. Change in HR impacts and is also impacted by change in the wider organisational system. A systems mindset is explained in greater detail in Chapter 1.
2. *See HR transformation as a process that needs to be worked through step by step.* This process is not predetermined. There is no schematic approach that sets out in advance every step: a form of 'painting by numbers' approach to change. The broad stages of change are clear and are reflected in the change cycle (see Figure 1.3) but the detailed steps needed to effect change will be unique to each organisation. When we refer to 'transformation', we refer to a significant shift in changing the way HR contributes in organisations. But this will not be an end-game – a final destination. There will always be another step beyond.
3. *Focus on the unique circumstances of each business.* Learn from the experiences of others, yes, but do not become obsessed with 'me too' external benchmarking. Too many organisations blindly follow supposed 'best practice'. What is right for one organisation is not always right for another. The most powerful results will be driven through a strong identification with the unique circumstances faced by your organisation at this point in its history. This highlights the need for an approach to change that is highly contingent, with the focus being on shaping HR in ways that will help the business now at this point in time.

So how do you combine the trends described previously with the practical steps set out above to ensure purposeful envisioning? In our change tool kit, we have a number of tools and frameworks which organisations have found helpful in creating an environment for effective envisioning. Four of the tools are now presented in the section below: Envisioning Tools.

Envisioning tools

Much of what we have presented, so far, in this chapter sets the context for envisioning the kind of HR function you need to become. In this section, we want to turn our attention to practical tools and frameworks that will help you work with individuals and groups to envision the new world of HR. If you have not already read Chapter 1, we suggest that you familiarise yourself with the content, as the chapter sets out our underlying approach to transformation and change. Understanding our approach to organisational transformation and change will help you to understand better how to use these tools and frameworks.

In this section, we aim to achieve two objectives:

1. to explain the tools and frameworks themselves;
2. to explain the use of these tools and frameworks in practice.

As with all the tools and frameworks presented, they are there to be tailored. We are great believers in using language and presentational formats that are right for your organisation. With this in mind, we will also show how we have tailored some of the tools and frameworks to respond to different circumstances.

Why use tools and frameworks? We would like to offer you four good reasons:

1. *They are solution neutral*: The tools are there to help you understand where you are now and what you need to become, given your particular business context.
2. *They enable conversations to happen*: Each of the tools and frameworks is designed for use with individuals or groups to stimulate debate and discussion. We believe that developing a shared vision amongst critical stakeholders is the necessary goal of the envisioning process, and this means that there must be a dialogue.
3. *They accelerate the envisioning process*: Having a common tool or framework actually accelerates envisioning because there is a common point of reference. In this way we accept that debate is, to an extent, contained. However, having a common framework within which points of agreement and disagreement can be identified and, where necessary, worked through is hugely beneficial.
4. *They work*: We have used these tools and frameworks in many different environments, and they are extremely powerful in helping groups to engender speed into the envisioning process and create purposeful outcomes.

The four tools and frameworks we present in this section include:

- business drivers,
- organisational levers,
- HR value pyramid,
- visualisation.

Business drivers framework

When should we use this framework?
HR transformation and the envisioned new world of HR must be hard wired to the critical business issues. Our starting point is, therefore, to consider critical business drivers. Why? Without this thought, it will be impossible to:

- make a coherent case for HR transformation;
- identify HR's priorities;
- link the new world of HR to the realities that face your business.

Put another way, identifying your critical business drivers helps the HR function to answer:

- What is wrong with the way things are?
- Where is the focus for the future?
- How will the proposed way of delivering HR help the business to perform more effectively?

What does the framework look like?
Figure 5.2 represents visually the business drivers framework. This framework has been used in the private, public and not-for-profit sectors; hence its broad applicability has been proven.

The framework considers the three main drivers of organisational effectiveness: revenue growth, cost efficiency and brand identity. Each of the drivers is then considered from three perspectives (you may wish to tailor these, but we have found that they tend to work well).

Figure 5.2 Business drivers framework.

For *revenue growth* we consider:

- *Customers*, who are the recipients of the products/services provided by the organisation (who are they, how do we retain them, how do we attract new customers in existing markets and will we need to move into new markets and attract new types of customer?),
- *Geography* (where do we operate now and where are we likely to operate in the future?),
- *Innovation around new products and services* (what do we need to do differently to compete effectively or satisfy customer requirements?).

For *cost efficiency* we consider:

- *Productivity* (how productive are we compared to relevant benchmarks? Where do we need to raise performance and productivity? How well do we measure and reward productivity?),
- *Work process efficiency/effectiveness* (how well do key processes work? What are the areas of strength, areas for improvement and future needs?)
- *Capital project returns* (What are our key capital projects? What is our track record in delivering anticipated benefits?).

For *brand identity* we consider:

- *Brand values* (what do we stand for as an organisation and how well do we demonstrate our values internally and externally?),
- *Image and reputation* (what is our current image and reputation, what might undermine it and how can we protect/enhance it?),
- *Consistency* (to what extent are we acting in a consistent way with our customers and employees and how might future challenges help/hinder our ability to deliver consistently?).

How do I use this framework?

This framework is best used in a workshop setting. We have also found it useful in one-to-one discussions to get individual perspectives and stimulate debate, but ultimately there needs to be a sharing of perspectives on critical business drivers, and this is best achieved when people are in the same room and are able to engage with one another.

To have a meaningful discussion about business drivers requires some preparation. You should draw on current knowledge of the business to populate these areas in advance of the workshop or, if you are confident that workshop attendees will have sufficient knowledge, you can populate these areas at the workshop. Where we have doubted that sufficient information will surface at a workshop, we have used a combination of pre-briefing people, inviting a senior internal client to talk about key organisational issues, and allocating pre-work so that participants can research an area.

Once there is a shared understanding of the critical business drivers, this then enables the key HR leaders and stakeholders to address three questions:

1. What are the critical people priorities that emerge from these business drivers?
2. How well are we currently equipped as an HR function to deliver these priorities?
3. How does the HR function need to change to help the business succeed?

Discussion of these areas will move you a long way towards defining the HR transformation agenda and priorities.

Organisational levers model

When should we use this model?
This model is extremely useful when applied to any significant change effort. It is applicable not only to HR transformation, but also to any organisational change. It is a foundation model and helps to explain the impact of change within the context of the broader organisational system.

Its value is to engage key stakeholders in a dialogue concerning 'current HR' and 'the future world of HR'. It is also a powerful way of capturing and presenting the outputs from discussions.

The organisational levers model has already been introduced in Chapter 1. If you have not already familiarised yourself with the model, we strongly suggest that you do so now. We do not intend to repeat the description of the model in this section, but will instead focus in greater detail on its application.

You should note that you might come across other versions of this model with slightly different labels. This does not matter. Taking a systems perspective is the important part of this model, and we would encourage you to use whatever terminology fits best with your business.

How do I use the model?
The examples below show how the organisational levers model has been used in a variety of ways (and alongside the other envisioning tools) to develop a 'whole system' approach to HR transformation and build a coalition of support around the new world of HR.

The two main ways in which the organisational levers model has been used to support envisioning are as follows:

1. *As a pre-prepared input to an envisioning workshop*
Prior to an envisioning workshop, a series of one-to-one discussions is held with key stakeholders to discuss 'current HR' and 'the future world of HR'.

Interviews are structured using the organisational levers model (although some of the other envisioning tools presented above can also be used if appropriate). The outcome of the interviews is the preparation of a 'straw man' set of descriptors relating to 'current HR' and 'the future world of HR', linked to each of the six organisational levers, namely external forces, performance outcomes, technology, processes, structure and people/culture. These descriptors are displayed in a workshop environment, typically on large sheets of paper; one sheet for each of the six levers.

Participants (hopefully most, if not all, of the key stakeholders you would have interviewed) are asked to challenge any descriptor that they either disagree with or are unclear about. They are also given an opportunity to add anything they believe to be missing from the straw man descriptors.

In debriefing the exercise, focus first on those descriptors where there are most challenges and work through them to seek clarification and gain agreement on the wording. Then follow a similar process with the suggested additions.

The outcome should be agreement of a set of 'as is – current HR' and 'to be – future world of HR' descriptors. This approach is particularly helpful when working with larger groups, and we have found that in a workshop setting agreement is typically reached within a matter of hours.

2. *Realtime in a workshop*

For smaller groups, you can achieve the above-mentioned realtime.

Ensure that your room has plenty of wall space and is divided into two areas: 'current HR' and 'future world of HR'. Display the headings of the six organisational levers under each.

Give participants two colours of Post-it™ notes. Ask participants to write (on one colour) descriptors that best describe 'current HR' for each of the six organisational levers. Repeat the process for 'future world of HR' using the other colour. Cluster descriptors where you can. Then work through each of the Post-it™ notes to ensure that there is agreement on any new descriptors that have been written (or agree a change to the existing wording).

What might an output look like?
In Appendix 1 we have shown an example from a client exercise. As you will see, the descriptors are succinct, but specific enough to enable the next steps in the process to take place – gap analysis and project planning. Just to illustrate that envisioning is not a one-off exercise, the example shown in the appendix was actually produced 1 year after the initial envisioning exercise as part of HR transformation review and taking stock.

HR value pyramid model

When should we use this model?
The aim of this tool is two-fold:

1. to engage stakeholders in thinking about where HR adds value;
2. to engage stakeholders in identifying where the balance of effort/resource in HR is now and where it should be in the future.

The model should clearly be used at the outset of the transformation journey in considering how the function adds value now and where it needs to focus in the future. We have also found the model useful in undertaking quick, high-level reviews during transformation.

What does the model look like?
Figure 5.3 represents visually the HR value pyramid. The HR value pyramid has four main propositions:

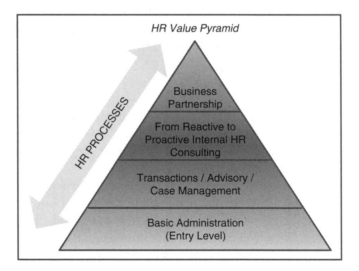

Figure 5.3 HR value pyramid.

1. There is a hierarchy of roles within HR.
2. The basic administration and transactional roles will be most impacted by e-HR (including employee and manager self service) and new organisational arrangements, such as shared service centres and outsourcing.
3. The HR processes impact roles within and outside of the HR function and an important task during the HR transformation process is to determine those activities which can be embedded within Web-based HR, who is accountable for data entry and where knowledge-based roles need to make their unique contributions.

104

4. The HR professionals will acquire widely sought after expertise when they become business partners, proactively engaging with critical organisational issues as part of the management team.

How do I use the model?

This model is helpful in stimulating initial debate with key stakeholders about what they want from HR. On a one-to-one basis, it is a simple model for stakeholders to engage quickly and can take discussions into a number of interesting areas, such as what service internal clients need from the administrative/transactional side of HR and the nature of business partnership.

In a workshop format, the model has been particularly helpful around sourcing and resourcing discussions; that is, what percentage of HR activity, resource or cost currently sits across the four areas and what percentages should exist in the new world of HR. We have found that this exercise stimulates quality discussion around themes such as cost versus headcount (e.g., you may have fewer people in the administrative/transactional space, but there are clearly costs associated with Web-based HR) and cost versus type of resource (e.g., you may have a lower overall headcount in HR, but the people you will have may cost more).

At the early stages of the transformation process there is considerable value in encouraging key stakeholders to play with these ideas and their implications. This helps people to work through for themselves what the new world of HR might look and feel like.

Visualisation

When should we use this tool?

The other frameworks and models presented in this section are generally aimed at the left side of the brain, which is the logical/rational part of our thinking processes. However, envisioning also needs to tap into the right side of the brain, which is the creative/playful side of our thinking processes. One of the best ways we have found to stimulate a more creative approach to current-state analysis and future-state envisioning is through visualisation.

We could say that you should use this tool with a degree of fear and trepidation – some of your stakeholders may need some encouragement to participate in a visualisation exercise. Do persevere, though, as visualisation usually produces some important and rich insights into the current and future worlds of HR. It is also valuable in engaging at the emotional level around HR.

What do the tools look like and how do I use them?

There are quite a few ways to engage people in visualisation, but the two types of visualisation exercise that we have found to work well are as follows:

1. *Free-form drawing*

A simple exercise to set up, participants are asked to draw a picture (or a number of images) describing (a) the current world of HR and (b) how the future world of HR would look if it was contributing most effectively to the organisation. Remember the focus is on content and not the quality of artwork!

In debriefing the exercise, ask each person in turn to present and talk about their 'current HR' picture. Typically there will be a richness of analogy and metaphor. Take time to explore the language and imagery, and do not assume that everyone understands things the same way. Often, metaphors will trigger interesting discussions, either around the original metaphor or through some tangential connections. Record some of the themes that emerge. Then repeat the exercise with the 'future world of HR' picture.

2. *Picture cards/collage*

If you are not feeling bold enough to run a free-form drawing exercise, then an alternative approach is to give people images to work with. This is inevitably a more structured approach and less spontaneous. Using the same questions as above, you can introduce images either through giving people some magazines with a good variety of pictures in them and asking them to produce two collages addressing each question, or by giving people a variety of picture stills (we have found that you will need between 50 and 60 pictures) and asking them to identify ones that speak to both questions. As an additional twist to this second exercise, the organisational levers model can be used to give structure to the visual presentation; for example, to pull out pictures that best describe current or future technology, HR people and culture, etc.

The debriefing of the exercise will be the same as for the free-form drawing exercise.

We have used these exercises when working with larger groups (more than 50 people) and with smaller groups (around 12 people).

Case studies

Organisation 1

Context

A large global telecoms company was in the process of integrating a number of its businesses into a global Internet technology business. An HR transformation programme director had been appointed, but there was not yet a proper HR transformation programme team in place or a coherent HR transformation vision.

Process
In the run-up to the launch of the new global business, a series of one-to-one interviews were held with the newly appointed HR leadership team and senior business stakeholders. The organisational levers model was the primary tool used during these interviews, which enabled us to prepare a straw man view of both the 'as is – current HR' and 'to be – future world of HR'.

A workshop was held with all the HR leadership team present, and in working through the process outlined above an HR vision was agreed around the organisational levers model. Additionally, an HR transformation governance structure was agreed to based on this work, which ensured that the HR transformation programme team was not solely focused on Web-based HR, but embraced transformation of the whole function.

Organisation 2

Context
A major energy utility had recently made a major acquisition in the United States, and the group-wide HR leadership team met to think through the implications for the HR function and to identify critical issues that needed to be worked on collaboratively.

Process
The team worked through a process using three of the tools set out above:

1. identification of critical business issues and the HR implications of these;
2. use of the visualisation technique mentioned earlier to encourage dialogue about the HR function;
3. use of the organisational levers model to develop a more structured view of the current and envisioned HR world.

This workshop identified a number of critical HR issues that needed to be progressed and also set the framework for the HR transformation agenda that has been implemented.

Fast tracking the envisioning process

When we discuss with clients the need for envisioning at the start of the HR transformation process, any resistance usually falls into one or other of these two reactions:

The first, and most worrying, reaction is that there is no need to envision because 'we all know what HR transformation is all about'. This is worrying because in our experience we have yet to be involved in any major change programme

(HR or other business changes) where there is a common and absolute agreement on the nature, purpose and vision of the change. It may be because individuals know what they want to achieve. But unless the organisation has a highly autocratic culture, there will be a need to engage with others to build a shared vision and a coalition of support for change. If you find yourself identifying with this reaction, we would encourage you to let go and to recognise that there is nothing to be gained in pressing on regardless – even if it does mean that the vision for HR transformation becomes a shared rather than a single vision and involves some degree of compromise.

The second reaction is that the envisioning process will take too long and end up in navel gazing, without much action. This is always possible, of course, but with good process and facilitation skills momentum can be gathered. Momentum building is extremely important from the outset, as envisioning can lead to prevarication. We have yet to be involved in an HR transformation programme that has dwelt too long on envisioning.

Indeed, using the tools set out above, the envisioning process does not need to be either a confrontational or long drawn out affair. A good example is how a large global business was able to reach a high level of agreement on 'current HR' and the 'new, envisioned world of HR' within a 4-week period. (Figure 5.4 illustrates

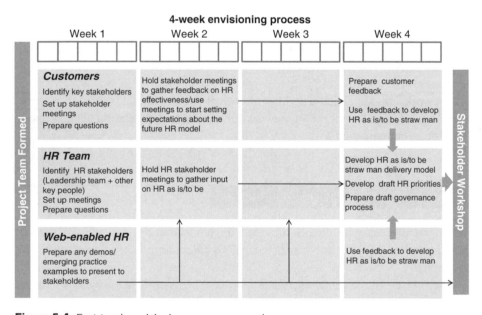

Figure 5.4 Fast track envisioning process: example.

this 'fast track' process.) This is not to say that no further work on the HR trans-formation vision was needed. But, applying the 80/20 rule, there can be sufficient definition to take the next practical steps in the transformation process; that is, to build a case for change.

We believe that if there is good cooperation from key stakeholders, a robust HR transformation vision can be reached within a few weeks, culminating in a stakeholder workshop.

Who should be involved?

This will vary between organisations, but as a minimum we recommend that this initial phase includes:

- the senior HR leadership team,
- key people within the broader HR community,
- critical business stakeholders,
- a sample of line managers.

Most of these key stakeholders can be involved initially through one-to-one inter-views (drawing on the tools presented in this chapter), although in some instances we have used a short HR effectiveness questionnaire with line managers.

The outputs from these interviews will be used to prepare a number of inputs to the envisioning workshop (which should include the senior HR leadership team and, if possible, some senior business stakeholders). These inputs may include:

- a summary of customer feedback,
- a straw man 'as is – current HR' and 'to be – new world HR',
- draft HR priorities,
- draft governance process to oversee HR transformation.

Once there is broad agreement around the 'as is – current HR' and the 'to be – future world of HR', there are three final outputs that flow from this early envisioning work:

1. *Gap analysis*

The 'gap' is the distance that needs to be travelled between where you are now and where you want to be.

Having established your 'as is' and 'to be', you are then able to do a reality check to test whether this gap can be closed within the time and resource con-straints of your organisation. Part of this assessment will be your gut feeling about the readiness of the organisation to make the proposed change happen. Other tools that will support this assessment will be the change equation and a more structured look at business impact and change readiness.

The change equation is detailed in Chapter 1, and is not repeated in this chapter. The way in which you can use the change equation with your key stakeholders is as follows:

- Ask your stakeholders to rate the elements of the change equation from their point of view (and how they might judge the reactions of key decision makers outside of HR). These reactions could be: dissatisfaction with the way we currently do HR; level of clarity about what HR should be; level of clarity about the next practical steps and their will to make the change happen (high, medium and low will be sufficient).
- Then ask your stakeholders to identify the main costs, for example, financial, resources, time, etc.
- Then ask them to weigh both sides – in their judgement, where is the balance? Is the new world of HR that they have envisioned likely to get the support needed to make it happen?

If the assessment is favourable, then moving to the next task is straightforward. If the assessment is not favourable, then you need to look at:

- increasing levels of dissatisfaction with the way things are, that is, helping people to realise that the way HR is delivered into the organisation is not fit for purpose. Your 'as is' and 'to be' analysis will be a powerful aid in achieving this;
- how you might modify your 'to be' vision so that the gap that needs to be closed is smaller;
- how you might reduce the perceived costs of making the change – either through reworking what has to be done or by looking for greater organisational benefits.

2. *Building the case for change*

Having completed your gap analysis, you are in a position to put together a compelling case for change. Building a business case is explored in greater detail in Chapter 6. There is also another 'case for change' that needs to be made to a range of stakeholder groups. This case for change will be less detailed, broader brush. But it will incorporate all the key outputs that have been developed as part of the envisioning process. Figure 5.5 summarises its key elements.

3. *Planning and keeping on track*

The final outputs from this envisioning process are the next practical steps; in other words, the pathway from where we are today to where we want to be.

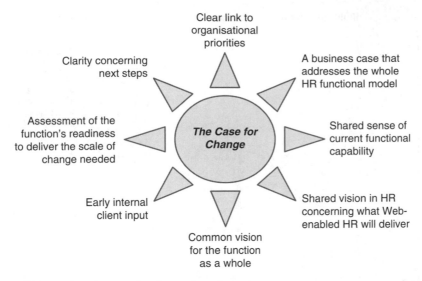

Figure 5.5 Building the case for change: key elements.

The programme/project management aspects of this are explored in greater depth in Chapter 9. At this stage, the senior HR leadership group will be in a position to do the following things:

- Set up a process of 90-day milestones to show how the function will bridge the gap from current to future HR.
- Commission (or establish and commission) the HR transformation programme team to initiate work streams/projects around these key 90-day deliverables.
- Establish appropriate levels of reporting between 90-day milestones.

Figure 5.6 shows an example of a high-level 90-day milestone developed by one organisation we have worked with. What this high-level plan does is to give the senior HR leadership group a sense of focus and enable issues around pacing and resource allocation to be aired in an environment where all have committed to delivery timescales.

The final word in this section is that the most powerful way of ensuring senior HR leadership group focus on HR transformation is to organise 90-day workshops around milestones so that there is a strong focus on reviewing deliverables, assessing progress and mobilising for the next 90 days. This reflects strongly the process consulting approach outlined in Chapter 1 and integrates with the need for strong programme management.

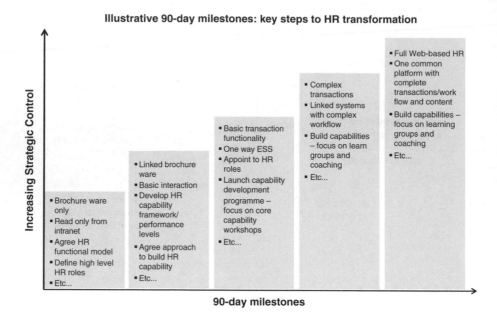

Figure 5.6 Ninety-day milestones: key steps to HR transformation.

Summary

The whole point of HR transformation is to make it happen; in other words, to implement it effectively and reap the benefits. The whole point of envisioning the new world of HR is to give focus and momentum to HR transformation.

Drawing on tried and tested organisational development tools, we have been able to help organisations develop and mobilise quickly around a vision for the new world of HR. In this chapter, we have set out the main drivers that suggest that HR needs to be done differently and some practical tools that help the process of envisioning.

What we have also shown is that envisioning is not an 'airy fairy' activity. HR vision needs to be hard wired into business reality and goals, and the point of envisioning is to get to grips with reality, enabling HR to make its most effective contribution within the constraints of the business and making changes happen purposefully and quickly.

6

The Business Rationale

This chapter deals with the construction of the business case. Chapter 5 talked about how to develop the future vision for HR, this chapter will focus upon taking the vision and building a strong rationale for change, being clear about the costs of implementing the vision and the financial and non-financial benefits it will deliver. To some in the organisation, the business case is the item that will persuade them that the changes that are being proposed are credible.

Key themes

- A business case serves three purposes. It makes the case in terms of the return on investment for the transformation; it is a tool by which HR can engage with business colleagues in shaping the future services and defining the value that HR delivers and it is the key control document by which the transformation and change programme guides action throughout the life of the programme.
- The proposed model for delivering HR services in the future is an important input into the business case because it will identify what will need to change in terms of organisation and technology. The service delivery model will be used in the business case to identify the costs and benefits of the transformation. The most significant areas of cost will be people and technology.
- The business case needs to address the hard return on investment (ROI) elements of the proposed transformation. Spending time and effort on both the costs and benefits of this will pay dividends both in terms of the credibility that this gives to your case and the baseline that this gives you for measuring possible benefit delivery.
- The business case is fundamental to making the case for change and as such is not just about numbers but also about understanding and articulating what

the nature of the change is and why it is important to the organisation. This needs to be made real for your business colleagues. Developing a roadmap of what will change, and when, provides a very tangible way of describing this change in practical terms.

Context

A compelling business case is an essential step on the way to achieving the vision of transforming the way the HR function works and to realising anticipated benefits.

This chapter examines how to make that case by defining benefits and costs – the so-called 'hard' elements of the case – and engaging the various stakeholder groups so that they understand, buy-in and commit to the business case – the so-called 'soft' elements. Soft elements are equally important because they involve stakeholders in making the case and establishing the case for transformation.

What is the purpose of the business case?

The purpose of the business case is four-fold:

1. the next step in the design process, where assumptions and high-level designs are turned into a delivery model, which describes how HR service will be delivered in the future;
2. the next step in the change process, where the business case and designs are communicated across the organisation to describe how transformation and change within HR will benefit the organisation as a whole and the delivery of overall goals and objectives;
3. the mechanism to obtain approval and funding to proceed with the transformation of the HR service;
4. the reference point for guiding all decisions and activities during implementation.

The business case is a document which needs to be more than numbers and a hard financial analysis. It needs to be a document which can articulate to colleagues from across the business the future vision for HR. Whilst you and your colleagues have developed and fully understand the vision, others need to understand it as well.

This means that business case needs to be able to explain the following:

- what the HR department will look like in the future, its size and structure;
- how the HR service will operate, that is, how staff will access support from HR; what information on HR policies and guidance will be available; how much will be provided through self service, a service centre and face-to-face advice; what strategic support will be provided to senior management;
- how the HR service will be measured and assessed to ensure that is delivering benefit and value.

A good method of communicating the vision for HR is to develop an operating model (Chapter 8 presents approaches to developing operating delivery models). This model will demonstrate how HR will be organised in the future and how it will deliver HR services. An example of a generic operating model is presented in Figure 6.1. This model is important because it is not only a communication tool but also identifies for the business case what changes need to be made within people, technology and processes. These changes can then be used to assess the financial impact of the transformation and its potential benefits. When presenting this model it will also be important to identify whether any services will be outsourced to another company, or whether services will remain within your company but moved to another team (such as a shared service centre) and/or country.

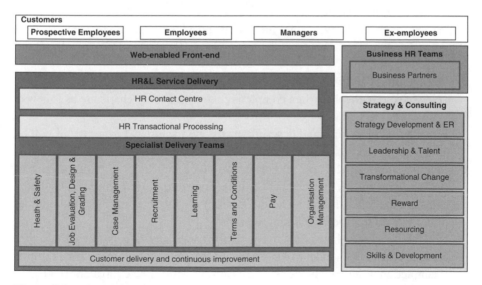

Figure 6.1 Example of HR operating model.

This information in the business case can then be communicated to your colleagues across the organisation. This process of communication helps to identify the advocates of change, those who are ambivalent and those who oppose the proposed transformation. Identifying the members of these different camps, and taking appropriate action at an early stage will significantly increase the likelihood of success. How to address these groups is explained in Chapter 7, where the steps in moving from commitment to resistance are explained in more detail.

In addition to its role in the change process, the business case will also become a document around which future programme management decisions should be based. The business case should be used as a reference point all the way through the programme, not just as a tool to get permission to start. For example, when the going gets tough it can be used to galvanise stakeholder support by reminding them of the commitments they have made.

Often it is prudent to develop an 'initial' business case prior to a more detailed 'full' business case. The objective of the initial business case is to obtain permission and funding to do more detailed work. As a result, every aspect does not have to be designed in extreme detail. The second, and more detailed, full business case is the document used to secure funding to do the main implementation, and to act as the reference point for all decisions and activities during the implementation, as long as any assumptions on which it is based, for example costs estimates, remain stable. Of course, not all assumptions hold true, and the business case becomes a document which is updated and refined throughout the life of the programme. This matter is also covered in Chapter 9, where programme governance issues are examined further.

An approach for developing an initial business case is to complete an 'Opportunity Chart', for each of the areas where HR transformation will deliver benefits.

An example of an 'Opportunity Chart' is provided in Figure 6.2.

Key issues to remember when completing the opportunity charts are as follows:

1. Provide short headings and descriptions of opportunities, further detail will be added in the full business case.
2. Identify some benchmarks and/or performance indicators to baseline current performance and set improvement targets. For example, in Figure 6.2, key measures are the ratio of training administration staff to total staff and the number of days taken to process training requests.
3. Use the difference between current performance and targets to estimate percentage of saving and identify key areas for savings. In Figure 6.2 for example, it is noted that the potential exists to save seven full time equivalent (FTE).
4. Not all benefits will be financial. Again in Figure 6.2, the time taken to process training requests will be significantly reduced.

Opportunity	**Reduce costs and time taken to manually book training courses by providing staff with an on line course booking system.**
Description of the problem	14 full time staff are employed to receive forms requesting training and these staff have to chase missing information on the forms, check that courses are available, manually input information from the forms into the training system to book the courses, manage waiting lists and notify staff when they have been booked onto a course.
Indicators used to measure the problem	• Number of working days to process training forms • Ratio of training administration staff to total staff
Current level	• 5–7 working days to process training forms • 14 training administration FTE supporting 4500 staff – ratio of 1:321. Target benchmark is 1:600
Target level	• 1 working day to input approved training request into self service and to get confirmation of booking or notification that staff member is on waiting list • 7 FTE to manage technology courses on self service and monitor waiting lists. Ratio 1:642
Financial saving	• 7 FTE
Non-financial benefit	• Eliminate administration and time lag when booking training courses
Costs	• Configuration of training administration system • Development of on line courses and guidance documents for all staff on how to use self service to book training courses • Development of courses to train HR staff to use and manage new self-service functionality

Figure 6.2 Opportunity chart.

5. Identify key costs such as configuration, training and communications. These can be estimated by contacting relevant software providers or by estimating the time that the IT team would need to configure and test a new self service function and the time that would be needed to produce training and guidance materials.

When a chart has been completed for each opportunity, they can be aggregated to produce the initial business case.

Case study

A local Authority was undergoing significant and radical change in the way that it provided services for its customers. The nature of this change meant that the Authority had to think much more radically than it used to, as it positioned itself to become an innovative, integrated and customer-focused authority. The HR community was identified as having a key role to play in supporting, driving and sustaining this change agenda.

The challenge for the HR community was to undertake a fundamental review of the HR service and ensure that it was capable of supporting the Authority with its transformation. This involved reviewing every aspect of HR and identifying those opportunities that would support the organisational transformation agenda, improve the performance of the service and reduce costs. In order to identify these opportunities they performed feasibility study which was divided into four stages:

- *Stage 1 – Baseline performance and costs.* This involved:
  - Identifying the total number of HR, payroll, health and safety and learning and development staff.
  - Identifying the cost of providing the HR service. This included salary costs, on costs, accommodation costs, IT costs and procurement spending.
  - Producing an inventory of HR processes and activities, assessing their performance against a range of benchmarks.
  - Identifying the number of staff supporting these processes and their indicative costs.
  - Undertaking a survey across the Council to test views on performance and quality of HR service.
- *Stage 2 – Identify opportunities.* This involved completing opportunity charts for areas where benchmarking, feedback from surveys and consultation with HR staff had identified the potential for service improvements and cost reduction.
- *Stage 3 – Prioritise opportunities.* A workshop was convened with senior HR staff and representatives from all Authority departments to identify those opportunities which would support the Authority's objectives for the organisational transformation programme, improve the quality and performance of HR services and reduce costs. Three key opportunities were identified:
  - the creation of a new HR model;
  - better buying (within recruitment and training);
  - implementation of Web-enabled HR systems and the automation and streamlining of processes.
- *Stage 4 – Produce initial business case.* The costs and benefits of each of the selected opportunities were aggregated into an initial business case which summarised the value of the HR transformation programme both in terms of

financial savings and its contribution to the Authority's overall transformation programme. This initial business case, which estimated annual savings of between £1 and 1.5 million, was approved by the Authority leadership team who were able to quickly and easily understand key opportunities and benefits. The initial business case was then used to develop a detailed business case and to initiate the HR transformation programme.

What are the key steps in producing a business case?

The previous discussion highlights the purpose of the business case as being:

- the next step in the design process;
- the next step in the change process;
- the mechanism for obtaining funding and approval;
- a reference point for decisions during implementation;

The development of the business case clearly needs to address each of these elements and may be developed in the following four steps:

1. Define target benefits and associated costs. This first step involves detailing the value that the transformation programme will deliver to the business and specifying how a transformed HR service will enable the organisation to deliver its corporate strategy and goals.
2. Conduct cost–benefit and risk analysis. This step takes the financial costs of the proposed operating model and demonstrates how it will deliver financial efficiency savings and business benefits. This provides the case for obtaining funding and approval to proceed.
3. Produce transformation roadmap. This step delivers an overview of all of the activities that are required to deliver the transformation and specifies when activities need to be delivered and how they are linked, thereby providing the reference point for implementation decisions.
4. Gain buy-in and ownership. This step focuses on communicating the transformational change to the business and involving stakeholders from across the organisation. This involves taking differing perspectives from frontline delivery staff, finance staff, IT staff, etc. and gaining their buy-in and support for change. Change within HR services often comes as a shock and is automatically resisted. Working early on with the business to explain what will change and the benefits this change will deliver is key to overcoming resistance.

Case study

The HR leadership team of a major UK government department wanted to seek ways of reducing resources engaged in routine administrative tasks, and to concentrate resources on supporting departmental managers in delivering government targets.

Therefore the objective of the business case development phase was to provide:

- the identification and detailed financial analysis of the benefits in relation to the HR process areas;
- the integration of the related people programme initiatives into the implementation plan setting out the linkages with the business case;
- HR organisation structure proposals and benefits integration with the business case.

The department was able to produce a three-tier business case that included:

- *Executive summary* – setting out the key factors for executive decision-making regarding this programme;
- *Main body* – defining the specific costs, benefits and risks associated with the project in the context of the proposed delivery approach;
- *Appendices* – providing the detail behind the body of the report, including detailed cost analysis, benefit calculations and assumptions.

Following approval of the business case, the programme team used it as the key control document throughout the implementation.

We now consider each step in producing this case in more detail.

Define benefits and associated costs

A key element in establishing the value of HR is to demonstrate how a transformed HR service will better enable the organisation to deliver its overall goals and objectives. It is, therefore, important that the benefits of HR transformation are clearly linked to the corporate and HR strategic objectives. The process for establishing this link is an iterative one, working from the whole to the part. The process starts with the strategic objectives for the organisation and involves:

1. taking the strategic objectives for the organisation as a whole and identifying the customer requirements for the HR service;
2. identifying how the HR transformation objectives will address customer requirements;
3. identifying the benefits that will be delivered by each of the HR transformation objectives.

The above approach will provide a clear flow from strategic objectives to transformation objectives and benefits and demonstrate how the transformation programme will support the organisation's overall strategy and goals.

An example of how to link HR transformation objectives and benefits to the organisation's overall strategic benefits are provided in the case study below.

Case study

An international services company needed to clearly demonstrate how its HR transformation programme would support the company with the delivery of its corporate strategy. The HR transformation programme began by taking each of the strategic objectives and defining the requirements for the HR service, as illustrated in Figure 6.3.

The transformation programme then identified how the programme's objectives would meet the strategic objectives and customer requirements, as demonstrated in Figure 6.4.

Finally the transformation programme linked the benefits of HR transformation to provide a clear flow from strategic objectives to benefits, demonstrating how HR transformation would support not just HR but the entire organisation (Figure 6.5).

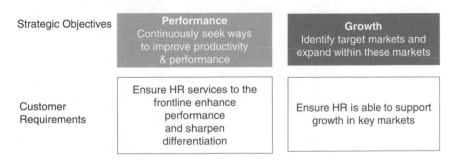

Figure 6.3 Defining customer requirements.

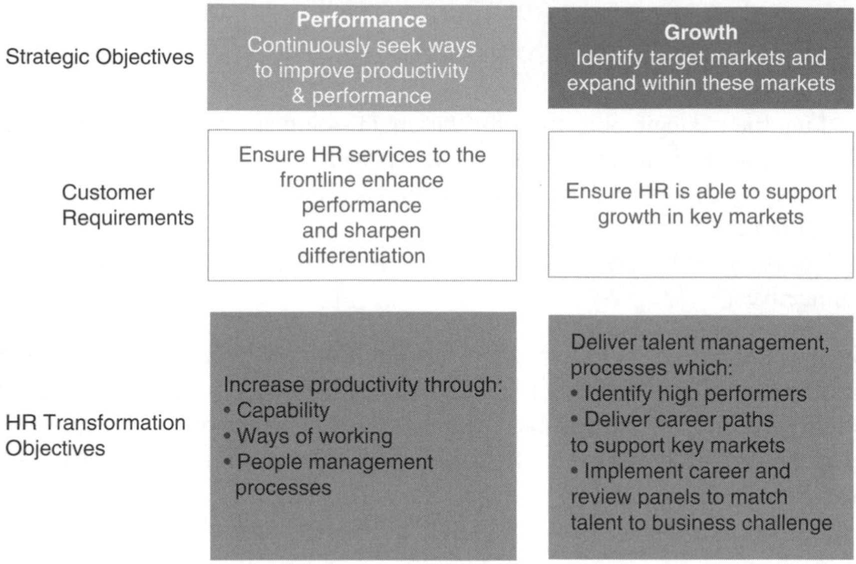

Strategic Objectives	**Performance** Continuously seek ways to improve productivity & performance	**Growth** Identify target markets and expand within these markets
Customer Requirements	Ensure HR services to the frontline enhance performance and sharpen differentiation	Ensure HR is able to support growth in key markets
HR Transformation Objectives	Increase productivity through: • Capability • Ways of working • People management processes	Deliver talent management, processes which: • Identify high performers • Deliver career paths to support key markets • Implement career and review panels to match talent to business challenge

Figure 6.4 Aligning customer requirements with transformation objectives.

Strategic Objectives	**Performance** Continuously seek ways to improve productivity & performance	**Growth** Identify target markets and expand within these markets
Customer Requirements	Ensure HR services to the frontline enhance performance and sharpen differentiation	Ensure HR is able to support growth in key markets
HR Transformation Objectives	Increase productivity through: • Capability • Ways of working • People management processes	Deliver talent management, processes which: • Identify high performers • Deliver career paths to support key markets • Implement career and review panels to match talent to business challenge
HR Transformation Benefits	• Increase frontline productivity • Efficiencies and financial savings delivered in key people management processes such as recruitment, learning & development and sickness absence	• High performing, talented staff in key markets • Clear career paths to develop talent in key growth areas

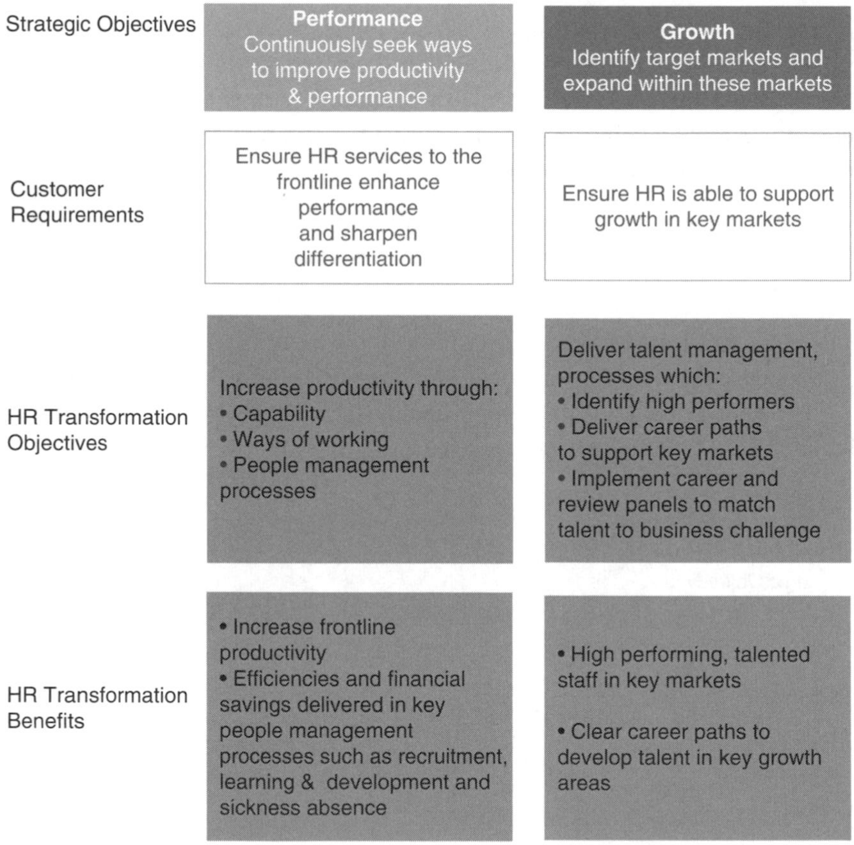

Figure 6.5 Aligning benefits.

When defining benefits it is also important to attach measures and targets to ensure that these benefits can be tracked and realised. An example of measures and targets for benefits could be a reduction in the HR budget of 30% or a change in the ratio of HR staff to employee base from 1:70 to 1:150. The key in setting measures and targets is to make them challenging enough so that it is not possible to achieve them without significant change (otherwise why would you embark on the HR transformation?) whilst ensuring that they are realistic enough to be achieved, as this will be a measure of the success of the transformation. To assist in setting measures and targets it is often help-ful to compare yourself to leading practice found elsewhere. Benchmarking where you sit in comparison to other organisations will give you an indica-tion of what would be realistic targets for your transformation programme. However, the risks with using benchmarks is that you may have to dig very deep into another organisation to find whether you are comparing like with like. So we advocate using benchmarks as a guide only, and spending enough time collecting your own baseline data so that you know where you are now and can then set targets in relation to that baseline. Once the targets are set, the next stage is to break them down to determine the detailed benefits that will collectively contribute to meeting the overall target. An approach to turning benefits into detailed measures and targets is presented in detail in Chapter 12.

Before considering what those benefits are in detail it is worth spending some time defining what we mean by a benefit, particularly the difference between tangible and intangible benefits.

Tangible benefits

Tangible benefits can be measured and attributed to the transformation pro-gramme, and crucially to particular budget holders. Therefore, as well as iden-tifying the benefit, it is important to determine the recipient or recipients of that benefit and ensure that they buy-in to it, as they need to be accountable for the delivery of that benefit.

For example, if we consider online recruitment, who will be the beneficiary of reduced agency fees: the HR function or a business unit? The answer depends on how costs are allocated in the organisation but, whichever it is, a tangible ben-efit will accrue to the budget holder(s) for those costs. The following table shows examples of tangible benefits for a selection of HR services' constituent processes and potential beneficiaries.

HR service	Constituent process	Tangible benefit	Beneficiary
Resource management	Recruitment and selection	Reduced agency fees	Business unit heads
People development and performance management	Learning and development	Reduction in external training costs	Vice President, L&D
Retention and reward	Reward strategy and reward levels	Manual reward data processing eliminated	Compensation and Benefits Manager

Intangible benefits

Intangible benefits can often be estimated but not attributed to particular budget holders. They would not normally be included in the cost–benefit analysis, as accountability for the delivery of that benefit is diffused across the organisation, making it extremely difficult to attribute the achievement of a benefit to a particular change that the HR transformation programme has made.

Again, if we consider a move to on line recruitment, there should be a reduction in the time from a vacancy arising to when a new recruit arrives, starts their induction process, and subsequently contributes to the business. In this case, it is harder to pin down to whom this benefit accrues. The following table shows examples of intangible benefits for the same selection of HR services' constituent processes. However, whilst beneficiaries are identified, it is at the business function rather than budget holder level.

HR service	Constituent process	Intangible benefit	Beneficiary
Resource management	Recruitment and selection	Reduced time from vacancy to hire	All business units and functions
People development and performance management	Training and development	Improved match of skills to roles	All business units and functions
Retention and reward	Reward strategy and reward levels	Improved retention	All business units and functions

Whilst intangible benefits are not included in the cost–benefit calculation, beware of thinking that they are not as important as tangible ones. Intangible benefits that contribute to the development of improved public services for example, are often strategically significant. Therefore, it can also be useful to further distinguish intangible benefits in terms of their strategic importance. In the case of transforming the HR function, these are often the benefits associated with how the HR function will add value to the products and services that the company delivers to its customers. Often the benefits sought in this area are delivered through the business partner role, and it is here that measurement of these benefits usually takes place. However, this area of benefit is one that does not lend itself directly to quantitative measurement, and comparative and qualitative data are often used here.

Having considered the changes that each process will undergo and determined what the benefits are, whether each benefit is tangible or intangible and who the beneficiaries are, the next step is to determine when you expect each benefit to be delivered and what its magnitude is. The milestone plan described in Chapter 5 provides a starting point for estimating when benefits will be achieved, taking into account the fact that usually benefits are not realised immediately upon implementation, but there needs to be a period of transition.

Estimating the magnitude of benefits depends on the nature of the benefit. For example, reductions in cost may be calculated by estimating how much less effort the new way of working will involve, and multiplying that by the number of transactions made and unit cost of performing each transaction. In order to do this, it is critical to have baseline measures of process performance from which estimates can be made.

In determining and estimating benefits a number of assumptions will be made which need to be recorded. If these assumptions change through the course of the programme then that particular benefit may need to be revised. Taking the Web recruitment example, typical assumptions include:

- How much do you plan to use the Web to recruit rather than agencies?
- Will agencies perform any pre-screening?
- Will you to continue to use specialist agencies?

Once the benefits identification and estimation process is complete across all process areas, then the individual benefits should be aggregated together to determine if the targets set at the macro-level can be supported by the benefits at the detail level. Typically, this process of aggregation and benefits identification and estimation is iterative.

Finally, one of the main levers for influencing achievement of the targets is flexing the scope of HR transformation. Clearly, increasing the scope should increase benefits and decreasing the scope should reduce benefits. However, this will of course have an effect on costs.

Costs

Benefits are only part of the story in the business case. All benefits need to be balanced with costs. When identifying costs it is important to consider both one-off costs – that is, those attributable to the delivery of the HR transformation programme – and those costs that are ongoing – that is, those required to maintain the HR transformation solution. The following table provides guidance on this classification and example technology and people-related costs.

Cost	Description
One-off/transformation programme-related costs	
Capability development	Redeployment and redundancy costs
Programme resource	Internal and external labour costs on the programme team, also including wider business costs covering development-related costs such as design workshops, testing and training
Content	Development of initial self-service content
Hardware	Server and associated implementation costs
Network	Costs of capacity to deliver HR to the desktop, telecommunications-related costs for service centres
Method of access	Providing sufficiently high-specification machines and software to access HR functionality
Licences	Initial software licence costs
Ongoing/maintenance costs	
Content	Maintenance of content
Capability development	Development of skills and expertise to manage and maintain processes and systems
Support	Both IS/helpdesk support and business support
Operational	For example: software upgrades and licence maintenance costs, costs of running a service centre, outsource charges, HR staff costs, etc.

Often some of the most significant one-off costs are those surrounding the people element of the solution or the capability development costs that support the main tenet of HR transformation – that is, the move from the administrative and transactional to business partnering.

The components of the capability development costs typically include:

- *Increase in resources to support senior managers.* HR transformation will result in an increase in resources dedicated to senior management support in the form of internal consultancy and business partnering. Some of these resources may already exist within the organisation, some may require a capability development programme, and others may need to be recruited externally.

The cost implications are that whilst a smaller number of business partners may be required than the current HR generalist population, the total employment costs for this group may be as great as or greater than the current HR generalist population.

■ *Redundancy and redeployment.* The combination of a reduction in administrative and transactional resources and an increase in consultancy and business partnering resources implies a reduction in the requirement for traditional HR management and HR transaction support. Clearly, some HR managers will move to business partnering roles and some transaction focused staff may move to service centre teams, but this will not be the case for all, and provision needs to be made for the costs of redeployment or redundancy.

■ *An increase in the capability and skills of HR staff.* The implementation of new strategic roles, such as business partners and new roles in the service centre, such as helpdesk support will require HR staff to adopt new ways of working. These roles will also require new capabilities and skills, which HR staff may need to develop. It is, therefore, important to understand existing capabilities and to estimate the cost of investing in development courses and programmes to address any capability gaps.

■ *An increase in line managers' capability.* Investment in line manager capability and increasing the amount of people management undertaken by the line can be a key factor in some HR transformation exercises. The degree to which line managers have become or are becoming responsible for people management processes such as sickness absence, performance management, career development and managing disputes varies across organisations. In some organisations, there is an increasing move to develop line managers into people managers who require limited support from HR. In other organisations, this is not the case.

However, regardless of the degree of people management responsibilities transferred for line managers, it is important to clarify to line managers exactly what people management processes they are responsible for delivering. It is, therefore, important to define the role of line managers and understand the level of training and support that line managers require to successfully deliver this role. This can include:

■ training to use self service, delivered either through a classroom, interactive Web training or computer based training packages;
■ training on how to manage specific issues such as sickness absence or performance management. This can be delivered through a classroom or through on line courses where line managers are shown scenario's and asked questions relating to the scenario's and given direction on correct responses to different situations and pressures;

- management and leadership training or training on such skills as how to manage conflict and resistance;
- HR guidance training where managers are advised through short courses on the people issues that they will have to manage, given the latest policy guidance and shown where, when and how to access support.

Capability costs are, however, only part of the investment requirement. HR transformation may also require an investment in HR technology. This provides a good opportunity to engage with colleagues from the IT function at an early stage. Key questions for IT include, do you enhance what you have by upgrading or is a new system the only feasible option? Working with your IT colleagues here will assist in getting the right solution and builds buy-in with the IT community.

Technology providers will usually be pleased to demonstrate their products and this can be an excellent way to capture the imagination of colleagues. However, do make sure that the technology provider covers their implementation strategy and other non-technical areas, as the technical elements of the solution are only one part of the costs. Key technology costs include:

- *Labour.* This will involve HR, IT and business staff as well as, usually, external consultants on the core programme team. It is also important to estimate the costs of providing cover or backfill for the HR and business people seconded to the programme team which may be needed and not to overlook 'hidden' costs such as HR and line people participating in workshops, testing and training.
- *Developing content.* HR technology is of no use unless the content supports the new ways of working, for example, online learning materials or performance management tools. There will be both one-off and ongoing maintenance costs associated with content.
- *Software licences.* It is important to consider the net effect of these, which is netting them off against the costs of the systems that are being removed. This is usually done by including the removal of the other systems in the benefits calculation.
- *Hardware costs.* Look out for opportunities to share costs and economies of scale with other programmes that are in progress.
- *Method of access* in order to interact with an HR system. Clearly, it is critical that employees have access to it. Costs will potentially need to cover laptops, desktops and other mobile devices, kiosks and possibly even home PCs, depending on the access solution defined.
- *Ongoing support and maintenance* of the solution. There will also be contractual costs if there are any outsourced arrangements here as well as the costs of system upgrades and other maintenance going forward.

Case study

The HR leadership team of a UK government department wanted to seek ways of reducing resources engaged in routine administrative tasks, and to concentrate resources on supporting departmental managers in delivering government targets.

The solution was to implement new HR technologies and a new model and governance structure for the HR service. The key changes within the HR service included:

- re-engineering HR processes to use HR technology and self-service tools to improve the performance of administrative processes and reduce costs;
- the development of an HR shared service centre;
- the creation of expert policy teams and centres of excellence to harness scarce HR expertise and provide strategic HR advice to the Board;
- the establishment of a small group of strategic business partners to work with leadership teams within the department's different business units.

The business case costed each of the above changes. The key costs that were analysed are listed in Figure 6.6.

Conduct cost–benefit and risk analysis

By this stage, you should have a financial estimate of benefits and costs, and when these will be incurred. These are now brought together in a cost–benefit analysis. The cost–benefit analysis will determine the value for money of the transformation programme.

Staff Costs	Infrastructure Costs	IT Costs	Consultancy Support
• Salary costs. • Pension. • Allowances, for example, car allowance. • Time devoted to processes by grade of HR and business staff and cost of this time. • Redundancy costs. • Redeployment costs. • Development costs for staff taking on new roles such as business partners.	• Accommodation – cost per square metre, including lighting, heating and furniture and fittings. • Telephone costs, including mobile phones. • Office supplies. • Procurement costs – agency staff, training and recruitment.	• Desktops. • Laptops. • Printers. • Peripherals. • Servers. • Network. • Software licences. • Software installation & development. • Software integration. • Build costs. • Implementation. • Helpdesk. • Document Management. • Desktop maintenance. • Software licence maintenance. • Other software maintenance. • Network maintenance. • Server maintenance.	• IT consultancy. • Training. • Change management. • Programme management.

Figure 6.6 Cost categories.

A variety of measures exist to analyse costs and benefits. These include such measures as Return on Investment (ROI), internal rate of return (IRR) and net present value (NPV). The measure that is most widely used across both public and private sectors is the NPV.

NPV is widely used because it provides a more accurate tool for evaluating costs and benefits over a number of years. A traditional analysis of a programme's costs and benefits simply adds together each year's cost or benefit and subtracts total costs from total benefits to produce a total net benefit figure for the programme. This analysis does not recognise that a £5 million saving today will not necessarily be a £5 million saving next year or the year after because the financial value of costs and benefits changes over time.

The NPV method addresses this problem of fluctuating costs and benefits by converting the value of future costs and benefits to today's actual value. The NPV delivers this analysis by applying a discount rate to the costs and benefits in future years of a transformation programme which compensates for the fact that costs and benefits will fluctuate over time.

For example, Figure 6.7 uses a business case produced by a public sector organisation and applies a traditional analysis. This analysis identifies that the HR transformation programme is projected to realise a cumulative saving of £4 million over 5 years. However, this analysis assumes that the value of costs and benefits will not fluctuate over the 5-year period.

The NPV approach applies a discount to years 2–5 in Figure 6.8 to compensate for the fact that the value of costs and benefits will change and to show in today's values the actual costs and benefits for future years. The discount that is applied will generally be provided by your finance department. Figure 6.8 below applies a discount to years 2–5 and demonstrates that when compensating for changes to costs and benefits in future years the cumulative saving is £3.5 million over 5 years.

| | Year 1 | Year 2 | Year 3 | Year 4 | Year 5 |
	£	£	£	£	£
Costs of Future HR Model and Service – including implementation costs in Year 1 and Year 2	7,000,000	6,600,000	4,800,000	4,800,000	4,800,000
Current Cost of HR Model and Service	6,400,000	6,400,000	6,400,000	6,400,000	6,400,000
Net Benefits	–600,000	–200,000	1,600,000	1,600,000	1,600,000
Cumulative Benefits	–600,000	–800,000	800,000	2,400,000	4,000,000

Figure 6.7 Cost–benefit analysis without discount factors.

	Year 1 £	Year 2 £	Year 3 £	Year 4 £	Year 5 £
Costs of Future HR Model and Service – including implementation costs in Year 1 and Year 2	7,000,000	6,600,000	4,800,000	4,800,000	4,800,000
Current Cost of HR Model and Service	6,400,000	6,400,000	6,400,000	6,400,000	6,400,000
Net Benefit	−600,000	−200,000	1,600,000	1,600,000	1,600,000
Annual Discount Factor (3.5%)	1	0.9962	0.9335	0.9019	0.8714
Discounted Cash Flow	−600,000	−199,240	1,493,600	1,443,040	1,394,240
Cumulative NPV	−600,000	−799,240	694,360	2,137,400	3,531,640

Figure 6.8 Discounted cost–benefit analysis.

Therefore, when using the NPV there are three key steps:

- forecast the costs and benefits for each year of the transformation programme;
- apply a discount factor to the forecasted costs and benefits for future years;
- add the cumulative savings after the discount factor rate has been applied.

The cost–benefit analysis is, however, not the only factor that will be taken into account in approving the business case. The risks in achieving the predicted benefits need to be considered. An example of a risk analysis is presented in Figure 6.9. It demonstrates that when assessing risks there are a number of factors to consider, these include:

- *Defining the risk.* This should provide a clear statement of what will happen if the risk is not managed.
- *Mitigation.* This should summarise the actions that are required to manage the risk and prevent it from happening.
- *Probability.* This is a subjective assessment of the likelihood of the risk materialising and could change when the risk register is reviewed. Typically these are classified as:
  - 0% – will not happen
  - 25% – unlikely to happen
  - 50% – equally likely to happen or not to happen
  - 75% – likely to happen
  - 100% – will definitely happen

Risk Description		Impact (Pre-mitigation)			Mitigation
	Probability	Time	Cost	Performance	
Key staff unavailable to support programme. Workload conflicts can lead to the unavailability of key staff. This will slow down and potentially compromise the successful delivery of the HR model, HR technology and new processes.	75%	High	Medium	High	• Identify key staff at the start of transition to 'win hearts and minds' and motivate people to stay on. • Knowledge transfer is also essential in terms of minimising risk to the ongoing service.
Poor communication, leading to misunderstanding, mistrust and negative perceptions of the shared services programme and active resistance.	75%	High	Medium	High	• Put in place a detailed communication plan for HR covering all channels and recipients. • Use a range of information dissemination techniques such as newsletters, Intranet articles, publishing progress reports, workgroup meetings, presentations at larger meetings, representation at management team meetings etc.
Loss of key staff and skills during the transition to the new HR model	50%	High	Low	High	• Identify key staff at the start of transition to 'win hearts and minds' and motivate them to stay on. • Knowledge transfer is also essential in terms of minimising risk to the ongoing service.

Figure 6.9 Risk analysis.

- *Impact*. This is an assessment of the impact that the risk will have upon the programme if it materialises and involves determining whether the impact is high (red), medium (amber) and low (green). The impact is also considered in three areas:
  - time, that is, will the risk extend the deadlines and time required for the programme;
  - cost, that is, will the risk require additional expenditure to manage if it materialises;
  - performance, that is, will the risk adversely affect the ability of the programme to deliver its benefits and hit its financial and non-financial targets.

Produce HR transformation roadmap

The transformation roadmap is a single high-level view of the key activities that are required to deliver an HR transformation programme. The purpose of the roadmap is to define the key milestones that are required to bridge the gap from current to future HR. There are many different approaches to producing transformation maps; this chapter presents two potential options.

An example of a transformation roadmap that was developed to support an HR transformation is provided in Figure 6.10. The challenge facing HR within the company was how to communicate the aims, objectives and key changes that would be introduced by its transformation programme to staff from a variety of professions and backgrounds. The transformation programme found that it had a

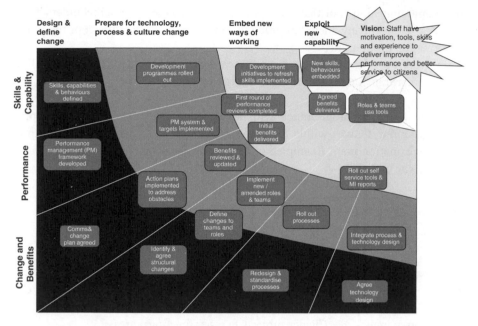

Figure 6.10 HR transformation roadmap.

large number of traditional project plans with considerable detail and high-level presentations but it had nothing that could communicate to staff and senior stakeholders what HR transformation would deliver to them, their managers and their employees.

The company, therefore, developed a transformation roadmap which is divided into:

- streams such as skills, performance, change, structures, process and technology. However, the map could also be divided into the organisational levers that were discussed in Chapter 3, that is, technology, structure, processes and people/culture;
- timeline which can be divided into 90-day periods or years and in every period there are specific milestones for each stream;
- objectives for the programme which are located in the top right-hand corner.

This map satisfied three important objectives for the company:

- a picture of key activities and deliverables for the different work streams within the programme to provide the programme management team with a tool for viewing and controlling what would happen and when;

■ a communication tool that could be used to engage with stakeholders from across the company, including trade unions, to explain the impact of the transformation programme.

■ an overview of the HR transformation programme that could be used to link into other transformation programmes taking place.

HR transformation programmes will have interdependencies with other programmes and initiatives within the organisation and these can be integrated into the transformation map. Examples of common interdependencies include those shown in the table below:

Interdependency area	Description
Technology	Linkages to programmes that upgrade network capacity and PCs
Interfaces	Systems interfaces with other core systems, for example, finance, procurement (especially workflow/organisation structure)
Change programmes	Change projects in other functional areas

The above transformation can, however, also be expressed in an alternative format, as demonstrated by Figure 6.11. In this version of the roadmap,

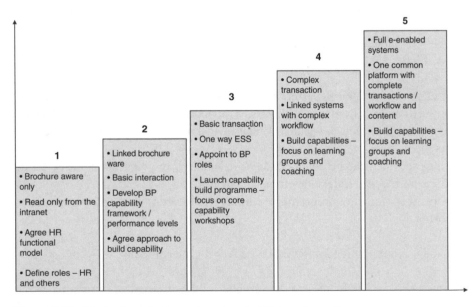

Figure 6.11 Ninety-day milestones: key steps to HR transformation.

initial high-level milestones are broken down to the next level of detail. The headings of process, people and technology are used to segment the roadmap horizontally so that in every 90-day period there are specific milestones for the process, people and technology elements of the programme. Further views of the roadmap can also be developed. For example, a view that defines when the different elements of the new HR service delivery model will be delivered from a senior management, line manager, employee and HR practitioner perspective for each 90-day period provides a tangible plan by which expectations can be set across each of those groups. Through creating these different views, the roadmap becomes an important communications tool in engaging people in the programme.

In the first part of the roadmap, it is often preferable to split this into individual months for the first 3 months of the roadmap in order to provide month-by-month clarity over that period. Similarly, for the later parts halfyearly periods may be more appropriate. After the business case has been approved and the roadmap becomes a working plan, keeping the first part at an individual month level of detail for a rolling 3-month period is very effective for managing expectations across the business and the programme team.

In the first parts of the roadmap, the delivery will typically be around 'quick wins' or 'early implementations'. Quick wins typically begin to put the new process and people elements in place supported by existing technology that has been tuned and modified ahead of the longer-term, enduring technology implementation (if this is what is planned). This provides the opportunity to deliver benefits early, build the credibility of the programme and encourage behaviour change throughout the life of the programme rather than in a 'big bang' at the end.

Gain buy-in and ownership

One of the main tenets of this book is that successful HR transformation is achieved through the effective management of change. In order to do this, the principles and practice of change management must be an integral part of each element of the transformation, in particular through the adoption of a process consulting mindset (see Chapter 1). The development of the business case is no exception and in this final section, we explore the elements of change management that are particularly pertinent in business case development.

In business case development, it is important to identify who the main benefit owners are as they must buy in to the benefits predicted in the business case and will, therefore, be highly influential in driving the change to achieve those benefits. The mechanism for achieving that buy-in is their involvement in developing the business case so that it is something developed collaboratively rather than imposed.

The impact of HR transformation on both HR and the line managers in many cases goes to the very core of people's working lives, and therefore taking the opportunity to involve individuals from these groups in the business case development process will begin to lay the foundations for them embracing the changes that HR transformation will bring and reducing resistance. However, gaining the 'buy-in' of stakeholders is not a one-off activity. Maintaining the 'buy-in' of stakeholder groups across the organisation is an ongoing task. This task also has to be a collaborative process where stakeholders are able to shape and influence the benefits that will be delivered. Imposing the business case will only entrench resistance.

Through this process of involvement, it is useful to identify change sponsors and change leaders. They are the people who are going to play key roles in implementing HR transformation within the organisation, and will occupy a range of roles throughout the business rather than being members of the programme team itself. It is vital to get them involved in the development of the business case so that, by the implementation phase, they are fully engaged and able to demonstrate their understanding of the impacts of change to their functions and to the wider business.

Change sponsors provide 'public' support – both in their actions and in what they say. Sponsors must be capable of representing the transformation to colleagues in a convincing way. They are usually in senior roles, and as such often provide staff and resources to support the change within the business. They must demonstrate 'publicly' that they buy in to the consequences of the change proposed in the business case, and often members of the programme team will support and coach the change sponsors in the execution of their role.

As you cascade further through the organisation, you will identify change leaders who are usually part of the change sponsors' organisations and who are in a position to help drive the change within their areas. Change leaders will be in a variety of roles, for example, business partners or line managers, but they will all be respected by their colleagues and be working at the local level. If they can be identified and involved in the business case, they will be able to work with you in moving from planning towards implementation from their positions at the heart of the business. The role of change leaders is addressed in Chapter 11 and the relationship between sponsors the organisation is illustrated in Figure 6.12.

Here are some practical approaches to involving HR and line managers in developing the business case that we have found to work effectively.

■ *Speak the business' language*

It sounds simple, but unless you communicate in a way that your business colleagues will understand, the message you are trying to give will be lost. Consider

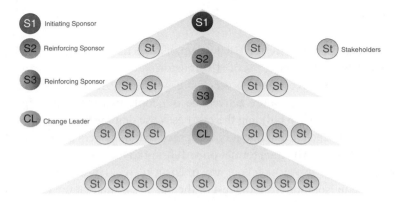

Figure 6.12 Relationship between change sponsors, change leaders and stakeholders. Source: Sponsorship and change leadership, based on Daryl Conner, *Managing at the Speed of Change*, Wiley, 1998.

involving a group from the target audience to check and rewrite the message. Why not ask them to take responsibility for it? In doing so they will become engaged in the programme.

■ *Place yourself in the business' shoes*

The impact of HR transformation is often misunderstood or is seen as much larger in the minds of managers than in HR. Requiring managers to phone a service centre when they used to be visited by HR is a significant change and can create feelings that HR has 'abandoned' the business and is too far away to understand frontline issues. It is, therefore, important to consult with the business on what is important to them.

For example, the CEO will be focussed on delivering strategic objectives, the FD on financial savings, operations staff on delivering products or services, the IT Director on the benefits of using technology such as self service.

In a large government department, the HR transformation phase began by holding focus groups with each of the main professions, delivery units and back office support teams. These sessions were designed to drive out the key issues facing these staff groups and define what they wanted from HR. This enabled the programme to be clear on what could be provided and what benefits would be delivered to each group and to define what couldn't be provided and set clear expectations. This helped to dissipate many of the objections and resistance.

- *Lead by example*

This is an ideal opportunity for HR to demonstrate its changing leadership role in practice. Many of the benefits of HR transformation lie in how effectively line managers and employees take on greater responsibility for the management of their careers, as well as a more active role in people management. Engagement with line managers when building the business case demonstrates that HR is both serious about the change and that it is concerned that managers believe in and buy into the benefits that HR transformation will bring to the organisation.

This approach is also an excellent way of ensuring that HR does not develop the business case in isolation from the rest of the business, and that the business stays involved after the initial engagement. This reduces the risk that the business perceives that the programme has gone into a black hole and is then suddenly hit by implementation. This approach also tests the HR transformation solution from the business perspective, providing the mechanism for the business to raise potential design issues early in the process.

- *Use demonstrations of new service delivery channels*

Demonstrations given very early on can be extremely powerful in getting people excited about what the transformation could look like. They help people really to understand what the HR systems delivery channel in particular will look like and what their role in that will be. Demonstrations can be easily organised – in fact, many software vendors will stage them for you.

Similarly, opportunities exist to demonstrate shared services and outsourced delivery channels. Site visits provide a good opportunity here, as do conference room pilots (physical demonstrations of how a process will work with simulated hand-offs and processing).

- *Ensure the commitment of those who have responsibility for benefit delivery*

Ensuring that benefit owners include in their budgets the effect of the anticipated benefit accruing to HR transformation is a highly effective way of demonstrating their commitment to HR transformation and of concentrating their minds on the implications of the changes. This approach is particularly effective where cost savings are concerned and where benefit owners need to commit to business case cost savings.

- *Deliver some changes early in the programme*

Delivering change early sends a message that change is possible and is beneficial. For example, delivering HR self service in phases enables staff to become comfortable with basic tools, such as updating personal information. Later phases of self service then gradually introduce staff and managers to tools that will enable them to book courses on line, more accurately record and manage sickness absence or better manage performance. This approach enables staff to become comfortable with self service and to start taking responsibility for managing their career and staff, whilst also delivering early savings within areas such as HR administration.

This approach enables transformation programmes to not only deliver concrete benefits before the whole programme is completed but also starts to change behaviours early, so that when the larger changes happen, people are ready for them.

Summary

This chapter shows that robust business case development provides a firm foundation for HR transformation, both in terms of the 'soft' and 'hard' elements. For instance, thorough preparation of the business case significantly increases the likelihood of meeting or exceeding the benefits case, whilst the inclusive and consultative approach taken in developing the case continues the focus on HR transformation as a process of change, developing real commitments to the changes proposed.

Through the development of the business case, the design of the HR transformation solution is taken to the next level of detail driven by what is required to achieve the target benefits. The cost implications are then determined and the process of assessing the comparative costs and benefits completed.

In a similar way, the initial transformation plan first developed during envisioning is taken to the next level of detail to form the HR transformation roadmap. The roadmap enables senior stakeholders to see what HR transformation will deliver to them, their managers and their employees over each period, becoming a key tool for communications with stakeholders across the organisation.

7

Stakeholder Engagement and Communication

In preceding chapters, we have identified the crucial importance of securing the commitment of managers and employees to the HR transformation process. The formalisation of this should be a feature of the HR transformation business case, covered in Chapter 6.

We advocate that stakeholder engagement should not be conducted in isolation but as part of an overall governance approach. More is said about programme governance in Chapter 9.

We have also noted in Chapters 5 and 8 the importance of stakeholder engagement in the design and delivery of HR services. Successful outcomes are affected by appropriately designed HR services architectures and the associated reactions of the users of those services.

Key themes

- A review of some perspectives on human change and how these can help to map out the stakeholder topography.
- How the stakeholder mapping process can inform the change sponsors and agents about the most effective ways to manage resistance and reduce negative impact on the programme.
- Using a variety of methods, including Web 2.0, to secure receptive and positive stakeholder outcomes.

Context

You will know that the ability to manage change effectively is regarded as a crucial skill. Vast amounts of resources are expended by organisations to adjust employees to a new way of achieving desired goals. The natural propensity for individuals and groups to 'defend the status quo' presents a set of challenges that HR management must overcome in order to bring about desired change. In addition, your management must also seriously take into account and consider the myriad of problems that may result if they are not responsive to issues in the workplace.

The change cycle model and process consulting mindset described in Chapter 1 also touched on these points and contribute to the view that in the context of HR transformation, change management includes:

- getting all those involved and affected to accept the changes and the results of the change process;
- the effective management of resistance.

We argue that viewing resistance and commitment together leads to a better understanding of the nature and dynamics of these factors in change management and the tools and techniques required to deliver successful outcomes.

We also stress the point that stakeholder engagement is not conducted in isolation but as part of an overall project or programme governance model. This reinforces the advice given in Chapter 1 about adopting a systems mindset, so that you are keenly aware that a number of inter-related elements need to be managed well to bring about successful HR transformation.

The case illustrations provide examples of how the use of different stakeholder engagement approaches can materially affect the outcomes of HR transformation.

Stakeholder engagement tools

Resistance and commitment to change should be seen as a dynamic continuum. This is illustrated in Figure 7.1.

Aggressive resistance is regarded as a destructive opposition, reflected in destructive behaviour such as purposely committing errors and spoilage, subversion and sabotage.

The neutral or apathy zone represents a situation where people are informed about changes, but their perceptions and attitudes regarding the changes are

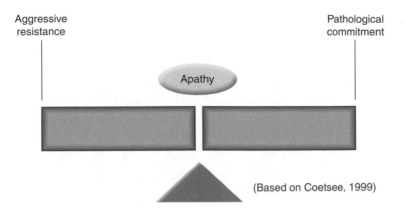

Figure 7.1 Securing commitment.

neutral and their behaviour is characterised by 'passive resignation', representing a transition between resistance and acceptance of change.

Pathological commitment represents the final phase of acceptance to change. In this context, it is characterised by passion for the change process, associated perhaps with obsessive and compulsive behaviours.

Between these poles are various 'shades' of resistance and commitment.

We believe this model provides a diagnostic framework to identify the extent of acceptance or rejection of change in your organisation. Mapping individuals, groups or business units onto the continuum may be difficult and should not be attempted lightly. But it is a powerful tool if used wisely. For example, following the use of one of the survey/measurement tools described below, you could map individuals or groups onto the scale. This provides a basis for meaningful discussion about what needs to happen in order to move those stakeholders into the more positive, commitment end of the continuum, if it can be shown that unacceptable levels of resistance are evident.

You should, of course, be prepared to justify the reason for any assumptions you have made when plotting stakeholders onto the continuum.

The stakeholder topography

This is the means by which you can construct a view of the stakeholder population which allows individuals/groups/business units affected by HR transformation to be characterised in terms of their importance to the change process and how they are impacted by it. This is assisted by using the stakeholder mapping framework shown in Figure 7.2. A sample is shown in the following table:

Stakeholder group	Example impacts
Employees	Maintaining their own data rather than relying on HR administration to do it for them
Line managers	Increased people management responsibilities supported by Web-based HR rather than HR consultants
HR consultants	Move to added value business partner roles rather than administration comfort zone
HR administration	Expert support rather than re-keying administration
HR specialists	Demand driven by business partners rather than line managers
Payroll	Data from Web-based HR system rather than separate re-keying
External recruitment	Reduced number due to e-recruitment functionality

Those individuals or groups that are seen to display high impact and high importance are the most significant in terms of securing acceptance of the change process. Those positioned elsewhere in the matrix present different levels of significance. In these cases, it may be acceptable simply to achieve modest support or even neutrality.

To expand on these points, let us look in more detail at some of the stakeholder groups illustrated in the earlier sample:

■ It is evident that line managers are both highly important to the transformation process and highly impacted by it. As such they warrant careful and

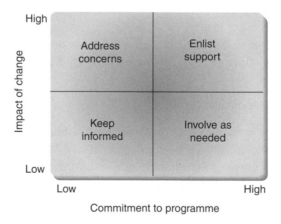

Figure 7.2 Stakeholder mapping.

considered attention. A failure to engage properly with this group and secure a good degree of acceptance to the transformation process will create significant issues, such as poor utilisation of Web-based HR and a failure to adopt more people-centred practices within their role profile. These will at best stifle the transformation process or at worst sabotage it completely.

- The HR administration team are important and may be highly impacted if the intention is to reduce headcount based on the assumption that more HR administration is performed by managers and employees using Web-based HR. This could raise morale/retention issues at a critical time when the new services are being introduced, requiring higher levels of support to users. In this situation, it may not be possible to persuade this group to warmly embrace the transformation process, but it will be necessary to move sentiment into the mildly resistive/ neutral zone of the continuum in order to maintain decent service levels.
- The reductions in the number of external recruitment suppliers may antagonise those suppliers eliminated from the new list, but conversely may also provide an injection of encouragement to the group chosen to continue (and possibly enhance) their contribution. These different impacts need to be managed. Those suppliers who are expected to maintain their contracts post HR transformation must be clear and accepting about what is expected of them. The rejected suppliers need to understand the rationale for their exclusion, but may never be accepting of them. This will not impact the HR transformation process in the short term, but may be an issue in the longer term if you seek to re-engage their services.

These examples show the value of stakeholder mapping as a way of categorising the different groups, and informing you about the level of effort and priority that needs to be invested in ongoing activities to bring about desirable outcomes necessary to support the HR transformation programme objectives.

How to enlist support and overcome resistance

You should be prepared to invest in meaningful stakeholder engagement at the start of the change cycle and continue, relentlessly, throughout. It will be worth it.

The biggest single contributor to success is securing the unwavering commitment of the senior change sponsors. Without this, the HR transformation programme becomes vulnerable to attack and disruption. We strongly recommend getting this in place early as a priority.

You may have to be creative to win an audience with the most senior stakeholders. If you can, arrange one-to-one meetings and use these opportunities to present a compelling factual case in support of the programme. If this is not possible, then gain access to the next reporting level and seek to influence this group of people so that they in turn can upwardly influence their superiors.

Whilst one-to-one meetings can be extremely impactful, think creatively about other channels:

- team meetings/workshops;
- invitation to a steering group;
- making sure the Personal Assistant (PA) includes a brief on the HR transformation programme in essential reading material;
- requiring a response through an auditable process, such as electronic tagging, so that the respondent is aware that simply refusing to reply will create an automatic elevation to the steering group or higher;
- using various Web-based tools to engender engagement, such as surveys, discussions forums, blogs and wikis.

Of equal importance to understanding how individuals or groups show their attitudinal stance for the change initiative, it is necessary to monitor and measure behaviour. You will almost certainly identify what we call 'secret subversives' – people who appear to be on your side, but then undermine the programme. They should be identified and dealt with as quickly as possible.

Developing a list of actionable items that demonstrate behaviour is essential. It should include:

- demonstrating that they are accurately communicating the change initiative to their teams;
- showing endorsement of the newly created HR processes;
- signing off on key documentation that allows financial investment.

It is important to stress again that investment of time and effort in the segmentation and characterisation of the stakeholder community, combined with techniques to understand their position on the resistance to commitment continuum, will repay itself in terms of dividend many times over. *This is not a task that should be undervalued, misplaced or subordinated to a low level in the priority order.*

Often in change programmes these 'soft' or human issues – which is essentially what stakeholder engagement is all about – become subordinated to the technical issues and considerations surrounding system choice and implementation. Beware of allowing the technical issues to take over for too long. Without the people on board, no system will deliver the benefits you promised in the business case.

Once you have mapped out the stakeholders, the next task is to understand where they lie on the resistance to commitment continuum, and this in turn will determine where effort should be prioritised.

How do we test the 'temperature' of the business?

There are various techniques that can be used to test the temperature of the business and in particular the stakeholder groups that have been identified using the tools described earlier. A number of different types of survey tool can be used to capture information about attitudes and behaviours. Figure 7.3 illustrates some of the different types that can be used.

The techniques that combine both qualitative and quantitative outputs can be very useful indeed. So, for example, a survey could be constructed that requires the respondent to indicate their perspective on the change process by answering questions based on the Likert scale (strongly disagree to strongly agree). In addition, free text boxes can be used to allow the respondent to provide a more in-depth response around particular issues or concerns. Analysing these responses will provide a good indication of the issue types and the strength of feeling or importance surrounding these.

This kind of survey works well in a Web-based format. The results provide a preliminary indication of any issues and/or concerns and allow a judgment to be made in respect of the position of individuals/groups on the resistance to commitment continuum. It may then be appropriate, particularly with the significant stakeholders, to probe these issues in more detail. This is usually best done in the form of focus groups or one-to-one interviews but can also be performed using Web-based tools such as discussion forums.

Examples of these approaches, linked to case illustrations, are described later. It is also very important that appropriate ethical behaviour and standards are observed at all stages of the process. For example, if you say survey results will be treated in confidence, make sure they are.

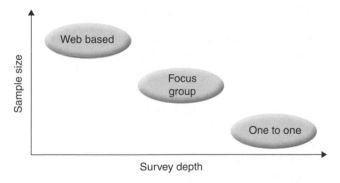

Figure 7.3 Testing the temperature.

The global dimension

The different segments of the stakeholder population within a global or multinational programme could have radically different views of the same change process. This means that the stakeholder engagement activity needs to address those different entities or jurisdictions, and you should not slip into the comfort zone of thinking that a very professional and comprehensive assessment of the situation in, say, the United Kingdom can then naturally map onto Japan, United States or other countries in continental Europe.

It may well be the case that data protection issues receive a more heightened degree of focus in Germany than they might in the United Kingdom. A global HR process that would allow, for example, someone in Italy to view the personal details of a German employee might cause enormous consternation. The degree of ambiguity around different aspects of the programme may raise concerns in one area, but be accepted as the norm in others.

You should investigate these factors thoroughly. It is stressed again that the *stakeholder engagement process needs to be applied with equal rigour to a multi-jurisdiction programme.* In this way, you get an informed opinion on issues in each of those jurisdictions. Subsequent efforts to address those issues can then be more closely tailored.

Case studies

These case studies are informed by previously published material written by one of us. In particular, more details concerning case study 1 can be found in Martin, Reddington and Alexander (2008) and case studies 3, 4 and 5 can be found, with a selection of others, in Martin, Reddington and Kneafsey (2009).

Case study 1: UK subsidiary of global mobile phone company

This case illustration demonstrates the use of a Web-based survey tool combined with focus group work, to ascertain the level of line manager sentiment towards a range of Web-based HR tools, which were an important element of the overall HR service delivery model in this organisation. A significant investment had been made in the technology platform supporting these tools through an upgrade to the latest enterprise resource planning (ERP) system, as the previous version had reached the end of its commercial life and eventually would not be supported by the supplier. This led to the development of a common HR portal, through which all online services could be accessed. The intention of this portal was also to help HR to create a greater sense of corporate identity among employees in the extended enterprise using an internal employer branding strategy (Martin & Hetrick, 2006). The real benefit being sought was an improvement in HR service quality, providing more accurate and reliable data, and enabling more informed management decisions.

The organisation agreed, as a stakeholder engagement exercise, to support a piece of research which allowed us to test the perceptions of HR and line managers towards these tools. The research aimed to achieve a meaningful assessment of the impact of Web-based HR on both the HR and line manager population, with a view to improving the service offering, where practicable, in the future.

Although it was conducted with levels of methodological rigour associated with academic research, the application of the methods should be both accessible and helpful to the practitioner.

Approach to data collection and analysis

The stakeholder engagement exercise was carried out by one of us during 2006 and 2007 and comprised two stages of data collection. The first tranche of data were collected using a Web-based survey of HR and line managers. The total number surveyed was 94, representing about 10% of the overall manager population. Seventy managers responded, yielding a response rate of approximately 75%. Within that total, 65 responses were from line managers and 5 from HR managers, which was broadly representative of the ratio across the wider organisation.

The survey was designed to elicit information on three aspects of the Web-based HR implementation, including line managers' views on usage and benefits of the HR tools, data quality and maintenance and the effectiveness of communications, support and training connected with the Web-based HR system (see Appendix 2 for a list of illustrative survey questions). These aspects were designed to enable key impacts of the investment in Web-based HR to be investigated, leading to clear indicators in respect of where improvements could best be targeted.

The survey was followed up by three focus groups, involving a total of 15 line managers, to probe some of the findings of the survey. A qualitative method was used in the form of a case study approach to create an in-depth, rich account (Yin, 2003) of how one organisation has implemented a Web-based HR system and what line managers think about the organisation's efforts.

Respondents were selected using purposive sampling; participants were purposely chosen because of their relevance to the research. Each respondent had completed the Web-based survey and confirmed his or her willingness to be chosen for subsequent follow-up research aimed at obtaining more detailed insights into their views of the Web-based HR system.

Focus group respondents were provided with a list of topics for discussion beforehand and permission was granted to tape-record the sessions for analysis purposes; confidentiality throughout the process was assured. The transcript of each session was sent back to participants for validation. Summary reports of the main findings were sent to the host HR function as a basis for discussion and the identification of follow-up actions.

Table 7.1 Results of survey among HR and line managers on Web-based HR

Dimension	Aggregate (%)			Line manager (%)			HR manager (%)		
	F	N	U	F	N	U	F	N	U
Use and benefits	54	24	22	53	24	23	69	24	7
Data accuracy and maintenance	73	13	14	71	14	15	90	8	2
Communications, support and training	45	28	27	44	27	29	60	37	3

Results of Web-based survey

Table 7.1 provides a summary of the results of the questionnaire based on a simple aggregation of percentage of favourable responses to each of the questions corresponding to the three dimensions. The favourable percentages combine the favourable/agree and very favourable/strongly agree scores; the middle percentage represents neutral scores, while the unfavourable percentages combine the unfavourable/disagree and highly unfavourable/strongly disagree scores.

A cursory examination of the headline data shows that HR managers recorded higher favourable percentages on all aspects of the Web-based HR implementation. This topography of sentiment revealed in the Web-based material serves to highlight the importance of obtaining results from both HR and line manager communities. The dangers of omitting line managers from research work aimed at assessing the future direction of change initiatives were also articulated in a CIPD Report (2002), which refers to the:

> *Weakness of research that asks a senior HR manager to complete a questionnaire about HR in his or her firm and then relies on those responses for analysis.*

(CIPD, 2002, note 13)

It is also clearly apparent from a closer inspection of the Web-based survey results that perceptions of data quality and maintenance dominate the favourable results, whilst perceptions of communications support and training are least favourable.

It was also very telling that within the line manager community only 34% reported an appreciation of the benefits of Web-based HR, from the perspective of return on investment. There were similar reservations about the impact of Web-based HR on HR services; only 30% reported that Web-based HR had increased the effectiveness of HR management in their organisation. These results, amongst others, were probed during the focus group sessions. The nature and extent of the inter-related implications, both for HR and line managers are now examined in more detail and we found

150

it helpful to adapt and reorganise the impacts revealed in our study into three main categories, as featured in the report by Parry et al. (2007).

■ the impact on HR activities and processes,
■ the impact on employee communication and engagement,
■ the impact on the changing roles and skills of HR and line managers.

The impact of Web-based HR on the efficiency of HR activities and processes
It is understood that the introduction of new technologies, such as Web-based HR, to deliver HR advice and services to line managers, as well as generating significant organisational benefits, can also cause potentially negative consequences if the implementation process is not managed effectively. For example, Whittaker and Marchington (2003) conducted research finding that there were concerns among the line manager community that the HR function lacked visibility and that it had become remote with increasing usage of electronic data systems and self-service HR. They commented:

> *... having the chance to talk with someone from the HR function was regarded as essential, if only to seek clarification face-to-face about how to deal with specific problems.*
>
> (Whittaker & Marchington, 2003, p. 258)

This lack of emphasis on 'the human side' of HR was reflected in our study, which highlighted the need for HR professionals to remember that they are dealing with individuals and they are providing a service; their work is about people, not processes. Line managers made the following observations:

> *It would be helpful if they [HR] came and talked to you like a human being ...*

> *[I] actually speak to HR and say, 'this is the situation, am I right in this or am I wrong in that?' Usually, that's the best way and it also keeps up the human contact, which is important.*

> *I think they've [HR] got to be consultative, they've got to be visible and they've got to be accessible to managers at a particular level but also, I think, from an employee perspective.*

The organisational benefits of Web-based HR implementation should not, however, be forgotten. At the host organisation some of the tools were quite heavily used, providing significant support to both line managers and employees. This is revealed in comments such as:

> *There's a lot of good material in there, there's a lot of good material on the Web site ...*

More specifically, line managers praised the HR email service as illustrated in the following remarks:

I find they're really responsive [the HR e-mail] ... they connect right away and give you the information and if you go back to them [with further queries,], they'll come back to you.

... more staff are now starting to use the e-mail system because they know they get a response quite quickly.

One important factor in the HR transformation process, which is often neglected by both academics and practitioners, is that Web-based HR needs to be considered in the wider context of HR service delivery. If change occurs in organisations it does not do so in isolation; it affects all other elements of the service delivery model:

The adoption of e-HR ... triggers a chain reaction of other consequences that have a profound bearing on the way organisations do HR ...

In our study, participants observed that the implementation of a new Web-based HR system signalled the need for a cultural shift within HR in order to ensure that the function was not just paying 'lip service' to line managers' expectations and aspirations. As one line manager remarked:

... I think there needs to be some shift where you get like a 'wow' factor; if you contact HR for any reason through any channel you should feel, 'wow that was great!' That's how we should feel ... I think at the moment that wow factor isn't there, it's here and there, now and then, but it's not consistent.

From this it is apparent that overall perceptions are very mixed towards Web-based HR, in terms of its impact on the efficiency of HR activities and processes.

The impact on improving employee communication and engagement
Our research demonstrates the importance of effective communication in ensuring that both line managers and employees 'buy-in' to Web-based HR. This is illustrated in the comments as follows:

New systems ... should be communicated well and users need to understand why these things are happening. This would lead to less resistance.

... the message that comes across is mixed and it's not a constructive message. I think they've [HR] got to develop how to execute that message and once they get that right then I think things will come through ... we're having to find [things] out for ourselves and it leads to people using different methods and certain tools in certain ways and it becomes a kind of a mixed bag.

Participants also highlighted the importance of intuitive systems and comprehensive training in order to secure line manager and employee engagement.

The tools should be intuitive and designed around us, the internal customer, so that tasks that are done very often, like approving leave and expenses, should be the easiest but often they seem really difficult. . . . Maybe it's a criticism of [the system] that we have to adapt to it rather than it adapting to us ... Why don't we have something that is more suited to us?

When we implement new systems ... every department should send someone along to be trained up to use it.

HR could ... get floor walkers, for example, on the day it goes live. You could have one experienced user per floor to show people how the new system works ...

I think the super user concept wouldn't be a bad thing ... if people are confused, then the super user is best placed to learn the nuances of it (new tool).

Linked to this, we found that there was often line manager and employee frustration regarding the usability of the system. The solution, as advocated by the users, was to create a more personalised and tailored HR solution. For example, whilst participants praised the email service provided by the HR team both in terms of the speed and quality of responses it provided, they acknowledged this service was only helpful in answering simple, self-contained problems and line managers experienced difficulty when they required more detailed advice from HR.

[The email service] is really good because all you do is send an e-mail, ask the question and they [HR] tell you what to do.

[The email service] can be great for certain things. An example would be if I had a direct report with a sick child, but no holiday entitlement left. I can [send an] e-mail ... and I know that I will have the answer. So that sort of very simple, self-contained problem can be easily answered. However, as soon as it's something less specific or more open ended, it's very difficult to know how to get that information out of HR.

It is essential for line managers to be involved in the implementation process in order to ensure that the new HR delivery model is client-centred. This can be achieved in a variety of ways: through early consultation with all managers; active, hands-on senior level involvement in the project team and a customer references panel that engages with the proposals throughout. As one line manager explained:

[A] good parallel is when we think about launching things to customers. The way it should work is ... figuring out how they want to do business with us and then we adapt to them because that's how you'll be a successful company. The same philosophy should apply to our internal offering – the HR tools and services. The tools should be intuitive and designed around us, the internal customer.

In spite of these criticisms regarding the impact of Web-based HR on improving employee communication and engagement, it is clear that line managers at the host organisation were making a significant effort to engage their teams, encouraging them to discuss areas that could be improved.

> *... what we do try and do is to get the engagement of the team. We ask the team, 'you tell us what we can do differently to get this working; what can we do?' I think the team as a whole can see that you try to take action on their issues and this creates an improved employee engagement score.*

From the evidence presented, it is clear that the perceived impact of Web-based HR on improving employee engagement and communication is disappointing. Despite this, the line managers presented a range of constructive suggestions to alleviate the issues identified.

The impact on the changing roles and skills for HR and line managers
In a transformed state, the HR function is unlikely to place a premium on administrative skills and the HR positions available will be strategic in focus requiring a higher capability of candidates. This is supported in research conducted by Bell et al. (2006, p. 303), and they found that:

> *Information Technology has allowed the HR function to focus less attention on routine, administrative tasks and dedicate more energy to delivering services that add value to the business.*

Thus, it is clear that Web-based HR can leave more time for HR to focus on expert or strategic issues and is therefore one way of facilitating the transition from operational to strategic HR.

Indeed, many line managers emphasised the important contributions made by the HR team and praised their ability to carry out job roles effectively.

> *I think there are brilliant staff [in HR]; I know who to go to and I've been really impressed by their customer focus. I think they're right on ... giving advice and I would definitely give them accolades.*

> *I find the learning and development team fantastic ... If I've got an issue to discuss (with L&D), I'll go and talk to [someone] and [they] will then sit down with me for an hour and talk me through the courses and tell me specifically what courses might be suitable for my people.*

> *I find the [people] in recruitment are fantastic; I deal with two of them on a regular basis.*

However, as one line manager commented:

If you're not careful HR is viewed with a degree of cynicism or scepticism it probably doesn't deserve ...

This is illustrated in our study by the following negative perceptions of the HR function:

Everyone knows that the HR function is an overhead (cost to the business) ... Very rarely, it seems, you get someone who says something good about HR; more often than not it's seen as the part of the organisation which stops you doing things.

I really don't know what HR does. I only think of them as people who pay us or tell us we've got the sack ...

This selection of comments illustrates that the views of line managers towards the HR function are quite patchy and that if, as Ulrich (1998) states, HR should be defined not by what it does but by what it delivers, the quality of HR service delivery needs to be high to ensure that the perceptions of line managers are largely positive. The HR function is required to improve and market convincingly its value contribution to the business in order to diffuse the type of negative sentiment revealed here by the line manager community. Indeed, as we have noted in Chapter 3 the challenge for each HR function is to define for itself a way of making a value-adding contribution that is right for its organisation.

Thus, in order to manage this challenge effectively, HR needs to be clear about how it can add value in a way that is appropriate to its organisation's unique context. If HR fails to achieve this, the threat is that the business will turn elsewhere for that contribution and the in-house HR function will become insignificant and impotent.

The line manager community surveyed in this study argued that the creation of SLA (Service Level Agreements) could provide one way of measuring HR performance and therefore help to define its value contribution.

My perspective as far as service delivery is concerned is that HR needs to have a strategy backed up by SLA's (Service Level Agreements) ... If they don't operate like that, how do you measure the performance of the department? ... HR needs to be accountable.

In addition, line managers felt that performance assessment criteria should make their own people management responsibilities more explicit.

There isn't a very clear way for [line managers] to understand their responsibilities; no-one really knows what their responsibilities are.

The aim of the [performance management] guidance is that we should have five objectives [but] there's not a lot of suggestion as to what those objectives should comprise ...

If you manage people then you're the first line of HR in any business and I think we could save ourselves a lot of time and trouble or even money if we got that little bit right.

Linked to the issue of establishing clear accountabilities for both HR and line managers, participants emphasised that partnership needs to be built between HR and the line to ensure the effective delivery of HR services. As one respondent commented:

It's a matter of having to try and advise each other as to how we can reduce each other's burden by making sure that once we understand what the issue is, whose responsible for dealing with it, then we get on with it ...

Overall observations

The application of Web-based survey tools and focus groups worked well in combination as a stakeholder engagement tool, revealing the topography of sentiment towards the newly implemented Web-based HR tools.

These findings illustrate that the impact of Web-based HR on the changing roles and skills for HR and line managers is a complex picture and encompasses a broad range of aspects that must be appreciated and successfully addressed, if positive outcomes are to be achieved. We believe that our study has underlined an important point; line managers want and value high-quality HR services and would be prepared to work collaboratively with HR to improve overall service delivery. HR should therefore seek to use the intrinsic goodwill that can exist among the line manager community to guide future HR activities. We recommend that the reader should consult other parts of this book to seek insights into how best the stakeholder discoveries can best be converted into measurable, beneficial outcomes.

Case study 2: Her majesty's revenue and customs (HMRC)

This case illustration demonstrates the value of an extended face-to-face dialogue with managers affected by the transformed HR service delivery model, following the merger of two 'titans' – the former Inland Revenue and Customs and Excise – in 2005.

The HMRC Operating Model and launch of new HR policies brought a shift of responsibilities for some HR functions from the centre to managers. When the Filling Vacancies policy was launched in February 2006, it exposed a lack of confidence in managers who felt ill-equipped to make difficult decisions affecting their staff. The Head of the Strategy and Policy Team immediately recognised that, with HR Service Centres not yet fully operational, the lack of effective management capability to deal with the cultural change meant that HMRC was exposed to a serious business risk.

Key stakeholders were consulted and the concept of a Taskforce to provide a mobile face-to-face service for HMRC's 17,000 managers was agreed as an innovative and essential tool.

The strap line for the change had been publicised as 'Managers Decide – HR Supports' but managers clearly felt in need of more support than was immediately available. The Taskforce was setup and mobilised within 6 weeks of the concept being proposed, including the recruitment of 20 'core' members from across the business.

To give the team impact and identity, people were appointed with proven leadership skills, who were eager to be involved in change management and could deliver a quality, professional service to their customers, and reflect the community of customers they would serve. This involved the creative use of resources within HR and Learning including restructuring and capitalising the skills of pre-surplus staff.

The Team Leader worked with the HR team subject experts to develop materials for delivery to managers; trained and upskilled team members to give them a clear understanding of the new HR policies and canvassed managers in business areas to gauge the support required. By 30 June 2006, the Taskforce had actively engaged with almost 90% of business units and by 30 June 2007 had delivered 773 events to 11,746 managers.

Reflecting on the formation of the Taskforce, Martin Warlow, who was the team leader, remembers clearly the unusual speed with which the Taskforce was assembled. Martin remarked:

From a standing start to becoming operational, we had a great deal of work to accomplish quickly in terms of getting our ideas, materials and logistics sorted out. Mobility was very important; being able to respond efficiently to the needs of managers was a high priority. We relied to a large extent on a 'pull through' effect – the HR Business Partners operating across the organisation would act as the gateway to their manager communities.

Nick Tooley, another core Taskforce member from HR, recalls how some of the early sessions in particular were treated by managers as surgeries where they expected the Taskforce presentation team to have ready-made answers to their operational issues.

We had to assume an assertive stance in these situations and make it clear that we were there to advise them on how to make judgements and decisions, not to take them on their behalf. This required persistence and practice and eventually the penny dropped and managers started to engage with the Taskforce in the right way.

The success of the Taskforce has developed and improved HR's standing throughout HMRC; provided a conduit for real-time feedback about the effectiveness of policies and has proved a positive platform for HR to demonstrate a truly customer-focused approach. As previously noted, a strong customer relationship was developed with the HR Business Partner network, the primary customers for the service, who work with senior Directors to identify the need for Taskforce interventions and to prioritise requests across their business areas. The context of the sessions was developed around the 'Raising the Bar/Driving Up Performance' theme, underpinned by a passion for and an ethos of continuous improvement.

Management guidance in the form of a set of materials called BOOST was developed and deployed to support managers in their day-to-day role as coaches and motivators of their people. Intended to supplement but not replace other published guidance, it was essentially designed to help managers to work with both individuals and teams to build positive working relationships to ensure high performance, and to tackle under-performance, built on a practical, commonsense approach to the broad principles of good management practice.

An example of its use in supporting managers about the best way to praise and acknowledge good performance is shown in Box 7.1

Box 7.1 BOOST example

Elaine had been in post for 5 years and her performance was above average but she sometimes had difficulty in resolving customers' enquiries quickly and effectively. Helen, her manager, had observed this. She worked with Elaine to identify the problem by coaching her for a short time each week to help her improve. With Helen's encouragement and support Elaine was soon making good progress and Helen was quick to praise her for the extra effort she was making. Within 4 weeks Elaine was managing all her customer calls much better and Helen gave her some very positive feedback. At the team meeting, Helen also praised Elaine's effort and achievement and other team members also said 'well done'.

Use this activity to check how you give praise or acknowledge good performance in your team.

1. How many times have you given praise or acknowledged good performance in the past month?
2. Think of the last time you gave praise to a member of your team …
   ■ What was it for?
   ■ How did it make you feel?
   ■ How did they react?
3. How could you improve the way you praise people in your team when they perform well?

A bespoke, but simple, database is used to identify the most appropriate service (e.g., presentations, coaching, mentoring, workshops, master classes, etc.) and to allocate resources, mixing and matching team skills to provide the best possible service delivery.

In addition, the Taskforce is the public face of HMRC in international relations and has delivered special one-off events for the Royal Institute of Public Administrations, foreign delegations including the Ethiopian Ministry of Revenue and delegations from France and Poland.

Measurable benefits

The Taskforce programme has delivered a range of benefits to HMRC, summarised as follows:

- Reaction sheets completed at Taskforce events show:
  - the content of interventions 'useful or very useful' – 97%;
  - overall 'good or very good' – 89%;
  - Taskforce team member's delivery 'effective or very effective' – 90%.
- Detailed evaluation carried out after managers have had the opportunity to put their learning into practice confirms that they are better equipped to understand their role in implementing the new policies.
- Taskforce interventions covering the new HR policies for managing poor performance and attendance and managing sickness absence have contributed to the reductions in sickness absence levels across HMRC, that is:
  - Days lost 12 months to January 2006 = 1,138,587
    - average 94,882 per month
    - average 11.68 per employee per year
  - Days lost 12 months to January 2007 = 966,252
    - average 80,521 per month
    - average 10.34 per employee per year

Testimonials – examples of unsolicited feedback from different parts of HMRC
- Tax Credit Office:

  ... the workshop has equipped managers with the tools and confidence to implement HR Policies positively ...

- Central Compliance:

  ... it was brilliant. All of it. From the way the material was used to deal with the issues they had at the beginning, to the way they were guided through the policies so they now understand how everything fits ...

- Debt Management and Banking:

  ... our people have valued these events. .... it's essential we continue to offer this support across HMRC – there is the demand and need ...

- Director of Studies at the Royal Institute of Professional Administrations (following a Taskforce presentation on 'Leading Strategic Change'):

  ... your excellent presentation ... was extremely interesting and relevant. As you will recall, the participants asked many questions during the visit and I believe we could have continued with more ...

- Detection:

  They were impressed by the speed with which the event had been arranged; We have generally developed good HR working practices but we need to per- sist and further improve. Your session was critical to this process and I am looking to use the HR task team to roll-out the HR changes to all Regional managers; Speaking as a manager I feel I now have a far clearer under- standing of the key issues. I feel more in tune with what is expected of me as a manager and how to achieve this with HR supporting my management decisions. I think the concept of a task force is an excellent one and I hope this method will be used in other areas in the future.

- Comment made at a People User Forum:

  the Taskforce event was the best HR event I ever been to in all my years in the Department.

These results demonstrate that the use of an intelligent blend of face-to-face events in the form of presentations, coaching, mentoring, workshops and master classes served to engage managers in a major transformation of HR service deliv- ery and helped to equip them to carry out their people management responsibili- ties. Identifying the managers as key stakeholders and then responding efficiently with interventions that were appropriate to their operational circumstances were the foundation stones of the Taskforce approach.

Case study 3: Pfizer

This case illustrates the use of an Enterprise 2.0 tool, in the form of an inter- nally developed wiki, to engage internal stakeholders in collaborative knowledge exchange.

Pfizer is the world's largest research-based biomedical and pharmaceutical company. It has a corporate headquarters located in New York, with several major research and development sites around the world, including one in Sandwich, Kent, United Kingdom which employs approximately 4000 staff.

The pursuit of innovative solutions and a knowledge sharing culture encourages Pfizer to embrace well-conceived and creative approaches to business practices. About 3 years ago, a small number of research scientists developed an internal shared knowledge repository using wiki technology (also see Chapter 4), to help them work more effectively on their project. From those early origins, a company-wide application called 'Pfizerpedia' was developed.

Pfizerpedia (see Figure 7.4) acts as a central Web hub that colleagues can use to link, generate and search content authored by the global Pfizer community. Project teams may use the Pfizerpedia to share non-sensitive information both within the group and with the rest of the organisation, but it is not intended to be a system for sharing data or summarised/interpreted results related to specific compounds or projects.

Its popularity has grown and it is fast becoming an online resource of first preference for R&D employees, seeking knowledge pertinent to their job role. Pfizerpedia now has over 2500 contributors creating over 5000 content pages. More than 3000 pages have received at least 1000 hits each. In total, there have been over 11 million page views and approximately 100,000 page edits since it was setup.

As the screenshot says, it is important to note that the Pfizerpedia does not replace any document management systems within Pfizer. Rather, it complements

Figure 7.4 Screenshot of Pfizerpedia homepage.

these systems by providing a way to easily link into them, while maintaining the security and authorisation controls to the primary documents.

The development of Pfizerpedia

At its heart a wiki is just a Web content publishing tool. The concept was originally conceived as a means of providing the simplest and quickest way for non-technical users to publish Web content. The features that differentiate a wiki from most other Web publishing platforms provide some good clues as to where and how wikis are best used.

Enterprise wikis such as Pfizerpedia are often used for:

- collaboratively building documentation,
- creating and maintaining knowledge bases,
- project management,
- gathering tacit knowledge (knowledge not related to any specific project but essential to getting things done in an organisation),
- meeting management, from agenda to minutes and action items.

Popular pages on Pfizerpedia include: (i) a 'one-stop shop' for navigating the acronyms commonly used by the business; (ii) scientific 'centres of expertise' knowledge bases; and (iii) the Learning & Development 'homepage' with regularly updated information on training opportunities.

John Castledine, the Director of Learning and Development for Pfizer's Global Research and Development (PGRD) Division, reflected on Pfizerpedia's growing prominence as a learning tool by suggesting that:

> For organizations that need to create and nurture an innovative culture, the development of an internal 'wiki' site can be an important element. It is certainly the case at Pfizer, where increasing evidence points towards the usefulness of Pfizerpedia in enabling our employees to share and access knowledge more quickly than before. The ability to publish freely attributed information online can help overcome any tendencies that may exist towards 'silo protectionism' or a bureaucratic approval process.

There are, however, important challenges, not least of which is dealing with the change ramifications of promoting organisation-wide access to new 'bottom-up' collaboration tools such as Pfizerpedia. This may also be viewed as an opportunity for HR professionals. John Castledine returned to this point:

> There can be little doubt that for an organisation to encourage the adoption of enterprise 2.0 there must be a perceived overall benefit in doing so. To achieve sustainable change, it is vital that these benefits are presented

from the frame-of-reference of the key stakeholders. We can partner closely with IT colleagues to help achieve this goal. For example, information over-load is a major concern for most colleagues. Hence without understanding RSS feeds, blogs become yet more websites to add to your favourites list. Similarly, wikis and social bookmarking (tags) offer welcomed options to reduce e-mail traffic within teams.

HR and Enterprise 2.0

John identified three steps that can be taken by HR to help drive the uptake of these Enterprise 2.0 tools.

First, early adopters (from both the scientific and IT communities) typically welcome wider interest. Hence there is a wealth of advice available within organi-sations for those seeking to better understand how to use the technology. HR col-leagues should seek out such information, and experiment with applying these tools in their day-to-day roles. This builds awareness and credibility to partner effectively with the early adopters in wider deployment of these technologies.

In the case of PGRD Learning & Development, this approach also provided a 'quick-win' for enhancing communication with internal audiences. Creating an L&D page on Pfizerpedia provided an additional channel for advertising the training available to colleagues. With all L&D team members able to contribute to the site, more information is being shared than through traditional Web sites (e.g., all Level 1 training-class feedback metrics), and updates are published on a regular basis. This has proved popular with about 1500 hits every month.

Second, by definition the early adopters view new technologies from a differ-ent frameof reference to the majority of the workforce. Their enthusiasm alone is rarely enough to achieve a tipping point for organisation-wide uptake. Hence, the expertise within HR to guide culture-change programmes should not be overlooked.

Finally, there is a lot written about the changing expectations of Gen. Y versus previous generations entering the workplace. There is no doubt that a growing number of new starters will be familiar with Web 2.0 tools. Given that HR have a central role in talent acquisition and integration, there are clear opportunities to use knowledge of the available Enterprise 2.0 tools (such as Pfizerpedia) to help attract talent to the company.

Case study 4: Westminster city council

This case illustrates the use of online discussion forums to enhance stakeholder engagement across the organisation.

Westminster City Council is a unitary authority providing local government ser-vices to 232,000 people and 47,000 businesses in London. Rated 'excellent – four stars' by the Audit Commission, Westminster is a pioneer in the provision of leading-edge solutions for local government. The council's 60 elected members serve a community that is highly diverse with complex needs, and which generates 2% of the United Kingdom's gross domestic product. The HR function, led by Graham White, has invested in the use of an online discussion forum, as part of a multifaceted stakeholder engagement programme.

The value of staff engagement

'*To sustain our status as a four star local authority, it is vital that we nurture and develop an engaged workforce*', said Graham White. '*One of the ways we are doing this is to allow our employees more opportunities to voice their opinions online, to help them better engage with key organisational issues. This fits in with other aspects of our strategy, such as staff development, talent spotting and building real values*'.

The Enterprise 2.0 solution

Many local authorities operate staff portals, where information is deposited on numerous subjects for staff to view. In these instances, where staff require further information, follow-up usually consists of reference to online support material, which is often set-piece, 'viewable only' information; alternatively, email or telephone assistance may be available, or staff may be referred to their respective line manager. All of these channels are regulated and do not foster spontaneous, conversational discussion that can be seen by the rest of the organisation.

At Westminster City Council, the decision was taken to adopt an approach which would allow employees at all levels to engage in online discussion on a variety of topics, some of them determined 'top-down' by key officers of the organisation, and others created 'bottom-up' by the employees. The pre-allocated subjects arise from a variety of inputs: council objectives, senior management meetings; subjects raised by individuals through a 'sounding board' email channel; engagement groups, open-house sessions or simply by one individual feeling strongly about a particular element of how the council is doing its business. An example of a pre-allocated discussion topic concerns Reward Strategy. In this case, the Council is implementing a new remuneration scheme for all staff that will introduce exciting, broader salary bands to ensure all staff in Westminster have the potential to earn top quartile salaries in the greater London area. The opening position statement, posted by a senior finance officer, draws attention to a central feature of the new proposals, which is the intention to ensure that no members of staff will receive less through the new scheme than they do at present.

The ensuing discussion thread unfolds as employees post their attributed comments, in full view of the rest of organisation. Graham White explained:

Our new Reward Strategy is an important component of the organisation's forward-looking approach to attract and retain the most talented people, but our explicit commitment to employee engagement, evidenced by the discussion forum, is also an important part of the overall mix of measures designed to enhance the Council's reputation.

More broadly, the system easily allows HR to track the level of interest in the different topics, by evaluating the number of 'viewing hits' a particular topic receives and also the number of responses. Graham White continued:

The authority employs over 5,000 staff and we are extremely pleased with the level of enthusiasm and engagement demonstrated by the online discussion forum. The comments posted by our staff not only help to refine the thinking of our senior management team on a particular topic but open up new avenues for discussion. Also, as we seek to downsize the number of employees physically located in our buildings and encourage more flexible working methods, the online discussion forum is a way of creating social interaction.

The online forum also allows topics to be generated spontaneously by the employees. Examples include subjects as varied as childcare vouchers, windows vista and the quality of the shower room. In one example, an employee raised the issue of making cycling to work easier for all staff. Over 280 staff reviewed the site and a number of them made further comments. This lively debate has now been picked up by the organisation, which is looking into the provision of better services for staff who cycle into work.

Policing the Enterprise 2.0 applications
The policing of the new Enterprise 2.0 applications has been carefully considered by Westminster, in recognition that it does have the potential to create reputational damage if it becomes a source of malicious or abusive intent. As Graham White explained:

We are conscious of the potential threat but this did not distract us from seeking to achieve the potential benefits. One of our rules is that all comments posted must be attributable. We also carefully monitor our discussion forum for any signs of misuse and employees know that such action will not be tolerated. I'm pleased to say that the forum is used in a responsible way. The key to achieving and sustaining this is in part attributable to maintaining good standards in the way the site is managed but equally importantly the employees need to see evidence that their comments count. In other words, the discussion forums do place an extra responsibility on the organisation to show it is prepared to act on good suggestions, where practicable.

Future developments
Looking to the future, the positive outcomes and experiences emerging from the use of the discussion forums has now stimulated internal debate regarding potential new developments in the suite of Enterprise 2.0 applications used at Westminster City Council. Graham concluded:

> *We are constantly looking at potential new ways of using these new technologies to enhance the level of engagement of our staff with the organisation. Our belief is that there is considerable scope for further enhancements, to give our people a greater sense of voice in shaping the Council's activities. We shall also look carefully at how lessons learned internally might be applicable to our customers, strengthening and extending the organisation's value proposition to new audiences.*

Case study 5: KPMG

This case illustrates the use of a variety of Enterprise 2.0 tools in enabling better communication and knowledge sharing amongst KPMG consultants, which in turn translates into more effective engagement with their clients.

KPMG is a UK limited liability partnership and a subsidiary of KPMG Europe LLP. It is a leading provider of audit, tax and advisory services. KPMG in the United Kingdom has over 10,000 partners and staff in over 22 office locations and recently merged with the German, Spanish and Swiss member firms. KPMG Europe LLP is part of a strong global network. Combined revenues for KPMG member firms increased to US $19.81 billion for the fiscal year ended 30 September 2007.

Due to the scale, complexity and geographical spread of KPMG's business operations, collaboration and knowledge sharing amongst KPMG's primary asset –its people – is a vital component of its success. Underpinning its drive to constantly improve this aspect of its business, aspects of Enterprise 2.0 applications are being adopted, to varying degrees, with the key aim of delivering better services to the firms' clients.

Using Enterprise 2.0 to improve knowledge sharing
Building on the theme of knowledge sharing, many assignments involve the formation of groups who work together around a common goal; effectively there are communities of practice – bringing together people with shared interests and passions whether they be from an industry perspective, particular KPMG service, client or geography.

As Ceri Hughes, Director, Global Advisory Knowledge Management/IT/ Research at KPMG in the United Kingdom explained:

> *In these situations, some teams have a naturally high level of face-to-face contact, where information can be readily shared. However, in those cases*

where, for example, we might have teams separated by geography, time zones, and office locations, we need to facilitate convenient and effective ways of stimulating and maintaining knowledge sharing and group working. In these cases we are beginning to turn to a variety of enterprise 2.0 applications.

The points made about convenience and effectiveness resonate with widely published research relating to the propensity for users to adopt new technologies and their subsequent reactions. The crucial element in all of this for KPMG was unremitting attention to making sure, where possible, that the new Enterprise 2.0 tools could be assimilated easily into the natural way of working for their people, without the need for significant support.

Ceri Hughes explained the steps taken to bring this about:

In order to make our new tools as simple, intuitive and familiar as possible; we have tried to make the initial access to them as straightforward as possible. To do this, we make as many of the tools as possible available from our KPMG Portal – our single knowledge sharing platform, built using Microsoft SharePoint 2007. This means our users have a single point of access to the tools to support their collaboration activities.

In-house support

Enhancing the critical 'pillars' of easy access and intuitive operation, KPMG has a network of knowledge managers who assist the organisation to optimise the use of the Enterprise 2.0 tools. These managers are confident in using the different capabilities and understand their most appropriate application. They provide support to the client-facing teams by raising awareness of the tools and providing direct support if required.

'A key role for the knowledge managers is recognising opportunities to use the tools to maximum advantage', said Ceri. 'This is the proactive side to the knowledge managers' role – building relationships with their internal clients and recognising opportunities where the tools can help these teams with assignment or project'.

The spin-off from this is that the client-facing teams get to experience a broad range or blend of tools that support their business processes and they can then take the knowledge of those tools into future assignments.

If knowledge managers are not available at the point at which support is needed, the users can turn to online support in the form of 'smarter working' toolkits which allow them to access the various tools available to support them by browsing various business scenarios available on the knowledge-sharing platform and selecting the one closest to their own which then leads them to the tools available to help them. These scenarios comprise a range of material that explains how to operate the tools in different client-centred situations and can take several forms from simple guidance cards that can be downloaded and printed as aide memoirs, to 'talking heads' type video clips, which explain how to setup and use the tools.

Commenting on these different support approaches, Ceri stressed the importance of maintaining momentum and interest.

It is critical that we build self-sufficiency and confidence in using the enterprise 2.0 tools. Not only do they enhance the way that we can work together in distributed environments and foster greater team working and knowledge sharing but they reflect the way that information is increasingly shared in our lives outside of work. Our 'generation Y' employees expect to see these tools made available to them, but some other individuals and groups require more encouragement and are perhaps more sceptical at first about the potential benefits.

Measurement of benefits

There are currently few hard measures that effectively measure the potential benefits of using the Enterprise 2.0 tools. For example, while it is possible to measure the number of items created over a particular period, this statistic holds little value. As Ceri explained:

At this embryonic stage in our development and use of enterprise 2.0 tools, the use of hard numeric measures is not particularly powerful in terms of telling us how effective these tools are. Perhaps a year from now, it would be helpful to know how many pages, for example, had been sustained over time, in a sense kept alive by their communities of shared interest. We could then probe more into why this had happened and infuse that learning into the wider organisation.

Currently, it is far more beneficial to ascertain via regular team meetings and post assignment de-briefings how the effectiveness of the different tools is perceived. This feedback can be converted into short, snappy case studies, which can be used by our knowledge managers and the online tool kit. We find that our firms' client facing teams are more likely to have confidence in trying out a new tool or way of working if they understand the value that it has already added to their peers or to another situation to which they can easily relate.

Future developments

KPMG will continue to monitor and evaluate its Enterprise 2.0 tools and seek where practicable to enhance their capabilities and penetration within the organisation. As the tools become more ubiquitous in everyday life, so employees will expect to have them freely available in their work situation. This point is recognised by Ceri:

With an increasing number of our current employees and prospective employees displaying high levels of familiarity with these types of tools, there is growing internal and external momentum surrounding their adoption. Indeed, we are conscious that our employer proposition benefits from displaying a willingness to embrace these tools.

Summary

The intended outcomes of HR transformation are largely dependent on the assumption that stakeholders will embrace the new ways of working. You should be aware that failure here could, of course, destabilise and reduce the anticipated benefit stream upon which the investment has been made.

This fundamental link between stakeholder commitment and benefit delivery underpins the importance of expressing stakeholder commitment in terms of its value contribution to the HR transformation process. For example, it is essential to secure the commitment of the key stakeholders who sign off the business case. Without the signatures of those principal sponsors in the first place and indeed their ongoing unwavering commitment, there would be an interruption to financial investment with an attendant knock-on to benefit release.

The maintenance and accuracy of the organisation structure, configured in the human resource management system, may be dependent on managers maintaining their particular part of it on an ongoing basis. This organisation structure will no doubt be used to feed many other processes and systems. Therefore, its accuracy and integrity are paramount. If managers fail to do their own maintenance, this will then create a higher maintenance burden for other functions in the business, adding layers of cost.

The use of newly emerging Web 2.0 technologies can radically transform stakeholder communication and engagement, giving rise to an improved employer brand and more effective organisational learning.

These are just some of the expressions of value that can be directly linked to stakeholder engagement – hopefully its value to you in your organisation can be readily appreciated.

Part 3

Planning and Implementation

Part 3 focuses on the Planning and Implementation aspects of HR transformation.

Chapter 8: Service Delivery Approaches reviews different approaches to HR organisation and some of the organisational interface issues that are being experienced. The Chapter also addresses outsourcing and provides guidance to help organisations navigate through outsourcing decisions.

Chapter 9: Programme Management considers how programme management approaches can be used to engage purposefully with stakeholders through ongoing communication and the use of governance structures. We also explore issues and risks around technology-led HR transformation.

Chapter 10: Implementation: Capability and Culture focuses on the roles and capabilities in the newly transformed HR function. In particular, we explore the capabilities needed in shared services and strategic partner (generalist and specialist) roles and the ways to build these capabilities. We also consider the impact of HR transformation on the role of line manager.

Chapter 11: Implementation: Process and Technology sets out the main considerations in delivering the process and technology aspects of HR transformation, including the impact of HR information systems on employees and managers. In addition, we explore how to track key benefit areas and how to measure and evaluate implementation effectiveness.

Chapter 12: Benefits Realisation looks at ways to track delivery of the business benefits of HR transformation, building on the content of Chapter 6.

8

Service Delivery Approaches

This chapter is concerned with the means by which the different kinds of HR services can be delivered into the business. The choices made will have a major bearing on likely costs, benefits and timescales of the transformation journey and therefore warrant appropriate attention.

Key themes

- The elements of Web-based HR, shared services and outsourcing can all play a part – how do you look at overall design considerations – who does what?
- The emergence of boundary issues associated with different structural approaches – how do you deal with these?
- If your organisation does want to move to outsourcing, what are the key considerations to make it work effectively?
- How does Web-based HR impact HR/line manager relationships?

Context

The considerations and issues associated with different service delivery approaches are related to the challenges that HR functions in organisations are constantly challenged to meet. These distinct, often competing aims are linked to the business drivers framework discussed in Chapter 3: to make itself more cost effective through reducing the costs of its services and headcount; to improve its services to increasingly demanding line managers and employees and to address the strategic and reputational objectives of organisations (Martin, 2005; Martin, Reddington, & Alexander, 2008; Snell, Stueber, & Lepak, 2002).

To help meet these challenges, the function first turned to organisational solutions in the 1990s, which included (a) outsourcing and, in some cases, off-shoring of key services, and (b) developing shared service models by centralising previously devolved HR operations (Reddington, Williamson, & Withers, 2005; Reilly, Tamkin, & Broughton, 2007; Reilly & Williams, 2006). Second, like other business functions, it turned to information and communications technologies (ICT), often in combination with organisational solutions, as a means to rationalise or even transform HR's internal operations (Gueutal & Stone, 2005; Kettley & Reilly, 2003). However, progress in Web-enabling the HR function and outsourcing has been piecemeal and fraught with problems. Some of these themes and issues are now unpacked in more detail.

The factors involved in the choice of service delivery approaches

Delivery channels – Who does what?

As we have already noted, it is evident that HR management in organisations is not just the domain of the HR function; there are many players in the delivery of HR in organisations:

- employees (through self-service),
- line managers (through self-service and their people management responsibilities),
- outsourcers (back office, recruitment, training, etc.),
- external consultants,
- different internal players in the HR function (shared service centre, specialists and generalists).

Collectively, we refer to these participants as 'HR delivery channels'. When designing the service delivery model, it is important to take decisions concerning where responsibilities for service delivery will change.

We can be certain that genuine, sustainable HR transformation will shift accountabilities for HR management. What each organisation will need to work out is how far these accountabilities shift and to whom. This is the purpose of this phase of work in the transformation process.

We do not start this thinking about future accountabilities with a blank sheet of paper. Some of the transfer in accountability will be directly related to Web-based HR and will be known. So, from a technology perspective, there will be core HR processes/activities that must be configured in the HR Information System (HRIS) backbone. These (such as responsibility for personal data) will be Web-enabled and move to employee self-service. There will, in all probability, be e-tools on top of the HRIS backbone that will embed other HR processes. There will be the opportunity for greater self-service concerning policy/procedural advice, and so on. These factors are discussed in much greater detail in Chapter 4.

In addition to these shifts in service provision that are linked explicitly to Web-based HR, we also need to take into account other organisational drivers that will shape the way HR has delivered. A useful starting point is to explore how to work through the 'who does what' question and, in particular, to ensure that the HR function ends up being focused on those areas that will contribute most value in the organisation.

Understanding that HR is delivered through a number of channels is the first step. The second step is to scope, at a relatively high level, the services embraced by HR management – not just what the HR function does – for your organisation.

Scope of HR services

The *scope of HR services* document is the second key input into this process. This is derived from the organisational levers model shown in Chapter 1, Figure 1.2. As a starting point, the HR services can be illustrated under five headings:

- people development and performance management,
- employee relations and communication,
- resource management,
- retention and reward,
- HR information.

In developing your scope of HR services document, the important things to consider are the following:

- Focus on the full scope of HR management, not just what the HR function does, and remember that HR management includes training and development.
- Do not aim for an exhaustive list of every activity undertaken in the realm of HR – keep labels at a high level.
- Aim for no more than 10 labels, and ideally around 5–10, for each heading.

A 'straw man' scope of services document is presented in Appendix 3.

As a precursor to organisational design, we have found it helpful to combine the work on HR delivery channels and scope of HR services to ascertain where responsibilities change for HR service delivery. Our suggested forum to complete this work is through an accountabilities workshop – see Chapter 10 for more details.

Structural issues

Where structural lines are drawn between HR delivery channels, the attendant issues will vary from organisation to organisation. The main questions that will need to be addressed are the following:

- What activities need to be centralised to take advantage of economies of scale and consolidation of expertise?
- Where do we need to decentralise to ensure that we remain close to the business and take account of the unique needs of different parts of the organisation?
- Where do we draw the line between those activities that are performed internally and those that are better performed externally?
- Where do we draw lines of responsibility for people management between internal organisational boundaries – both between the HR function and line managers/employees and within the HR function itself?
- How do we leverage technology to deliver HR services?

In answering these questions, there are many contingent factors, such as the ambition or ability of the organisation to implement Web-based HR solutions; current capability of line managers in people management; attitudes to in-sourced and outsourced provision; maturity of the HR function; suitable outsourcing options and so on. This means that your decisions around HR delivery will ultimately be the product of trade-offs and contingencies that reflect the situation your organisation faces.

We are seeing some significant changes in the way the HR function is working, what HR professionals are doing and how they are contributing. The key point to note is that it is not the labelling or even where organisational lines are drawn that is important. What is important about the structural dimension is the alignment of HR delivery with the strategic goals of the organisation and the focus on the internal business clients.

A useful model which illustrates the alignment or 'line of sight' between HR strategy and HR service delivery approaches or architecture is shown in Figure 8.1. The model draws upon the prominent, relevant literature and our own practical experience and research and shows four central elements – *HR strategies, HR service goals, HR service architectures* and *HR service outcomes*. In effect, this creates a 'line of sight' between the adopted HR strategies of an organisation and the HR service outcomes. The moderating elements reflect the changing and dynamic nature of HR service delivery in its varying organisational contexts. Consequently, every organisation can engage with this model at a different point. Some may already have advanced technology-based applications or tools in

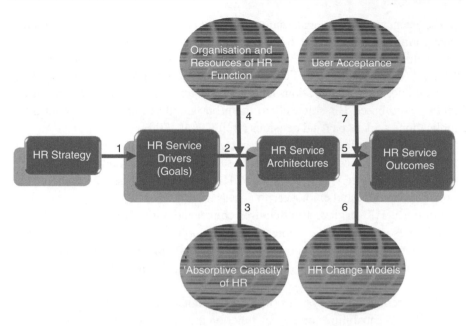

Figure 8.1 Framework linking HR strategy with HR service outcomes (adapted from Reddington, Martin, & Alexander, 2008; Reddington et al., 2005).

place, whereas other organisations may be engaging with these more advanced technologies for the first time, as HR seeks to move from a traditional support function to a more strategic partner.

The *HR service delivery drivers or goals* flow from the HR strategies discussed earlier (Relationship 1). These drivers can address HR's *transactional* or *transformational* goals (Snell et al., 2001). The former focus on reducing the costs of HR services or improving its productivity, and improving service delivery to managers and employees; the latter focus on freeing up time for HR staff to address more strategic issues rather than basic administration, and by transforming the contributions that HR can provide to the organisation (its 'business model'). The transformational goals involve extending HR's reach to more remote parts of the organisation to create a sense of 'corporateness' or internal integration in extended enterprises (e.g., through HR portals); enabling more sophisticated recruitment searches (e.g., through widely available social media to uncover people not actively seeking jobs) and (self) selection through online tools; creating new forms of organisational community and methods of communications through new applications of Web 2.0, for example, interactive employee engagement surveys, virtual communities of practice, 'blogging' and 'wikis' (Martin, Reddington, & Kneafsey, 2009). These and other technology-related aspects were covered in more detail in Chapter 4.

The extent to which an organisation focuses on any or all of these goals should, in theory, influence the types of *HR services architectures* it adopts (Relationship 2). The architecture refers to the *HR data, systems and technologies* but also how these are *sourced* and the choices made over the *human resources organisation*. For example, some organisations have set up in-house shared services centres and applied Web-based HR solutions to them but simultaneously outsourced major applications such as pay and pensions (Reilly et al., 2007).

It follows, therefore, that an organisation which places an emphasis on transactional goals, such as cost reduction, would seek to design and build a Web-based HR services architecture which streamlined HR processes and deployed self-service tools for managers and employees to access them.

Similarly, HR services architectures concerned with addressing transformational goals would involve elements such as sophisticated search technologies, career development tools, human capital management systems, social software, e-learning and knowledge management platforms and virtual meetings software.

The sourcing of these systems (in-house vs. outsource) and the implications for the skills and capabilities of the HR function are also important considerations – also see Chapter 4.

As the model shows, the HR services architecture will be *moderated* by the *absorptive capacity of HR* (Relationship 3) to seek out knowledge and exploit these architectures to the full. Absorptive capacity in this context can be defined as the *potential* for the HR function to seek out and assimilate knowledge about HR technologies and incorporate these into their vision for a changed HR function (Jansen et al., 2005). It can also be defined in terms of the capacity of the HR function to *realise* potential by good implementation practices and ongoing support.

One of the major debates in the practitioner world is whether Web-based HR technologies should be adapted to existing or revised HR processes (customisation) or whether HR processes should be adapted to fit usually bought-in technologies (the 'vanilla' solution). Evidence to date suggests that the vanilla solution is winning out because of the difficulties in changing existing Web-based HR technologies at reasonable cost (Shrivastava & Shaw, 2004). This realisation phase is also marked by the ability of the HR function to combine face-to-face and technology-mediated HR approaches to produce a new business model for HR previously discussed; that is, HR's ability to transform what it can currently do with available knowledge and technology into a more strategically oriented function that addresses the key strategic drivers of the organisation (Huselid et al., 2005).

The organisation and resourcing of the HR function (Relationship 4) refers to the different configurations of organisational structures used by organisations to deliver their human resources strategy, including decisions on centralisation of decisions, outsourcing and specialisation among HR professionals.

Different models are currently being adopted, all of which involve choices on the development of shared services, centres of HR expertise, managerial and employee self-service and HR business partnering (Caldwell, 2008). These developments are often associated with the research and prescriptions of Ulrich (tripartite model) though as Reilly et al (2007) and others have pointed out, there are many variations on this theme, with large HR departments still being organised along functional lines.

Finally, the adoption of specific HR services architectures should lead to specific *HR services outcomes* (Relationship 5). Note that these outcomes can be both intended or unintended, and also positive or negative (Fisher & Howell, 2004). It should also be noted that the positive/negative classifications will sometimes depend on where one stands. For example, the headcount reduction of HR is often used as a justification (positive outcome) by the organisation for adoption of Web-based HR but it also has potentially damaging consequences for organisational knowledge, as well as those HR staff displaced by the reduction (negative outcome).

Again it should be noted that these outcomes will be *moderated* by the *change models* (Relationship 6) and approaches adopted. The change management literature is extensive, analysing how different approaches to change produce better or worse results; controversy still exists over the merits of 'top-down' versus 'bottom-up' change, incrementalist approaches versus 'big-bang' and the pace at which change should be driven, including the competence of HR to manage such change effectively.

One of the most important factors shaping the success of technological change is *user acceptance* (Relationship 7). Thus, important moderating factors that need to be considered are architectural system design decisions and reactions to the Web-based HR technologies (Stone, Romero, & Lukaszewski, 2006).

Case example illustrating aspects of the model

This Oil and Energy Services company had grown both organically and through acquisition into a global organisation employing 64,000 staffs in 80 countries. To create high levels of customer service it depended on high levels of international team working and knowledge sharing. This reliance on knowledge and technology caused them to describe themselves not only as a leading oilfield services provider but also as information systems specialists, who could support their customers by translating data into useful information, and then transform this information into knowledge for improved decision making around the globe. Given their strategy of creativity, collaboration, and high levels of customer intimacy, the levels of understanding of customers' needs, managing international diversity and knowledge sharing required a great deal of international teamwork.

HR Strategy

The HR function was seen as pivotal to the development of international team-working and knowledge sharing. The HR function had a crucial role in developing culturally sensitive management and in so doing was required to shed its administrative workload to concentrate on culture management and change issues. The HR function was being gradually transformed into a more strategically oriented function, in which HR staff worked more closely with managers in the new operating structure.

To achieve this, the HR function was first divided into the now common shared services and business partner model (Ulrich & Brockbank, 2005). Shared services provided administrative and policy support with HR business partners providing direct support to business-facing managers in the field. Second, shared services adopted a global HRIS to allow it to become more efficient and effective in providing globally available data for all service lines and all business groups from the same database. This allowed consistency and integration of performance management and other HR practices and policies throughout the company. Third, Web-based HR was introduced to improve service delivery by opening up the access to the HRIS using manager and employee self-service applications.

HR service goals

Thus, the HR service goals were primarily concerned with improving service quality and freeing up time for HR staff to address more strategic issues.

So when we looked at it we realised that in order to do that we had to take off a lot of the administrative load from the HR function in each of the groups and let them focus much more on people and then...work with one another around people issues because that's the cultural driver and let all the support stuff be taken care of somewhere else.

(UK HR Director)

HR service architectures

First, these goals were to be achieved through the development of a common HR portal, through which all online services could be accessed. The intention of this portal was also to help HR to create a greater sense of corporate identity among employees in the extended enterprise using an internal employer branding strategy (Martin & Hetrick, 2006). Second, the company implemented a global HRIS, comprising a set of basic information systems and the first set of Web-based HR tools. These technologies were a combination of out-of-the-box applications, derived from the global HRIS, combined with bespoke tools, many of which were developed in-house'.

The parent company's internal analyses had shown that

There is a cost saving ...but that cost saving does not offset the cost of imple- mentation and investment cost. It might do in the long term but if you're looking at sort of two/three year returns it doesn't work. (UK HR Director)

The real benefit being sought was an improvement in HR service quality, pro- viding more accurate and reliable data and enabling more informed management decisions. The company, however, had a longer term transformational goal of introducing ICT to improve human capital management through the development and introduction of a bespoke global 'career centre'.

Service centres were established to handle transactional enquiries from line managers and employees. The emphasis was on the internal sourcing of HR tech- nologies, unless a compelling case could be made for outsourcing of services. As the HR Director explained:

I think outsourcing overall is quite dangerous because outsourcing is ... in many cases it's cost driven and if it's cost driven why should another organi- sation be able to take some cost out which you can't?

HR service outcomes

A mix of intended and unintended outcomes emerged. On the positive side, man- agers were satisfied overall with the level of transactional support provided by the shared service centre and the quality of data available via employee and manager self-service tools. There were issues, however, with some Web-based HR applica- tions, in particular the 'career centre' which was supposed to enhance opportuni- ties for international mobility but failed to live up to its promise. Managers also reported problems with 'service ambiguity', in the sense that they were not always sure what services to reasonably expect from different parts of HR, citing poten- tial conflicts and overlaps between specialists and business partners.

This example, supported by the framework described earlier, points to a num- ber of important points for practitioners to be aware of when considering different HR service delivery approaches:

- Consider carefully the specific HR services goals that define the purpose of the investment in the project(s)
- Design an architecture which is appropriate for the defined goals
- Implement the solution with a determination to achieve positive, intended outcomes which reflect the defined project goals
- Check carefully that a 'line of sight' has been established between HR strat- egy, goals, architectures and intended outcomes

Some of these architectural design decisions are now examined in some detail, as these are often a source of anxiety and confusion for HR professionals.

The opportunities and challenges associated with different structural models

Most people currently think of structural change in terms of introducing the so-called 'Ulrich model' or the 'three-legged stool' (i.e., shared services, business partners and centres of expertise). However, this structure is really designed for large complex organisations, especially those with geographically dispersed operations, and even here there is much adaptation. Organisations might introduce only one or two legs, particularly choosing to have business partners. Certainly smaller organisations tend to stick with a single integrated HR team where all activities are combined. If the organisation is somewhat bigger/more complex, separate teams may deal with some or all the HR issues for particular locations or business units.

The advantages and disadvantages of using the Ulrich model are shown in Table 8.1.

As we have previously noted, structural changes are usually accompanied by some process modernisation (reductions in 'handoffs', removal of duplication or redundant steps and simplification and standardisation of tasks) and some technological improvement (i.e., employee/manager self-service and improved HRIS).

As can be seen from the list of reported advantages, many of these accrue not just because of structural change but because of what the reorganisation allows to happen: the development of new 'mindsets' about what HR exists to do; a focus on improving HR processes and investments in new technology.

It is also worth noting that the tensions described in Table 8.1 were also identified in People Management (October 2006), which draws attention to recent research that questions the validity and effectiveness of the Ulrich model:

As HR has sought to become more strategic, value-adding and business-focused, the emphasis has increasingly fallen on the ideal structure for the function – a trend that has been particularly influenced by the writings of US academic Dave Ulrich.

His writings have built up the popularity of a three-legged model: an HR shared-service centre, centres of expertise, and business partners. In many large organisations, this model has replaced the integrated teams that previously carried out the full range of HR activities, from administration to strategic direction.

Though the three-legged model is often thought of as the norm, our research has highlighted the shortage of evidence – in the UK and Ireland at least – on the extent of its adoption and, more worryingly, on its effectiveness.

(People Management, 26 October 2006, p. 62)

The efficacy of the Ulrich model is also challenged in an article by Gratton (2003, p. 18), which concerns the perceived fragmentation of HR services after the Ulrich model had been adopted in an organisation:

> *During the past decade, we have fragmented the roles and responsibilities of the function. We have outsourced the lower value, operational work, and we are beginning to develop the staff profiling work that will enable us to act as 'employee champions'. We also putting the 'change agent' roles back into the stream of business to work closely with their line manager partners. Meanwhile, the 'business partners' are either going into the business or clustered around 'best practice centres' which may be located in different places.... this fragmentation of the HR function is causing all sorts of unintended problems. Senior managers look at the fragments and are not clear how the function as a whole adds value.*

As we have previously noted, not all organisations adopt the three-legged stool structural model. Indeed, the Reilly et al. (2007) report observed that among the organisations surveyed only 18% confirmed their restructured HR function incorporated all three elements of shared services, business partners and centres of expertise. The vast majority, therefore, had adopted either a partial Ulrich model (46%) or claimed to have no elements at all (36%). These latter cases reflected HR functions which had been conflated into single teams and the Ulrich descriptors were not recognised as distinct and separate channels of service delivery.

Informed by these observations, we now take the opportunity to examine in more detail the rationale and challenges posed by the introduction of shared service centres, business partners and centres of excellence.

Shared service centres

Shared service centres provide services needed by several, if not all, other parts of an organisation. Two distinctive features of HR shared service centres are:

- they offer a common service provision of routine HR administration and, sometimes, additional HR services;
- they are service-focused, enabling the customers of the shared service to specify the level and nature of the service.

An increasing number of organisations are exploring the option of HR shared service centres, including the use of 'off-shoring' whereby the service centre is located in a geographically remote location. As shown earlier in Table 8.1, the introduction of a shared service centre is just one element of a wider change to the way that the HR department operates and is structured. For example, a shared

Table 8.1 The advantages/disadvantages of the Ulrich model (Adapted from Reilly et al. (2007); Reilly & Williams, 2006)

Advantages	Disadvantages
Cheaper because of economies of scale in a shared services operation	Costs creep back after the initial reduction. This may be for good reasons that the service offering becomes more variegated to fit different customer needs or as a reflection of the relative shift towards higher paid professional staff However, costs may arise because inefficiencies develop and are not tackled as they were in the initial set-up phase
Improved resourcing flexibility because of larger pool of administrative staff	Only true if co-located but poorer career development because step up to business partners and experts is difficult
Better knowledge transfer within the administrative team	Only true if co-located, but potentially poorer knowledge transfer with business partners and experts
Faster service through automation and/or simplification of processes	Managers complain at the transfer of work where the self-service technology is difficult to operate and where the tasks were once performed by HR
Better performance quality through better specification of process ownership and process re-engineering	Customers complain that shared service centres are often remote and that contact is impersonal or too standardised. Managers also object to the perceived loss of a single contact point now having to get services through multiple channels
More time spent on business critical issues because process standardisation and automation reduce the proportion of time spent on administrative activities	Though there is evidence to support this contention, there is also evidence that senior HR staff do not focus on the key issues as they are distracted by operational support to line managers
Higher HR credibility because administration is done better than before and the business partner role with its focus on a strategic contribution offers greater added value to the business	The question mark regarding this benefit arises from the business partner role – is it working properly?

(Continued)

Table 8.1 The advantages/disadvantages of the Ulrich model—cont'd

Advantages	*Disadvantages*
It is easier to handle a merger with this model because of the separation of activities. Thus, service centres and centres of expertise can be combined and business partners retained to meet any revised business unit structure	No evidence to contradict this contention

service centre is often introduced at the same time as there is a move to introduce business partners and centres of excellence as there is a corresponding increase in the number of people management activities that are devolved from the HR department to the individual employee.

The content of shared services will vary from one organisation to another. A shared service centre can provide the full service from routine administration in, for example, recruitment, payroll and training, right through to supplying specialist HR information and advice on HR policy and practice.

HR shared service centres can be resourced by in-house personnel or they can be outsourced to specialist third party outsourcing providers. In practice, it is becoming more common to see hybrid models. One example of a hybrid model might be whereby the majority of the HR services are provided through an in-house shared service centre, with a few specialist areas being outsourced (e.g., employee 'wellness' or 'well-being'). A different example could be where the administrative activities are outsourced to one provider and other specialist areas are outsourced to separate specialist providers. A model of shared services which illustrates the benefits and challenges posed by different organisational models is shown in Figure 8.2.

Key architectural design issues

When setting up a shared service centre, a lot of thought needs to be given to the following areas:

- *Determine a clear case* for creating shared services that is based on the value-added to the business. How will shared services help the organisation manage its business more effectively? Decisions about whether a shared service environment is appropriate need to reflect a full stakeholder perspective – including leaders in individual business units, trade unions and employees.

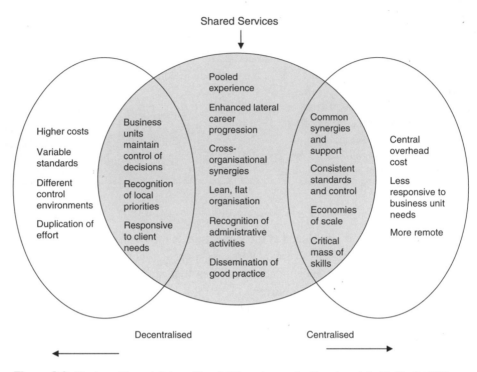

Shared Services

Higher costs

Variable standards

Different control environments

Duplication of effort

Business units maintain control of decisions

Recognition of local priorities

Responsive to client needs

Pooled experience

Enhanced lateral career progression

Cross-organisational synergies

Lean, flat organisation

Recognition of administrative activities

Dissemination of good practice

Common synergies and support

Consistent standards and control

Economies of scale

Critical mass of skills

Central overhead cost

Less responsive to business unit needs

More remote

Decentralised

Centralised

Figure 8.2 The benefits and disbenefits of different organisational models (Reilly & Williams, 2006).

- *Review and redevelop HR processes.* How do we organise our HR processes to most effectively deliver the service our customers expect? Simply pulling processes together in a central hub is unlikely to deliver a more streamlined, customer-driven service. Moving to a shared service provision requires a fundamental re-engineering of HR processes.
- *Explore options for the structure* of the shared service centre. How can the centre most effectively be structured to deliver its business objectives? Multinational organisations need to decide whether the shared service is most effectively delivered a number of centres based on, for example, business groups, regions or a global shared service. A key factor in helping managers to make this decision is the number of people employed in the operating countries. For example, Standard Chartered Bank introduced their shared service centre on a global basis, despite the company having a large geographical spread, because the numbers of people employed in each of the countries was relatively small. Others, for example, IBM, introduced their shared services on a regional

basis, or in the countries where they have the largest numbers of employees, as in the case of PricewaterhouseCoopers. National Grid, which has major operations in the United Kingdom and the United States, designed a model described in Box 8.1.

■ *Clarify the role, responsibilities and accountabilities of the HR shared service centre.* The content and scope of the HR shared services centre can vary between organisations, but they largely fall into two types: (1) basic administration of, for example, relocation services, maternity leave and recruitment services and (2) providing specialist information and guidance to employees and managers on HR policy and practice and employment law. The centre may also offer pooled internal consultancy and project support.

■ *Clarify and communicate the role and responsibilities of the customers (e.g., line managers).* If the shared service centre model will require them to act differently (which it is likely to, for example, through the introduction of Web-based self-service), they must be given the appropriate support.

Box 8.1 National grid shared services

An example of how an FTSE 20 company has evolved its shared services to meet changing business requirements is found in National Grid. In a move to bring clarity over each core people process from strategy/policy to administration, National Grid implemented a 'deep' shared services model. This model incorporated specialists into the shared services structure from areas such as resourcing, L&D and ER.

Since then, National Grid has set out a business strategy aimed at standardising policy and ways of working across its UK and US businesses as a whole. For HR it was decided that this would be best achieved by giving senior specialists Centres of Expertise roles outside of shared services with global rather than regional remits. As a result, regional shared services now focus on process excellence and transactional execution. This aligns with the broader business strategy of standardising processes where possible and creating a global approach to policy and thinking, whilst still allowing regional execution. This evolution of the shared services model has also allowed National Grid to revisit where responsibilities lie for what they term 'professional delivery' – areas such as graduate recruitment, technical training and professional recruitment – and to determine where the demarcation line is best set in terms of CoE or Shared Services responsibility.

- *Agree on performance indicators* to ensure the services are being delivered to plan by using, for example, service-level agreements and a performance management framework to measure the effectiveness of the service delivery.
- *Specify the scale of capital and the nature of the resources required* to get the right technology and organisation infrastructure in place. Don't underestimate!

Architectural design decisions in relation to business partners and HR specialists

In truth, this varies from organisation to organisation and the shades of HR organisational design are many. The roles and capabilities of business partners and specialists are covered in much greater depth in Chapter 10. A number of themes emerge and include the following:

- The primacy of the business partner role in managing the client interface. This is a significant change and shifts power within many HR functions away from the specialist to the business partner. As such, it is both a substantive and a symbolic change representing a cultural shift to a more client-centred approach. For many HR functions, this change has involved a difficult transition for specialists and can be a significant point of resistance during the early stages of HR transformation. We have found that this is particularly true of training and development areas, which may have previously had account management posts and may have been organisationally distinct from HR.
- The specialist role is being increasingly provided externally through outsourcers, consultancy and specialist providers.
- Areas previously staffed by HR specialists (e.g., HR policy) are increasingly being led by HR business partners. For example, in one organisation the development of new HR policy will be led by an HR business partner and run as a project involving a variety of stakeholders on the project team. In another organisation, HR business partners may have responsibility for leading an HR process or policy area, for example, resourcing, performance management and diversity.
- Whether HR professionals report through a business unit or the HR function, there is a need to develop an HR community – for development, networking, knowledge sharing and learning.

Managing the boundaries between the different HR service delivery channels

This is an area of difficulty often faced by HR functions. The underlying issue is primarily about which role is the tail and which is the head. Does it matter? Ultimately, the function needs to develop an HR agenda which will support and help the business succeed. So what matters is that the function works through issues around the client interface and how work is commissioned and then delivered.

In the Reilly et al. (2007) report, 56% of organisations identified 'boundary disputes' within HR shared services as the most prevalent problem affecting their operations. These can often relate to a lack of clarity about roles, responsibilities and accountabilities of the different parts of shared services and fragmented processes. Transferring HR activities to a shared service centre can have knock-on effects on existing career paths, creating tensions and conflicts between an apparent 'esteem' attached to business partners and specialists, compared with the 'institutionalised devaluation' often attached to HR staff involved in administrative and transactional support roles. This thinking can drive wedges among HR professionals and weaken the overall effectiveness of the HR function.

Indeed, Nick Worrall, HR Director at National Grid, identified similar issues associated with the development of its UK shared service centre. As he reflected:

When it became apparent that various people, including myself, were to be part of comprehensive shared service solution, we didn't exactly go home skipping that night. However, those initial thoughts were progressively dispelled as it became evident that the adopted structural approach allowed for end-to-end responsibility for many big ticket HR services, such as recruitment and learning and development, in addition to general transactional support.

Elaborating these insights, it is becoming recognised that one of the ways to mitigate these effects is to involve staff in the design of the centre and being explicit about career development and opportunities. Some organisations have opted to keep their HR service centre separate from the wider HR function. Others have encouraged those wishing to develop a career in HR to acquire wide-ranging HR knowledge in the centre through, for example, rotating around different business streams, and then moving to line or specialist roles in HR or elsewhere in the organisation.

There is also the potential for boundary issues between business partners and specialists. In our experience, if HR specialists are business-focused, boundary issues are less of a concern, as their work will be inexorably linked in with business priorities. Problems arise when HR specialists are semi-detached from the business, pursuing their own agendas and priorities rather than those of the business. For example, in one organisation some learning and development specialists had invested significant time in developing a whole range of training workshops which were not a priority. There are many other examples outside L&D, such as the development of inappropriate policy, investing in unnecessary external research, participating in external bodies of dubious value to the organisation and so on.

One of the ways HR functions are resolving these organisational boundary issues is through adopting aspects of the consultancy model, featured in Figure 1.1. In particular, there are three aspects that help business partners and specialists to work together more effectively:

- The acceptance that HR professionals need to be addressing those issues that are most critical to their clients. This is an important way in which value is expressed and is based on the principle that there will be a *commissioning* of work by the client.
- This work will be packaged as a *project*, with clear terms of reference – including deliverables, timescales, resources, costs, etc.
- HR participates fully in these business-critical projects because they have *valuable skills* that will help their client to make progress.

Whatever the structural solution, it is likely that boundary issues will arise and require resolution. Also see Chapter 10 for some useful insights into this area.

The role of Web-based HR

Developments in technology underpin, to varying degrees, the different HR service delivery approaches. However, introducing new technology is not an end in itself. It enables the organisation to complete work more efficiently through better processes and more effectively by improving quality control. However, it is an expensive venture to upgrade computing and communication devices and this has driven some organisations towards outsourcing, because they cannot fund the capital investment themselves. Outsourcing is covered in more detail below and the factors surrounding technology architectures and implementation are covered in more detail in Chapters 4 and 7.

As we have already noted, Web-based HR is a recent phenomenon (Guetal & Stone, 2005), emerging within the more established and broader context of technology, organisation and people management. The more visionary, advanced interpretations describe a fully integrated, organisation-wide electronic network of HR-related data, information, services, databases, tools, applications and transactions that are generally accessible at any time by employees, managers and HR professionals. So instead of a centralised personnel team handling everyday tasks such as approving pay raises, sorting out training and checking holiday entitlements, these can be handled by the employees themselves or their line manager – Figure 8.3 provides an illustrative screen shot of an employee self-service home page.

Part of the espoused case for Web-based HR (Ulrich & Brockbank, 2005) is that it offers the potential to transform HR's role. It promises to do this by increasing the HR function's influence as consultants focused on the needs of managers and employees and expanding HR's reach as the experts of the organisation's people processes and the developers of value propositions for different employee groups.

The emerging literature (Martin et al., 2008; Parry, Tyson, Selbie, & Leighton, 2007) and our own research and experience show that in order to meet or exceed

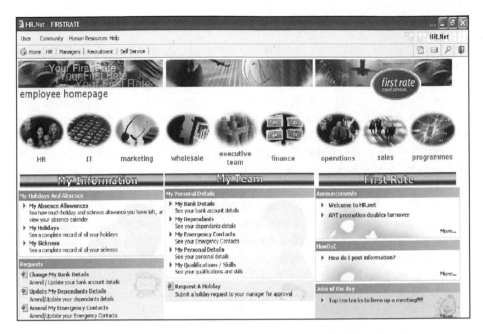

Figure 8.3 Illustrative employee self-service screen (courtesy of HR.net).

expectations associated with investment in Web-based HR, it is vital that a number of considerations are addressed at the outset:

- The focus on occasion is too much on the efficiencies of Web-based HR, that is, cost-cutting and not the longer term gains enabled by the new infrastructure. One clear cause for concern is that discussion at senior management levels regarding the transformation impact on the HR function's capability could be too little and too late.
- The extent to which Web-based HR software is over-engineered and designed by IT consultants and not HR practitioners.
- The fact that Web-based HR is designed for the HR function and not the line managers who should be the real custodians of people and performance.
- The difficulties in securing access to the information that people really want.
  - New technology does not remove poor-quality data.
  - Expect user resistance – unless the new Web-based HR-derived functionality is easy to use and seen to be relevant to the user, adoption rates are likely to be low.

In order to assess whether or not Web-based HR is meeting the promises, we should perhaps look in more detail at what has been achieved with the Web enablement of HR processes in practice.

Web-based HR processing practice

There is very little independent research on the take-up and impact of Web-based HR solutions by UK-based employers (Reddington, 2008). Most of the larger surveys are drawn from predominantly North American samples and are undertaken or funded by proprietary software suppliers or consultants.

These surveys suggest the most effective implementation of Web-based HR solutions depends on several factors. Key among these include standardisation of processes, to the greatest possible extent; available IT infrastructure; data quality and ongoing data maintenance. Where HR management is highly decentralised, it is much more difficult to implement shared core HR technologies, such as HRIS and payroll, or Web-based employee and manager self-services. In highly decentralised organisations, there is likely to be significant resistance to standardising processes. Without adequate IT infrastructure, implementing broad-based Web-based HR technologies is simply impossible. Managers and employees must have at least workplace Intranet access, and the supporting data and telecommunications network must have adequate capacity to accommodate the level of usage that results from implementing Web-based HR services.

Other studies support the main themes evident from the above reports and show us that:

- Web-based HR will not succeed unless it is part of an employee focus culture, where people are trusted to manage their personal affairs. A corporate Intranet with an employee directory will not of itself increase performance. It may save time, but it may not necessarily make people perform better (it may just give them more time in which to perform badly).
- HR needs to take ownership for establishing a relationship between the deployment of Web-based HR and enhanced organisational and employee performance.
- As the guardian of employee and organisational performance, the HR function will increasingly be caught up in the growing debate regarding the sustainability of the dependence upon new technologies in the workplace, such as Web 2.0 – also see Chapters 4 and 7. These developments are often associated with the research and prescriptions of Ulrich (tripartite model), though as Reilly et al (2007) and others have pointed out, there are many variations on this theme. It appears to be the case that significant numbers of large, complex organisations are using the Ulrich model in whole or in part, while smaller organisations have tended to stick with traditional models.

So what we see is that the advent and deployment of new technology that has enabled employers to change the structure of their HR functions by creating new options for delivering HR services. As we have noted, amongst these are, for example, call centres, Web-enabled self-service and shared service centres. These activities may be provided in-house or in whole or in part through third-party organisations, such as outsourcing, covered later in this chapter.

However, technology is not the only factor in determining options in HR service delivery. The different levels of access amongst sections of the workforce and the willingness of managers and employees to use them are just as important, if not more so.

It seems likely that most HR functions would prefer to offer multiple channels at least until self- and assisted service have become more culturally acceptable to the organisation. However, the key to success seems to lie in creating a strategy of self-service contact that is driven by business imperatives, whilst being responsive to users' needs. Our own experience and the published material considered earlier emphasise the need for technology decisions to be firmly rooted in business and functional strategies and HR practices, if they are to maximise the potential benefits. HR should expect senior management to exert more pressure on HR to justify investments in HR technology through return on investment analysis (ROI) and business case developments. Chapters 6 and 12 deal with these issues in more detail.

The role of outsourcing

It has already been stated that outsourcing can be part of the overall service approach mix. Outsourcing is a word that has come to represent a complete range of activities but we can trace the base concept back to a decision to place outside an organisation's boundaries a set of activities which were once contained inside the ownership structure of the organisation. That is, what was previously inside the tent is now outside. However, the term is also used to describe situations where resources from outside an organisation are employed in support of the core organisation's customer support when they were never ever inside the organisation's boundaries. Such an example could be the provision of technology-based applications hosted by an external organisation which represent entirely new services. The term we use to describe an organisation which provides the types of services noted above is an outsourced service provider (OSP).

There can be little doubt that HR outsourcing is on many organisations' agendas. In fact, a survey by the Conference Board in 2004 indicated that 76% of the 120 North American and European companies having annual revenues of at least US$1 billion have outsourced one or more of the HR functions. In that survey, the most popular activities outsourced included 401(k) retirement programmes, pensions/benefits, stock options, health benefits, training and development and payroll (Conference Board, 2004).

What to outsource?

The usual answer to this is non-core business and typically 'Back Office' support activities are seen as less risky but we need to think carefully about the choice. Outsourcing offers the chance to do a number of things, including cost reductions on normal activities; provide increased control information; build capability and possibly capacity with some new investment; enhance current contribution and value-added capability and create new business opportunities. Each of these requires different structures and governance processes alongside key performance indicators.

What many regard as outsourcing is captured in the announcement by DuPont of a major outsourcing deal in 2005:

Convergys will provide comprehensive Human Resources (HR) transactional services to DuPont's 60,000 employees and 102,000 retirees in 70 countries and 30 languages around the world. Convergys expects this contract to generate revenues in excess of $1.1 billion over its thirteen-year duration. DuPont expects to realize a 20 percent productivity improvement as services transition to Convergys, increasing to 30 percent after 5 years.

Convergys will provide DuPont with a comprehensive suite of HR transactional services such as Organization & Employee Development, Workforce Planning & Deployment, Compensation Management, Benefits Administration, Payroll, Integrated Health Services, Recruiting, Employee & Labor Relations, HR Process Support Administration, Work Environment Support, Performance Management, Employee Data Management, Vendor Management, and HR consultative services. Deloitte Consulting, LLP will support the implementation.

Convergys will implement, host, and maintain a state-of-the-art HR information system.

Jim Borel, DuPont senior vice president, global Human Resources, said 'Convergys brings best-in-class global services to its clients, and DuPont will benefit from increased business performance through improved efficiency, reduced administrative costs, and better utilization of strategic workforce information. DuPont will be able to utilize world-class employee and manager self-service tools as well as state-of-the-art service centers located around the globe. Convergys is the right partner to enable the transformation of our HR transactional services by standardizing, simplifying, leveraging, and automating a number of our HR processes'.

(http://www.convergys.com/news_release 2 November 2005)

It can also be planned in a sequential manner to sort a problem, develop new capability and then to bring the activity or function back inside to deliver a better and more controllable service. Alternatively, there might be an option to float off the new unit as a separate business entity with new clients and new focus on business growth. These possibilities already demonstrate the need to think more long term so that short-term decisions and processes do not restrict strategic moves later.

Of course the journey also depends on where you start from. It is likely that an HR function which has already coordinated activities across multiple sites perhaps into a shared services organisation is more ready to meet the challenges of outsourcing. Alternatively, such a structure might be so embedded that taking it outside the organisational boundaries would present a serious organisational challenge.

Without a complete understanding of the current state of expertise and potential reach, it will be very difficult for an external provider to know what they are being asked to take on and it will be extremely difficult for the internal decision makers to evaluate any external bid. The HR function, therefore, requires a level of process maturity and robustness to be in a position to consider outsourcing.

Outsourcing might be seen as a solution to a failing service which must be sorted at all costs. Such an open-ended commitment is not to be encouraged since the costs can escalate very dramatically. Without detailed internal understanding, any external Service Provider will need to consider a considerable consultancy effort to create the baseline performance level on which to build a bid for the contract. The base level description will allow the creation and evaluation of improvement agendas for support to the bid and to support the OSP's decision process that such business can be delivered profitably. Such a consultancy intervention might be even be worth the investment by the client to allow them to become an intelligent customer in evaluating the OSP's bid and might actually re-open the possibility of the in-house options.

Scope and scale decisions are also important. It is possible to outsource parts of activities (i.e., 'cherry pick' from the equivalent of the DuPont list above), complete activities or business processes (e.g., recruitment) or the whole of the HR functional business scope. This again might be a staged process to build experience and confidence without the risks of a complete functional outsourcing from which it may be difficult to retrace the steps.

In broad terms, the opportunities and threats created by outsourcing are summarised in Table 8.2.

The range of options or variations on the outsourcing theme which can be available are discussed in greater detail in Hermann and Macbeth (2006) and Macbeth (2008).

Some of the themes noted above and summarised in Table 8.2 were also evident in an article published in the *Sunday Times* (29 April, 2007), which drew attention to some of the threats and downsides, which arguably had overshadowed the perceived benefits:

Table 8.2 Client and outsourced service providers' opportunities and threats (Macbeth, 2008)

Opportunities for client	Threats to client
OSP provides focus	Loss of control
Investment in focal activity	Opportunistic pricing model
Technology support updated	Limited benefit share
Benefits of scale and scope	Loss of focus to other client's business
Dedicated skills and management	Reduced emphasis on performance and support over time
Overhead reduction	Rigid – specifically, rigidly adhered to increasing coordination costs with increased complexity
Provide operational data	Reduced compliance data visibility

Opportunities for OSP	Threats
Business growth and extension	Underestimating client complexity and underpricing
Leverage	Staff transferred are not/cannot be helped to be competent
High-efficiency utilisation	Service expectation creep
Lock in of client, barriers to entry to competitors	Contract re-tendered or re-patriated
Sell capability to other clients	
Capture undervalued skills from client	
Release creativity and motivation in staff	

In an industry full of jargon, there is one word that is becoming more popular: insourcing. Defined as the process of bringing a contract back in-house, which had first been outsourced, it is a phrase that telecoms giant Cable & Wireless (C&W) now knows well. One of the pioneers of HR outsourcing, the company surprised the industry last October by announcing that it would not be renewing its five-year contract with Accenture, but that it would be bringing its HR processes back in-house.

For an industry that mainly sees one-way traffic, the news was a shock. But C&W has not been the first company to do this: US computer firm

Gateway terminated a $400m seven-year deal with outsourcing firm ACS in 2004, a year after signing the deal, when the two reached a mutual decision to end the relationship.

The two deals have something in common: a huge change in the client company's business model. For C&W, its UK workforce had shrunk from 10,000 to 3,500, while Gateway had also slashed the size of its workforce, making the deal unprofitable.

C&W's international HR director Ian Muir was sanguine over the about-turn. 'The company had changed so much that the reasons for doing it in the first place had disappeared', he told trade magazine People Management. *'Every outsourcing provider is wanting to make a profit and the economics are not so compelling now we are a different kind of enterprise'.*

These examples illustrate the need to be very mindful of the potential downsides when entering into an outsource deal. Indeed, Francis Alcock brings an insightful perspective, having worked at Cable & Wireless when it outsourced a range of its HR services, and at BT and the BBC - both of which had outsourced services already in existence. Her observations are as follows:

- Often outsourcers talk about partnering and offering 'beyond the transactional' but at the heart of any outsourcing arrangement is a hard commercial deal where organisations want higher (or at least same) quality service at a lower cost and the outsourcer wants to make money out of the deal. So relationships often end up at the transactional/contract management end.
- Set-up of outsourcing contracts is key – with outsourcing being treated like a merger change project. Time must be spent on helping the organisations get to know one another and she sees the appointment of a relationship manager as key.
- HR needs to see the outsource partner as part of the core organisation not as an arms-length supplier. The business often cannot differentiate which is the supplier of its HR service and so the whole HR function has to accept that blaming the other party for problems doesn't serve the customer or their own reputation.

These perspectives are very helpful in highlighting some of the opportunities and challenges in pursuing the outsourcing option and we now set out some practical ways in which you can deal with them.

How to find a suitable outsource provider

So how do you decide whether to outsource HR services, and on what basis? Remember that outsourcing is not the only option. All sourcing options should be evaluated against clear objectives and with an understanding of how benefit delivery will be measured. Do not assume that existing suppliers will make good outsourcing partners, and be creative in the way you define projects of 'work packages' to meet business objectives.

A key decision must revolve around the perception of the degree of internal management control which is necessary to protect a vital interest or where the impact of failure is severe.

The treatment of core activities, seen as critical to the organisation or a source of competitive advantage, should be the central elements of any outsource decision. Some organisations may take the view that these should be closely guarded and kept in-house, whereas others would be only too ready to outsource these if the overall cost/benefit analysis proved favourable.

Having decided to outsource an activity, the next step is to establish your contract strategy. This helps you to decide what kind of provider you are looking for, how you make your choice and broadly, at this stage, the nature of the contract you want.

Providers offer the following broad range of capabilities:

- niche skills: for example, recruitment and learning;
- technical solutions: useful where technology is expensive, leading edge or complex such as supporting Web-based HR applications;
- broad-based capability: this is combined with sufficient technology.

There are several models depending on whether you use one single or several best-of-breed suppliers, or a main contractor with subcontractors, and whether you intend to contract out part or all of the function/process. Individual suppliers will probably not be the best at everything and single supplier deals are not always the most cost effective. On the other hand, there is much more work involved in managing multiple contracts and suppliers need to work together to provide the best service.

Also, in recent years, 'off-shoring' has become more popular. In this context, off-shoring describes the relocation by a company of HR services from one country to another. The architectural design decisions that come into play need to accommodate full consideration of both cost and service quality. It is important not to view off-shoring simply in the context of cost savings, as this could have serious service quality and reputational consequences.

Settling upon the right sort of contract

There are standard terms that an effective contract should cover, but overall its emphasis should be on rewarding the supplier for quality of service rather than penalising them for failure to deliver. Many contract-related problems in outsourcing relationships stem from a failure to create a living document which is flexible and reflects the expectations of both the parties. Effective contract preparation provides a sound basis for productive outsourcing relationships. The contract should cover:

- terms of the agreement,
- minimum service levels,
- ownership and confidentiality of data,
- warranty,
- exhibits,
- transfer of assets and contracts,
- staff moves,
- termination clauses,
- incentives,
- disclaimers,
- bankruptcy,
- force majeure,
- performance measures,
- anticipating change.

It is also critical to have a clear contract specification defining the scope of the work, covering the following:

- inter-relationship between processes;
- what work is handed over by whom to whom and at what point;
- if work is completely new, invite the potential contractor to propose the services they would choose, thereby standardising the production of an imaginative solution.

Hence it is at this stage, as part of the due diligence process, that you may want to ask the following type of questions. (This is not an exhaustive list, but provides examples.)

Commercial/pricing/cost savings

- Please provide details about any strategic relationships you have and how material those relationships are to your proposal.
- Provide a clear, transparent breakdown of your proposed price structure by function and activity and year. What assumptions have been made regarding headcount?
- Provide examples of the level of discount we could receive.

- What is your willingness to apply a variable pricing structure straight away, as opposed to 6–12 months from transition?
- Provide a detailed breakdown of your proposed set-up costs.

Term and effective date

- Please clarify the input and dependencies surrounding the time-related elements of the proposed contract.

Service levels

- Are you willing to agree to service levels upfront?
- Please provide specific service levels for review.
- Explain your rationale for your approach on service credits.
- What is your approach to operational assurance?
- What is your approach to handling ongoing and new initiatives?
- Explain your approach to and methodology of recruiting, including processes for identifying/attracting marketing candidates.

Other considerations

- In order to judge that other bids are acceptable, you need to have a detailed understanding of your current costs against your current services; otherwise it would be impossible to judge the quality of what you are being offered.
- Documentation should be in a form that makes sense to allow companies to meaningfully compare one bid with another.
- Selection of contractor will not only involve price and service offered, but also reputation, track record, one's own experience, if any, and the contractor's apparent financial stability.
- Also understand the motive of the contractor – why do they want the business, where do they expect to make money?
- Contractors may work to encourage the widest possible take-up of services made to optimise the higher value-added components. In other words, they may purport to be able to offer services at the top end of the service pyramid. Make sure you do very stringent diligence checks on these claims.

When designing the flexibility elements in the contract, make sure you account appropriately for reductions in activity levels compared with existing levels as well as increases. The potential contractor may seek to impose a minimum annual commitment, a financial sum that represents the minimum value of the contract per year. This sum may seem to be fair and reasonable on the basis of current activity levels being maintained in the future, but can become a financial burden if activity levels decrease significantly.

Determining the contract length

- Generally, shorter-term contracts are more appropriate for cost-driven approaches and tend to be favoured for lower skilled or less complex tasks.
- Longer term contracts are more appropriate for more complex tasks involving significant handover times and learning period for the contractor.
- The concept of a 'strategic alliance' becomes more realistic as contract times are lengthened. Contractors prefer longer contractual terms because of increasing efficiencies over time, and also the 'softeners' that can be offered in the early years.

Statement of key deliverables

These deliverables must relate to volume, training and quality of the output (see examples below). Importantly:

- These deliverables have to be buttoned down; otherwise ambiguities will later become apparent.
- If existing performance definitions do not exist, you need to establish a baseline through stakeholder perception analysis or by linking expected performance to benchmark performance of other service providers.
- Establish clear contractual key performance indicators (KPIs) to define the expected level of operational performance from the contract (see Figure 8.4).
- Consider contractual measures for dealing with success and failure; that is, withholding payments as service levels fall or providing bonus payments if performance levels improve. Whatever the regime, a regular reporting schedule is necessary, including indices of performance and progress meetings.
- There should be an escalation clause in the contract to resolve disputes and ultimately terminate the contract if things have degraded to a profoundly unsatisfactory level.

Designing the structure of the business relationship

The following list highlights some of the most significant and most frequently overlooked elements of a good outsourcing arrangement. It is vital to be clear about how the business relationship will be managed by both the supplier and the customer.

Service item	Service descriptor	Service measure
Resourcing services	Permanent employee – time from receipt of an approved hiring request form to offer acceptance	Average time to offer acceptance: within 20 business days
Resourcing services	Non-PAYE contractor – time from receipt of an approved hiring request form to offer acceptance	Average time to offer acceptance: within 6 business days
Learning services	L&D projects customer satisfaction	90% customer satisfaction based on post delivery survey
Reward services	Action authorised contractual salary adjustments by agreed cut off dates	90% of adjustments to be processed accurately for pay runs
Reward services	Ensure statutory compliance in all processes	100% compliance

Figure 8.4 Illustrative contractual KPIs

The *relationship plan* should establish how the respective parties are going to establish trust and how the initial controls will evolve to reflect the changing relationship. In most cases, controls can be relaxed as trust is developed, but they are essential in the early stages of the relationship.

The customer should have a role in agreeing the supplier's account management, and key managers on both sides should be involved in the contract design and negotiation.

The transitional phase relies heavily on *trust and collaboration* between those involved, and this is where most problems arise. At this stage, it is essential to establish roles, responsibilities and processes to enable a seamless transfer of service. If there is inadequate trust between the management and the supplier, things can go wrong quickly and with dire consequences.

If these issues are addressed effectively at the outset, the relationship is off to a sound start and partnership is a realistic goal. The best way to consolidate and build on such a relationship is to establish a unit in which both the customer and the supplier(s) have a stake – emotionally, professionally and financially, if not legally. This unit, which can be called the *management organisation*, is the champion of the outsourcing deal. Its objectives are determined and its performance is measured in the terms of the contract. Ideally, it is answerable to a joint group comprising representatives of all the stakeholders: the business and all outsourcing suppliers.

A culture of *open information* is essential if both supplier and customer are to get what they need out of the relationship. The supplier needs to make a profit and the operating side of the business might want a share of the management organisation's gains. Practical difficulties can arise from this: for example, the supplier may have data centres containing sensitive information for more than one customer. These issues need to be identified and resolved early on in the relationship.

People management

The timing of the outsourcing implementation plan needs to take into account the demand that this will make on resources, including people from:

- the function which is in scope,
- other parts of the business which are impacted,
- HR,
- legal,
- finance,
- facilities,
- PR.

Managing by contract

A project manager may typically have had between 50 and 200 people working for him or her prior to outsourcing. This will have conferred considerable power in a traditional and hierarchical sense. In contrast, the management organisation or retained function may consist of a small team of very experienced and competent people within specific domains, of which project management may not be one. Therefore, the management of transition to new roles within the retained function and introduction of new contract management skills is a key issue that should be planned before and during implementation. It cannot be assumed that the skills required to run an in-house function will necessarily be those appropriate to managing the contract.

It is important to retain the right people to manage the outsourcing process, that is, those with the right skills, attitude and personality. The management organisation is often required to switch from a task-led environment into a service-oriented culture. It may be necessary to retrain or transfer existing employees or even to recruit new ones. The new team needs to be built and developed as quickly as possible. External advisors with experience in outsourcing can help to transfer skills using tool kits, coaching, workshops, feedback and assessment.

Summary

It is self-evident that the overall HR service delivery model for an organisation will be an amalgam of service delivery approaches. It is also the case that each presents its own challenges and opportunities, and the practitioner needs to be cognisant of the associated benefits and pitfalls. A range of practical advice, supported by literature references, published research and senior practitioner insights provides a basis for an intelligent, value-adding design of HR service delivery. It is probably worth stressing that because of the myriad of options available, and the associated costs and reputational consequences, practitioners would be wise to involve external expertise in the architectural design, if only as a critical friend to help assure the overall approach.

9

Programme Management

The preceding chapters have made reference to the crucial importance of securing the commitment of managers and employees to the human resource transformation process and to do so within an overall project or programme management framework.

You may have everyone bought into the new vision of HR and built the finest and most watertight business case, but if you have doubts about the programme management capability, you should put off the start of the programme until you have the right person or team in place.

To achieve successful programme outcomes, particularly in respect of highly complex programmes extending over many months or even years, it is vital that appropriate disciplines are in place to ensure that costs, benefits and implementation time scales are carefully monitored and managed.

Key themes

- Good governance is a prerequisite of successful HR transformation programmes.
- All programmes give rise to conflicts with attendant risks and issues. Knowing how to manage through these is vital.
- Understand the relationship between people, process and technology workstreams and maintain a connected view of these aspects throughout.
- Do not be afraid to admit to problems and maintain close attention to programme health.

Context

We have noted previously the importance of a well-designed, evidenced and well-communicated case for HR transformation. We also recognise the point that stakeholder engagement is not conducted in isolation but as part of an overall project or programme governance model. This reinforces the advice given in Chapter 1 about adopting a systems mindset, so that you are keenly aware that a number of interrelated elements need to be managed well to bring about successful HR transformation. Our experience and case illustrations highlight a number of areas that are likely to be featured within any HR transformation programme. These are set out below and you are also advised to refer to other chapters of this book, which give these matters more individual and detailed attention:

- the importance of understanding stakeholder topography;
- supporting people through the change process;
- securing unwavering support to the business case;
- communicating the business vision;
- listening to, and monitoring issues and concerns, and doing something about them!

Programme governance is the overarching framework for success. For HR to be perceived as professional in its transformation efforts and establish itself as a role model for the business, adherence to good programme governance is a prerequisite. This is the means by which the different facets of the transformation programme are managed with the overall aim of achieving successful outcomes in terms of cost, benefits and time scales. These considerations are now explored in more detail.

Programme governance tools

Building upon the attention given in Chapter 7 to stakeholder engagement, it is worth being reminded that all of this activity should be housed within an overarching governance framework that provides a vehicle for effective management of HR transformation. We start with the business case for transformation, the constituent parts of which were described in some detail in Chapter 6, but now we view that activity from the perspective of the wider governance framework.

Business case framework

It is usual for business cases to go through a sequential phase of development. This is elaborated in Figure 9.1.

Reinforcing the points made in Chapter 6, the initial proposal may be a short document that highlights the overall costs, benefits and risks associated with the programme. If the proposal looks reasonably promising, it can then be developed into an initial business case, at the conclusion of which one should have a 60–70% confidence level in respect of the main costs, benefits and other outcomes. After that, a full-blown business case, with associated confidence levels in excess of 90%, can be worked up, and it is this that forms the ultimate touchstone for investment decisions and benefit expectations.

But who is applying the overall guidance and inspection needed to ensure that the HR transformation is not only well conceived but has a good prospect for delivering value to the business? How is the implementation monitored and measured? How are problems dealt with? To look at these matters, we need to delve further into the composition of the governance structure.

Steering board

We strongly make the point that programme governance should not simply be confined to the identified programme team, dealing with the day-to-day implementation. There should be other layers of governance, as illustrated in Figure 9.2.

The programme director should be answerable in the first instance to a steering board which provides a higher level inspection of costs, benefits and delivery

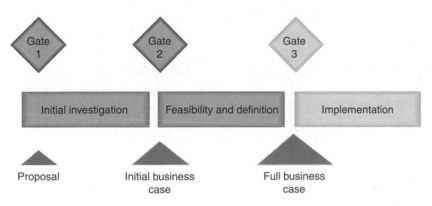

Figure 9.1 Programme business case framework.

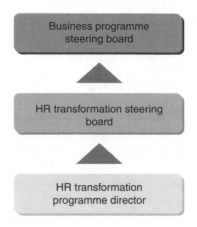

Figure 9.2 Steering boards.

milestones and becomes an issues and risks resolution forum if matters present themselves that are beyond the resolution of the programme director.

Chaired by the senior programme sponsor, the steering board should comprise a broad range of talent: senior HR people, internal audit, line managers and finance. At a higher level still, it would be beneficial to have an overarching business programme steering board that looks to see how the HR transformation programme dovetails with other change programmes that may be going on in the business at that time. It also provides a further opportunity to inspect cost benefits and delivery milestones.

The emphasis around periodic inspection of cost benefits and delivery milestones cannot be overstated. Whilst some may view this as an unnecessary administrative burden that simply detracts from 'getting on with the job', it is undeniably the case that without these disciplines in place the risks to the programme outcomes can become massively magnified.

Frequent inspection of costs, benefits and delivery milestones can provide comfort and assurance that the programme is basically on track. Furthermore, it can pick out those things that, if unchecked, are likely to destabilise the programme at a later point in time.

Early identification and remediation of these kinds of issues provide enormous dividends. Left unchecked, however, such issues could cause significant ramifications, if not a crisis, for the programme in its later stages.

Programme team

Extending the theme further, look at the composition of the team in Figure 9.3.

Clearly, the programme director has overall responsibility for managing the different elements of the programme on a day-to-day basis and keeping it in good

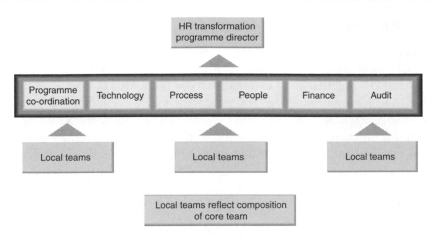

Figure 9.3 Programme team.

overall shape. This person will have a major influence on the way the programme is characterised. For example, if the person is known to have a particular leaning towards technical issues, it is possible that he or she will be allowed to be the dominant consideration and skew the activities of the programme team accordingly.

We are not saying that someone with a predominantly technical background is not fit to run HR transformation. Rather, we are making the point that the person chosen for this role must be capable of understanding the need to keep a number of workstreams properly aligned and not fall into the trap of allowing personal preferences or comfort zones to drive the programme in a particular direction, to the detriment of others. The best way of achieving this is to keep the overall customer experience 'front of mind' and use this as the basis for driving the programme forward.

Crucially, as we have discussed earlier in this chapter, the person must have exemplary stakeholder management skills; it is likely that these will be tested to the limit!

Reporting to the programme director, you would have, in an ideal situation, someone whose sole focus is on the day-to-day coordination of the plethora of activities that are associated with a major HR transformation programme. This individual would be very much at ease with one of the recognised programme management tools such as MS Project, and be in a position to advise the director of any apparent slippages or problems that might arise that would ultimately affect the declared programme milestones.

Chapter 1 raised awareness of the need to split HR transformation into three main areas of *technology, process* and *people*. Here, we look in more detail at the sorts of activities and people profiles that would typically align with those areas.

Technology workstream

The person responsible for technology would be expected to be a principal point of engagement with the systems integration provider, whether this is the internal IT function or an external party or both. This person is ultimately responsible for translating the HR processes into a technological solution, involving configuration of the main system. In addition, there would be considerations surrounding the suitability of the Intranet or people's ability to access that system through their desktops, laptops or phones.

Process workstream

The person responsible for the process workstream is the person who will effectively manage the process re-engineering work to ensure that in the 'new world' HR processes become as lean and efficient as possible. There are a number of ways of approaching this. One way, for example, would be to approach the work with literally a clean sheet of paper, calling upon various people in the organisation to contribute their view of a particular process and constructing the new process from scratch.

Whilst this has undeniable benefits in terms of creating a perception of inclusion, by engaging a wide stakeholder audience and appearing to be genuinely in line with the concept of meeting customer expectations or being customer driven, there are also a number of potential major pitfalls with this approach. One such pitfall is that, having created or crafted a new process based on this highly inclusive clean sheet approach, it then becomes eminently obvious in consultation with the technology department that to configure such a process in the system would require considerable time and expense. This realisation then might prompt the need to go back out to the stakeholders who contributed to the original process to say that it is no longer applicable – with the subsequent dissonance this would create.

Another way of doing it would be to adopt as a baseline the standard 'out of the box processes' that come with the new system, and only permit variants to those standard processes where it can be demonstrated that a significant business benefit would result. These variants may take the form of observance or compliance with legal requirements, or where a judgment could be taken that for cultural reasons it is necessary to do things in a particular way and that enormous disaffection could be caused by overhauling or retiring that particular process.

One of the drawbacks of presenting baseline core processes in the way described is that it could appear to senior stakeholders to be a *fait accompli* and might therefore create a backlash from stakeholders, with associated disruption to the programme.

On balance, therefore, it is probably the best tactic in most situations to engage the appropriate stakeholders on process grounds by presenting the overall picture. In other words, to explain that whilst their views are being sought to help refine and better the existing processes, there are nevertheless frameworks within which those betterments or changes need to take place to take account of the issues surrounding configuration within the main system. These issues carry a cost implication now and in the future.

People workstream

The people aspects of the programme deal with the human capability enhancements or changes that are needed arising from the business change process, and also address organisational design issues. As stated earlier, however, this critical area of an HR transformation is often overlooked or subordinated in favour of technical considerations.

Taking this a stage further, it may be tempting to confine the discussions and the initiatives around people enhancement to within the HR function itself. Quite properly, the HR function undergoes major change in an exercise of this kind, seeking to move from being predominantly administrative in its persona towards being a more strategic value-add contributor to the business – as discussed at length in Chapter 3. The skill sets, therefore, of the newly formed HR function are markedly different from the historic situation, and a good deal of time and effort and planning needs to go into securing these capability enhancements.

However, that is not the entire story. The line managers are an absolutely critical component in the overall success of the programme, because they will be in the front line for dealing with the business changes as they happen, taking more responsibility for day-to-day HR matters, using the new Web-based HR-derived tools, such as employee self-service and manager self-service, and acting as ambassadors for the change process throughout the business. It is critical, therefore, that line managers or representatives of the line become involved in the programme at an early stage so that their views are taken proper account of.

Crucially, the technology, process and people enhancement workstreams must be kept in close alignment; the importance of this will be demonstrated a little later in this section. As a consequence, it is highly desirable to have these three core aspects of the programme incorporated under *one* 'governance umbrella'.

Potential conflicts

It is worth mentioning again at this point that potential conflicts can arise between the technology, process and people workstreams. This is linked to a tendency amongst many programmes of this type to devolve towards a technology-based solution whereby the programme becomes a technology-driven implementation and the 'system' becomes the main focus of attention. Instead, of course, the programme should be characterised as a business change programme. As mentioned earlier, it is important for the programme director, at an early stage in proceedings, to stamp his or her authority on this situation to ensure that the programme is led very much from a customer perspective.

Certain solutions to fulfil customer requirements could prove to be very expensive to translate into practice, requiring system customisation, for example, that carries a heavy price tag, not only at the outset but also into the future. So one of the roles of the technology head is to ensure that the customer requirements are assessed in terms of cost and benefit and that the most appropriate technological solution is ultimately performed. However, this is different from the technology department deciding at the outset what the solution is going to be and then essentially requiring the customer to be a 'forced fit' into the technological environment.

Many so-called 'skirmishes' occur on this point. These can become a focus for inherent tension and conflict within a programme, and the programme director needs to understand this, to be prepared for it and to make sure that the technology function does not dictate the overall programme outcomes.

Other considerations

Equally importantly, the finance team, the audit team, the procurement team and other support services as deemed necessary should form part of the overall HR transformation programme team. These support services provide the disciplines around cost, monitoring and control, benefit measurement and the measurement of benefit realisation, the very ingredients upon which the business case depends for its validity and upon which the business took the decision to make the investment.

If the programme encompasses more than one country, or a series of sites in one country, it would be helpful to have locally based teams responsible for the delivery of the programme in those individual sites or in those individual jurisdictions. The local teams would need to have a skilled composition that reflects the overall mix of the core team that has been described earlier. There should be no dispute about the local teams acting as the principal conduit into those site-specific businesses or in individual jurisdictions; the main debate surrounds whether or not the local team should 'pull through' the final solution from the core team or whether the core team 'pushes out' the solution through the local teams and into those businesses.

The best advice here for the core team is to make sure that it sets up the appropriate common standards that will apply across all aspects of the programme. In other words, the overall governance framework, the style and tone of the programme emanates from the centre, but the local teams working within that framework fashion the solution to meet the local requirements – with those requirements being assessed, tested and analysed by the core team. In this way, the local implementation would appear to be more in touch with the requirements of the local business whilst at the same time being backed up and supported by other resources.

The problem of risk destabilising the programme outcomes is examined in the next section.

Managing risks and issues

Risk management

Risk is any uncertainty, potential threat or occurrence that may prevent you from achieving your objectives. It may affect timescale, costs, quality or benefits. All programmes are exposed to risk in some form, but the extent of this will vary considerably.

The purpose of risk management is to ensure that:

- Risks on programmes are identified and evaluated in a consistent way.
- Recognised risks to programme success are addressed.

You cannot use risk management to eliminate risk altogether, but it will enable you to avoid it in some instances or minimise the disruption in the event of its happening in others. When a programme sponsor approves a programme, he or she does so in full knowledge of the stated risks, and accepting the consequences should things go wrong.

The steps are:

- *Identify*: Log all the risks that may potentially jeopardise the success of the programme.
- *Estimate*: Review each risk in turn:
  - assess the likelihood of the risk occurring;
  - assess the severity of the impact on the programme if it occurs.
- *Evaluate*: Use a risk matrix to determine the 'risk category' (high, medium or low) to help you assess how acceptable the risk is.

Depending on the risk category, take action as follows:

- *High risk*: Take definitive action to prevent or reduce risk. Reconsider the viability of the programme before proceeding further.

- *Medium risk*: Take action to prevent or reduce risk where appropriate. Prepare a contingency plan if risk cannot be reduced. Manage risk and implement contingency plan where necessary.
- *Low risk*: Take action to reduce risks if cost effective. Monitor risk – it may become more significant later.

Taking positive steps to reduce the possible effects of risk is not indicative of pessimism, but is a positive indication of good programme management. Many possible options exist for reducing risk, including:

- *Prevention*, where countermeasures are put in place either to stop the threat or problem from occurring or to prevent it having any impact.
- *Reduction*, where the actions either reduce the likelihood of the risk developing or limit the impact on the programme to acceptable levels.
- *Transference*, which is a specialised form of risk reduction where the impact of the risk is passed to a third party via, for instance, insurance.
- *Contingency*, where actions are planned or organised to come into force as and when the risk occurs.
- *Acceptance*, where the organisation decides to go ahead and accept the possibility that the risk might occur and is willing to take the consequences.

Consider also:

- bringing risky activities forward in the schedule to reduce the impact on the programme outcome if they are delayed;
- modifying the programme requirement to reduce aspects with inherently high risk, for example, new, leading-edge technologies;
- allowing appropriate time and cost contingencies;
- using prototypes and pilots to test the viability of new approaches.

Issues management

An issue is something that has happened and threatens the success of the programme. Examples of issues are:

- the late delivery of a critical deliverable;
- a reported lack of confidence by users;
- a lack of resources to carry out the work;
- the late sign-off of a critical document or deliverable;
- a reported deviation of a deliverable from its specification;

- a request for additional functionality;
- a recognised omission from the programme scope.

When an issue is identified you should:

- record it in an issues log;
- agree and take action to resolve the issue;
- regularly update the progress commentary on the log;
- once the issue has been resolved, record the method and date of resolution in the log;
- report new, significant issues in a regular programme progress report.

You should expect a large number of issues to be raised at the start of the programme or at the start of a new stage within the programme. These will mainly be queries from people seeking clarification that aspects of the programme they are concerned with have been covered. This is a rich source of feedback on stakeholder concerns as well as a check on completeness of the programme plan and scope.

Make sure you record issues, even if you have no time to address them or cannot yet find a person to manage the resolution. Just making them visible is sometimes enough to start resolving them. Also, many issues cannot be resolved on their own simply because they do not reach the core problem; they are merely symptoms. Once other 'symptoms' appear as issues, it is possible to start making connections that can help to identify the core problem. Once this is solved, a number of issues can be struck off in one go.

'Scope creep' is a phenomenon where a programme over-runs its agreed timescale and budget due to many extra (often minor) 'features' being added in an uncontrolled manner. For this reason, it is often easier to bundle a number of small changes together and assess them as a whole, choosing to implement only those that will further the objectives of the programme. At the other end of the scale, it is wise to consider delaying the addition of a major change until after the programme is completed and introduce it as a second phase programme. Remember, the primary aim of a programme is to fulfil a stated business need. As long as this need is satisfied, fine tuning, enhancing or embellishing the outputs are potential wastes of resources.

At some point, a time may come on a programme when an issue arises that cannot be resolved whilst keeping the programme viable. Either a time window will be missed or costs will be so high that even a marginal cost analysis leads to the conclusion that it is not worth continuing. In these cases, a decision to terminate a programme might be treated as a success, as there is little point in continuing with a programme that is not viable in business terms. However, such a situation would demand serious questions being raised about the risk and issue management regime in place at the time.

Figure 9.4 shows how a well-managed programme retains a decent shape all the way through, meaning that key activities in the programme are being well managed and aligned and harnessed. Benefit delivery is good and on track and the governance structure is able to contain the complexity to within manageable proportions. On the other hand, if the complexity becomes unmanaged, what then happens is that a significant shortfall of benefit takes place: either benefit streams themselves are delayed, or costs rise significantly as efforts are made to contain the event or sequence of events that have created the unmanaged complexity situation.

This point illustrates something mentioned earlier about the need to retain a highly diligent focus on costs and benefits, and also to make sure that key milestones are achieved and to be in a position to have the processes in place to take swift remedial action if it is recognised or identified that things are moving out of kilter.

An unmanaged complexity situation can be very draining and very wearing on members of the programme team and indeed the higher steering boards. Therefore, it is highly beneficial and desirable to prevent those situations happening in the first place than to have to deal with them, although it is almost inevitable that there will be occasions during a complex programme extending over many years when unmanaged complexity will strike. The ability to be able to deal with that situation is absolutely fundamental to the overarching programme governance framework.

Returning to the theme of keeping major items in alignment, Figure 9.5 shows how the three core pillars of the HR transformation programme – technology, process and people – are kept in alignment around a particular milestone.

The point of this is really to show how a number of inter-related activities need to be carefully managed in the build-up to a critical go-live situation, and how

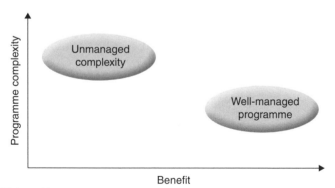

Figure 9.4 Risk and issues management.

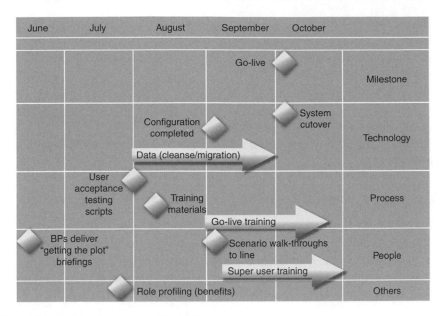

Figure 9.5 Making it happen – illustration.

the state of each of those major activities would need to be regularly tested and assessed as the days tick by in order to minimise or eliminate risk. Chapter 6 makes reference to organising these bundles of activities into 90-day periods, to give more visibility and focus around deliverables.

Finally, it would be highly recommended for practitioners to constantly review and assess a number of questions listed below. Having reliable answers to these questions provides an insightful perspective on the programme overall.

Business management
- Is the programme still a good business proposition; are the risks acceptable?
- Is the business ready to take on the operation of the solution?
- Are the benefits/results monitoring systems in place?
- Are current estimates of the costs and benefits in the business forecasts?
- Are all internal and marketing communications designed and ready?

Programme control
- Has a programme health check been done and found to be acceptable?
- Are you sure beyond reasonable doubt that the solution will work?

- Have all stakeholders reviewed and approved those deliverables requiring their input?
- Have all purchases that affect service delivery been properly completed?
- Are all support agreements in place?

Ongoing evaluation
- Are resources in place to monitor adequately the costs and benefits against the business case?

Case study 1: Scottish Executive (SE) e-HR and HR Transformation

This case study is used to illustrate how deficiencies in governance and related protocols, discussed in the earlier part of this chapter, led to a serious and disruptive delay in the deliverables of a major government HR Transformation programme. The lessons learned underpin the critical importance of a robust governance framework.

The SE, known as the Scottish Government since August 2007, is responsible for most of the issues of day-to-day concern to the people of Scotland, including health, education, justice, rural affairs and transport. It managed an annual budget of more than £30 billion in 2007–2008. It embarked on an ambitious HR transformation programme in 2005, consisting of e-HR and HR Transformation projects, which soon ran into major difficulties, prompting an official review conducted by Bill McQueen in 2006. The review was tasked with

> *Establishing the current state of the Scottish Executive's (SE) e-HR and HR Transformation projects, the circumstances and causes which threatened deliverability, whether the conduct and management of the projects was compliant with relevant protocols and best practice, whether the projects remained deliverable and to make recommendations.*

The following information draws heavily on the published review - McQueen (2006).

An overview of the state of the project

SE contracted with Fujitsu Services Ltd on 5 September 2005 to provide an e-HR system, using Oracle software providing 'best practice' solutions for better delivery of HR reporting responsibilities, including data integration and some self-service functionality. Within days of signing the contract SE sought, and Fujitsu agreed, a variation to the contract which changed the deliverables and brought forward the date of 'rollout' from November 2006 to May 2006. By December 2005 the risk status of the project delivering on time and budget was deemed 'Amber', by January 2006 it was assessed as 'Red'; in February the project moved into 'recovery' status. In May 2006, the project had been 'paused' pending consideration of this review: the outputs specified in the contract have not been delivered; however, a series of 82 HR business process maps had been produced, capable of configuration into e-HR software with minimum customisation. By June 2006 costs amounting to some £4.6 million of the originally approval £8.5 million (including moving to a new payroll provider) had been incurred.

A separately constituted HR transformation project, embracing major structural changes to HR – the establishment of Business Partners, the launch of a single entry point for the new HR Shared Service Centre and co-location of dispersed HR teams into one new location – was consequentially destabilised by the disruption in the e-HR project because the new HR operating model was not underpinned by the planned self-service facility for line managers or the improved level of management information that had been envisaged.

It was concluded that a 'number of individual factors combined over an extended period and in particular during the last 4 months of 2005 serve to explain the failure of the e-HR project to deliver on time'.

Governance

Governance arrangements fell short of best practice. Concerns were expressed on several occasions by external and Gateway reviewers and by the non-executive Programme Board members. These voices called for clarity and precision in the roles, responsibilities and accountabilities of key personnel. While governance was discussed frequently by all parties, proper, practical and convincing arrangements were not put in place in a timely fashion, with the consequence that there was not sufficiently adequate independent assessment of risk and oversight of progress. This was compounded by the Senior HR User assuming the responsibilities of Senior Responsible Owner. The departure of the established e-HR programme manager shortly after contract commencement and his replacement by two inexperienced successors within the next 3 months meant that project leadership was not sufficiently rigorous or effective.

Business case

The business case against which the e-HR project was approved was prepared between November 2004 and February 2005. There were calls for it to be revised to reflect the final costs and scope of the contract and the relationship between e-HR and HR transformation. The assumed cost improvements arising from e-HR in terms of headcount reduction in the HR function had already largely been realised by the time the contract was signed. The e-HR business case was not adequately reviewed and updated at the time of contract signing and whilst a draft Project Initiation Document outlining at a high level the additional benefits assumed to arise from HR transformation was circulated to Programme Board members in August, there was no detailed, revised, comprehensive business plan setting out the various critical dependencies, which could be formally evaluated, considered and agreed by the Board. This was regrettable and contrary to best practice: it made it difficult for the Board to undertake its role of understanding and challenging assumptions, assessing risks and deliverability and ultimately of championing the overall programme.

Scope of the e-HR contract and revision to timetable

Changes to scope and timetable were two significant factors contributing to non-delivery. In the run-up to signing the contract Fujitsu agreed to the senior user's request that it would be varied almost immediately to drop some elements and add others. There was at the time (and which remained some months later) confusion among the SE staff closely involved about precisely what has been properly, contractually authorised by way of change requests to the scope of the contract. In the original proposals, the timescale envisaged a start to contract in summer 2005 with Fujitsu's deliverables completed by July 2006 and rollout of service across SE by November 2006. The SE senior user brought the completion date forward to the end of May 2006. While there was discussion with HR team leaders and Fujitsu, no clear detailed plan showing milestones, interdependencies, resource input obligations and risks was prepared at the time, agreed with Fujitsu or shared with the Programme Board, staff and stakeholders. Fujitsu considered they had no option but to agree to the revised date and the local SE context was one which did not support informed, effective challenge to the senior user's estimation of what was possible. The reduction of 40% in the overall contract period, with a consequence of shortened timescales for workshops to develop the operating model, for testing and for putting in place the major communication and training effort, was over-optimistic and allowed only 9 months to complete the work. This was shorter than the equivalent periods allowed by other government departments involving Fujitsu in e-HR solutions and did not allow sufficient time for contingencies and recovery in the event of significant problems arising with work on the critical path; nor was it realistically achievable given the level of cultural awareness in SE about the changes envisaged, the work which would have to have been put in train to secure staff readiness, and was risky given what was known then about staffing resources going forward (e.g., impending departure of the programme manager, live vacancies and the likely impact of the pay review).

Reporting arrangements

Progress on the e-HR project was reported to the Programme Board and other bodies in different ways on a quarterly basis. However, the nature of such quarterly reporting meant that events were reported retrospectively and it was always possible to accurately ascertain the current status of a project operating within a tight timescale via this method of reporting. When the e-HR project was reported as being on target and within budget at the end of October 2005, concerns were already being raised within the project. There was no mandatory requirement for such concerns to have been brought to the attention of the Programme Board at this stage; rather, it was a matter of personal judgement about the extent to which problems needed to be shared with senior colleagues. Three Gateway reviews of the project were conducted in 2004 and early 2005. Whilst the findings of the Gateway reviews were made available to the Programme Board, a number of their specific recommendations were not translated into practical action.

Disharmonies

As we have noted previously, whilst it is not uncommon for tensions to arise within high-profile projects operating within tight deadlines, success is difficult to achieve without a common understanding of goals, a proper respect for team working and mutual trust between the individuals working on the project. The view articulated by many of those involved in the SE programme was that these aspects were not sufficiently present: the programme was lacking in effective, engaged leadership and characterised by poor working relations, both within SE representatives and between SE and the contractor, and low morale. There were problems at all levels, and at times within SE these included a lack of confidence in the project by Programme Board members and tensions between the programme manager and the senior user. More generally, while some staff were enthusiastically supportive of the SRO/senior user, others plainly found her leadership style difficult or felt unclear about the HR vision and project deliverability.

Communications

The lack of a clear, effective and timely communication effort to HR professional staff, line managers in SE and staff in SE and its related departments and agencies contributed to the failure to deliver. Fujitsu argued that the absence of clear understanding by stakeholders prejudiced the successful completion of the business process workshops and in turn meant that the e-HR software could not be configured in the tight timescale set. The major cultural change entailed by e-HR

221

and HR transformation needs to have strong stakeholder engagement and line manager buy-in if staff are to make a success of it. To achieve this a transparent and consistent message must be planned and conveyed and a significant training effort needs to be planned and mounted. That was not done.

Conclusions and recommendations

The review concluded that there had been substantial difficulties with the e-HR project and the factors which primarily accounted for these were identified as matters of governance, leadership, changes to specification and timetable, project planning and management consideration of risk in relation to cost, working relationships, communication and the performance of the contractor. Some of the difficulties could have been avoided if SE's established procedures and protocols for project management had been properly followed, but it seems the key action from which it was impossible to recover was the attempt to change the scope of the project so that it was better aligned to the HR transformation programme whilst simultaneously shortening the timescale for completion to May 2006. And all this without having undertaken full consideration of the associated risks and dependencies, rigorous project planning, meaningful and considered input from the Programme Board and without having the necessary building blocks in place to deliver related workstreams.

The recommendations were numerous and resonate with the good practice advice and guidance provided earlier in this chapter. An abbreviated list is set out below:

- Sound and clear governance arrangements need to be put in place, defining roles, responsibilities, accountabilities and authorities of staff at different levels, including 'agency contractors'.
- For any future e-HR procurement Scottish Procurement Division should be represented on the Project Board.
- The SE Centre of Excellence should issue advice and guidance about the composition of Programme and Project Boards and the roles of members, including the responsibilities of any 'non-Executive' members of such Boards.
- Absolute clarity must be achieved about what should now be included within the e-HR element and the HR transformation element. It would be sensible to undertake thorough site visits (to encompass the HR professional users, corporate users of management information, IT command and self-service users) in organisations with similar size, staffing structures, user requirements and culture to the SE before concluding what needs to be in the final scope cost and timing.
- The e-HR and HR Transformation Business case should be revisited in light of the current position on implementing HR transformation and after further consideration of the desired scope of any e-HR software solutions.

- Advice on best practice for establishing and maintaining effective joint teams of SE staff, agency contractors and suppliers should be drawn up for those involved in substantial projects such as this one.
- Communication and training strategies and detailed plans need to be worked up, and to maximise the chances of successfully impressing staff in the line the Programme Board will need to give a heavy emphasis to championing, with Departmental Management Boards and staff, the benefits of the new arrangements.
- The SE Centre of Expertise should consider whether to establish a more formal mechanism for drawing Accountable Officer attention to 'red' ratings in Gateway reviews.

In the light of the review and its recommendations, appropriate actions were taken to put the programme back on track.

Case study 2: The Metropolitan Police Service (MPS)

This case study illustrates how the Metropolitan Police Service (MPS) is managing a large, complex HR transformation and provides a more detailed insight into the governance arrangements that surround this £42 million programme.

The MPS is the largest of the police services that operate in greater London (the others include the City of London Police and the British Transport Police). It employs 32,000 officers, 14,000 police staff, 300 traffic wardens and 4,500 Police Community Support Officers as well as being supported by over 2,500 volunteer police officers in the Metropolitan Special Constabulary and its Employer Supported Policing programme. The Metropolitan Police Services covers an area of 620 square miles and a population of 7.2 million.

In 2006 the MPS embarked on a major HR transformation programme, as part of a wider *Met Modernisation Programme* (MMP) in order to:

- Further improve HR service delivery levels
- Streamline, and where possible, automate standard transactional and informational activities (self service)
- Provide quicker and more consistent HR support to Line Managers
- Remove duplication and bureaucracy and provide the benefits of economies of scale
- Move HR service delivery from being largely reactive to being strategic, proactive and aware of operational needs allowing for greater operational flexibility.

Martin Tiplady, the Director of HR at the MPS, recalls the rationale and origins of the programme:

We were characterised largely as an administrative processing and rather bureaucratic HR service and it was apparent that we had to do something about that in order to add greater value to the organisation. We also responded to Gershon's review of the effectiveness and efficiency of backroom services and basically we concluded that there were much cheaper ways of doing it.

I also recognised that unless we responded proactively then somebody from Her Majesty's Government might have come in to tell us how we should it. As it is, we are forecasting a saving of around £15 million per year, once the full effects of the transformation have come into force.

But this is simply the foundation layer that enables a different class of HR to emerge, which is about HR doing more of being in the driving seat in the business, securing better outcomes and customer focus; working with our managers to make then better leaders, better managers and easier ways of achieving more objectives and targets than anything else, that's the value added HR, which is what I'm used to and where I think we ought to be. Perhaps putting it another way, we should be more highly regarded for our input into the resourcing strategy for the 2012 Olympics than for our ability to design a new sickness form.

Structure of new HR service delivery model

The scheme of work involves setting up a new structure, which accommodates a higher proportion of activities being migrated to a 'HR Centre'. This centre incorporates both transactional and strategic elements – see Figure 9.6. Business partners and strategic HR advisors are assigned to the various MPS operating units. Web-based self-service tools complete the service delivery model.

The responsibilities of the different facets of the model are set out below:

HR Shared Service Centre

The operational hub of the model is the **Shared Service Centre**, responsible for delivering the policies and programmes developed in the **Strategic Centre**, and designed around tiers (0 – **Self-Service** (on-line answers and transactions); 1 – **Human Resources Advisory Centre** (24x7 service); 2 – **Expert Services** (specific queries, more complex or time-consuming transactions); 3 – **HR Operational Support** (deployed from the Expert Services, this group is based

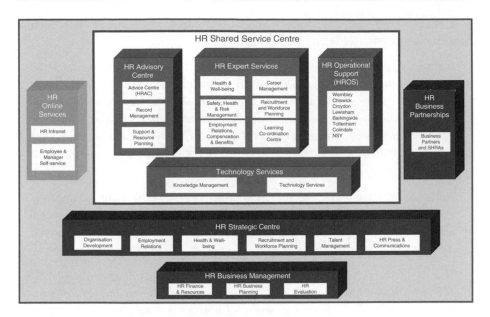

Figure 9.6 Overview of new organisation.

in the business; one-to-one interactions where sensitive or complex cases require this level of support)).

Business partners and strategic HR advisors

This area is responsible for understanding/defining HR requirements from a business perspective; ensuring the **Shared Service Centre** is meeting local SLAs in the delivery of HR services; developing business solutions to meet business requirements in conjunction with the **Strategic Centre** and working with SMTs to manage the organisation.

Strategic Centre

The Strategic Centre designs and develops policies, processes and programmes to support business requirements; utilising intelligence coming from the Service Centre and Business **(Business Partners / Strategic HR Advisors)** and understanding issues/gaps to design corporate HR solutions; proactively identifying trends across organisation; Interfacing with Training, Leadership and Organisation Development.

Reflecting on these proposals, Martin Tiplady acknowledged that gaining stakeholder buy-in had been challenging.

For many people, the intended changes to our service delivery model have been perceived as a centralisation programme, with all the connotations that brings in regard to taking away well-thought-of local resources and replacing them with a faceless, centralised bureaucracy. In fact it is not a centralisation programme; it is just that as a line manager the things you expect to be done by your HR manager 'down the corridor' will now get done in another way.

Allied to that, we needed to use technology rather better than we do, in a sense that we spend quite a lot of time in HR updating individual records and doing lots of checking. Well, the new model relies quite a lot on self-service and we shall be relying on our technological infrastructure rather more in the future.

If I'm frank, we have the support of our top management, the Board, who have undoubtedly questioned and challenged the programme but they have been willing to listen to the arguments and have been persuaded. However, when I go out into the Boroughs, and visit our Operational Command Units (OCUs) there is still a job to do winning over hearts and minds. It is there that the perception of centralisation is probably at its most acute.

Governance structure

The reader will have noted that the MPS HR transformation is a complex, large scale undertaking. Drawing on the earlier general guidance relating to programme governance, it is useful, by way of illustration, to see how MPS set up their governance structures for the design phase and implementation phases – see figures 9.7 and 9.8. You will notice how the structure is 'beefed up' to include additional elements relevant to technical system procurement and solution delivery. Included in these elements, a new strategy group and programme delivery board are constituted to monitor and guide the programme and you will notice that three of the four major workstreams change their title (and responsibilities) to signify the transition of the programme from design to delivery.

The constitution of the various governance bodies, their membership and roles and responsibilities, are set out in Tables 9.1 and 9.2.

The responsibilities of the workstreams are set out in Figure 9.9 below.

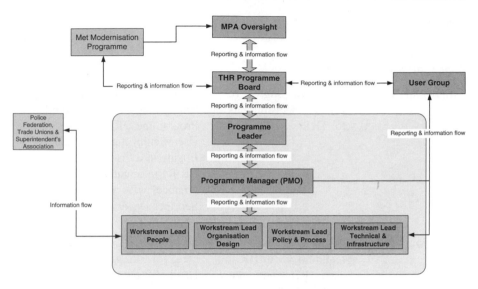

Figure 9.7 Phase 1 governance.

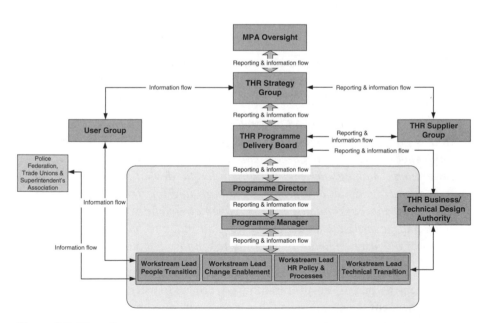

Figure 9.8 Phase 2 governance.

Table 9.1 Phase 1 governance bodies and forums

Governance bodies/forums	Purpose	Membership
Programme Board	Programme progress & strategic decision making for THR	Senior Responsible Owner, Programme Leader, Head of Programme Office, Senior User, Senior Supplier, Senior Business Advisors, Senior HR Representative, Business Finance, MPA member, Property Services Department, Programme Conscience
User Group	Gathering views and requirements of HR users. Represent views of stakeholders	One senior rep from each business area, THR Programme Leader, Head of Programme Office, Workstream leads
Trade Union, Federation & Superintendents Association	Engage with and consult with representatives of affected groups	Programme Leader, Workstream Leads, Union, Police Federation & Supt Association reps

Yvette Dorman, the change enablement workstream lead on the HR transformation programme, sums up the challenges inherent in this massive undertaking, echoing the sentiments articulated earlier by Martin Tiplady:

Convincing in excess of 50,000 people that a transformed HR function is going to deliver better HR is probably the biggest challenge I have encountered in my career. This is a vitally important part of the programme, making sure that people understand what is involved in the new operating model and preparing the ground for its implementation. The 'eyes and ears' intelligence is extremely useful to the programme team and governance arrangements are in place to make sure that the views of our user community are fully taken into account.

The views expressed by Yvette underline the importance of stakeholder engagement as part of an overarching governance structure which incorporates *all* facets of the programme. This is a useful comparator with the Scottish Executive example, where workstreams were de-coupled from a governance perspective, which then contributed to the myriad of problems exposed in the review.

Table 9.2 Phase 2 governance bodies and forums

Governance bodies/forums	Purpose	Membership
Strategy Group	Strategic decision making for Transforming HR Programme	Senior Responsible Owner, Programme Director, Programme Manager, Head of Programme Office, Senior User, Senior Supplier, Director of Information, Director of Resources, MPA member, Property Services Department, Programme Conscience, Business Finance
Delivery Board	Day to day delivery of THR decision making, risk management and progress	Programme Director, Programme Manager, Head of Programme Office, Programme Finance, Business Finance, Workstream Leads, Contracts Manager, Main Supplier Lead
User Group	Gathering views and requirements of HR users. Represent views of stakeholders	One senior rep from each business area, THR Programme Director/ Manager, Workstream leads, Head of Programme Office,
THR Supplier Group	Supplier performance & relationships	MPS Contracts Manager, Programme Manager, lead supplier, 3rd party supplier reps, Programme Finance
THR Business/ Technical Design Authority	Ensure coherence of technical and functional design	MPS Technical Design Authority, THR Business Architect, THR Technical Design Authority, Technology Workstream Lead, Service Delivery partner representatives, Business Change Manager
Trade Union, Police Federation & Superintendents Association	Engage with and consult with representatives of affected groups	Programme Director, Workstream Leads, Unions, Police Federation & Supt Association reps.

Figure 9.9 HR transformation programme workstream responsibilities.

Summary

Our own experience and the case illustrations supported by critical insights from senior contributing practitioners underlines the critical importance of good programme governance. You neglect this area at your peril. Ensuring, for example, that stakeholder engagement does not happen in isolation, but as part of the wider

HR transformation, is critically important and we have emphasised the need to put in place appropriate governance arrangements to ensure from the start that you monitor costs, benefits and key delivery milestones. Never be afraid to admit to problems before they reach a serious and disruptive level and make sure that that the conditions of success of the programme remain clearly articulated and understood.

10

Implementation: Capability and Culture

This chapter focuses on the capability development and culture change aspects of implementation. These areas remain significant and critical gaps in HR's transformational journey. As such, we will address the following questions:

- Why is HR capability development important?
- What does excellent business partnering look like?
- What new capabilities do HR professionals, shared services and line managers need to acquire?
- How do we develop these capabilities?
- How do we know when it has been done successfully?
- What are the key culture change challenges faced by HR functions?

Key themes

- Investment in capability development is essential if we are to change significantly HR's contribution in organisations.
- The impact of HR transformation on HR, line managers and others involved in HR service delivery needs to be assessed to identify and agree on role expectations.
- HR professionals will need to develop stronger capabilities in strategy and organisational development, client relationship/consulting and project management.
- Capability development needs to be sustained and cannot be seen as a once-off exercise.
- We need to be intentional about the way we shape the culture of HR, becoming more customer focused and with a stronger emphasis on internal consultancy and marketing.

Context

When HR functions have implemented new HR information systems, established a shared services centre to handle transactional and advisory enquiries and set up an expert team to manage disciplinary, grievance and performance cases, line managers are often still unclear about their role, the role of HR shared services and HR professionals. This is particularly true for HR professionals who are often posed with the 'million dollar question': 'So what do you actually do now?'

One of the main points we have made throughout this book is that HR transformation is about the transformation of the whole HR delivery model. It is not just about getting the technology and process management right. It is also about shifting capability and culture.

So, the question posed by line managers is fair and reasonable – what expectations are now placed on them as people managers; how will people working remotely in shared services help me and what value will I get from HR professionals if things I previously valued like case management and sorting out people problems are now being handled differently? And it is no good for HR professionals to be shrugging their shoulders and saying, 'Oh, I am going to be more strategic now'. This will not wash. We need to have an answer and be able to deliver on the promise.

So, why is capability development important? Partly, it is because line managers and HR alike are still confused about what is required of them in the brave new world of transformed HR – they want greater clarity on what exactly they need to do differently and, for HR professionals, how they contribute in a more strategic capacity. It is also important because of a simple reality – if you do not shift capabilities in parallel with other changes in structure, processes and technology, you will not shift HR's contribution in organisations. HR professionals cannot learn to work differently through a process of osmosis.

Historically, HR has focused professional development on service delivery areas and processes – creating efficient and effective processes in core people areas such as recruitment, administration, development, talent, reward, etc. or being experts in advisory services on policy and legislation. This expertise will remain core to HR's overall value proposition, but transformed HR requires HR professionals to add value in other ways too.

In Chapter 2 we have already noted that capability development remains a critical gap to be bridged if HR functions are to truly transform. Box 10.1 presents recent research in the United Kingdom and United States that underlines this point and highlights the capability gaps that currently exist.

The research shows that significant capability development areas remain. This suggests that there has generally been insufficient investment in capability development and that this gap must be bridged if HR professionals are to contribute differently and more effectively – and not just acquire a new job title.

Box 10.1 Recent research on the HR function

The changing HR function: CIPD 2007

This research suggests that there has not been much change since 2003 in the skills needed by the HR function: they remain those of strategic thinking, influencing, political skills and business knowledge. These are the capability areas considered most important in shaping the new breed of HR business partners and specialists.

Achieving strategic excellence: Edward E. Lawler III, John W. Boudreau, Susan Albers Mohrman (2006)

This longitudinal study reports that 'overall our respondents report significant movement toward HR becoming a strategic partner and doing higher value-added activities. However, before we conclude that this has actually occurred it is important to look at the results from 1994, 1998, 2001 (which are) *almost identical to the data collected in 2004*.

The research also goes on to assess HR skills in more detail and finds 'a low level of satisfaction exists with business partner skills. Deficits are still perceived in the substantive business support areas of strategic planning, organisational design and cross-functional and global understanding'. Change management capability also remains at best neutral.

The research concludes that 'HR suffers from a skills deficit. It is notable that there is only a moderate level of satisfaction with all HR skills and that most ratings fall into the neutral category. Of particular concern are the relatively low ratings given to business partnering skills, since they are related to HR's playing a significant role in strategy ... There is much work to be done to enhance HR skills as well as develop a common understanding about the nature and level of those skills.

Why this is the case is alluded to in the CIPD report which expresses worries that 'HR's change programme is disconnected both from the business strategy and any other structural modernisation taking place elsewhere in the organisation'. The absence of a systems mindset and a holistic and integrated approach to HR transformation appears to be at the root of this deficit.

In this chapter, we focus on the capability gap and cultural change in HR. We will explore what excellent 'business partnering' looks like and then set out a process to identify, baseline and build capability in line managers, shared services and HR professionals. We will present some examples of how organisations have approached capability definition and development. Finally, we will present a framework to enable you to be more intentional about how you shape culture, identifying three areas where HR functions need to particularly focus change.

Excellent business partnering

Before we set out a process to identify and develop capability, we want to explore what excellent business partnering looks like. The title 'Business Partner' is currently the title of fashion in the HR profession. We also know that during our 25+ years' experience of working in HR titles have their seasons. The profession has long been seeking to move into the strategic partnering space – indeed the shift from Personnel to HR Management was an earlier precursor of this. But there is still confusion about what this more strategic role (whether played out by generalists or specialists) looks like. As it is generally the current title of choice in HR, we will use the term 'Business Partner' for convenience. We predict that this title 'will, in time, fall...' out of fashion and will be replaced. So, irrespective of title, what we are more interested in is what this role really looks like. What do HR professionals do if they are working in this space? What does excellence look like?

Even David Ulrich recognises that there are quite different versions of business partnering in organisations. In a People Management interview (28 June 2007) he talks about the business partner title having broadened in organisations to a point where it describes a nearly impossible role: where HR Partners are expected to contribute across a very broad front and where, for many HR professionals, it has been easier to keep doing operational HR than the strategic.

Recent research (Box 10.2 summarises some key sources), along with our own experience of working with a wide range of organisations, suggests that excellent business partnering (whether HR professionals wear a generalist or specialist hat) embraces the following five characteristics:

1. *Understanding your organisation's business.* Without this understanding HR professionals cannot even begin to shape a business-focused people and organisational agenda. This means being fluent in the metrics and the language of your organisation. We must understand what it takes for our organisations to perform and be able to hold our own in conversations about customers, markets, stakeholders, financials, operations, etc. This requirement was identified by a number of our senior practitioners. Alison Grace (Rackspace) identified business awareness, commercial acumen and mental agility around numbers as key HR capabilities. Ian Muir (ESAB) also underlined the need for commercial fluency, including numeracy and financial literacy. Jerry Arnott (DWP) stated that 'what has increased in importance is an absolute necessity for HR

professionals to understand their business and metrics/numeracy. These are areas that need to be beefed up considerably. The problem is that in many instances HR does not identify with the business or understand it'.

2. *Building strong relationships* with business colleagues. Much research and writing about business partnering focus on the need for HR professionals to demonstrate personal impact and credibility. The essence of partnering is an ability to change the kinds of conversations HR professionals hold with business colleagues. This means being confident to challenge colleagues, bring new thinking to the table, influence effectively and ask the kinds of questions that make people think differently. Strong relationships are relationships of equals. Ian Muir (ESAB), recalling his time as HR Director for Cable and Wireless International, stated that 'success as a Business Partner is much more the product of intellectual, physical and commercial alignment to the client. Building this relationship is critical and this happens on the fly, in corridor conversations as much as in more formalised surroundings. My desk was within 5 metres of the CEO's desk in an open plan office'.

3. *Acquiring a new toolkit of expertise.* Expertise must be developed in core HR disciplines such as talent acquisition, capability development, employee relations, etc. and in the areas of business change and organisational development. This means developing a strong understanding of change management tools and project management approaches alongside traditional HR subject areas.

4. *Bringing this toolkit of expertise to the table in a way that is problem-led* so that we work with our business colleagues to identify a solution rather than telling them, as 'the expert', what the answer is. We need to work in ways that build business commitment to and ownership of outcomes. Many authors are clear that excellent business partnering requires strong consulting, coaching and facilitation skills. (Reference Chapter 1 and the process consulting mindset.) Frances Allcock (BBC) pointed out that HR activity must be aligned to the organisation's strategy. If no time is made for senior HR professionals to engage in strategic conversations with business colleagues and to understand business problems, there will be resistance because HR will be seen as imposing solutions and how these products help the organisation to deliver its strategy is missing.

5. *Focusing on the organisation's change agenda* – shaping and delivering the strategy, developing and building organisational capability, addressing systemic organisational issues. Business partners need to be able to shape small- and large-scale organisational changes and bring the toolkit of change management and organisational development skills to help the business move forward successfully.

Box 10.2 Research on the role of the business partner

Corporate leadership council – Building the next generation of HR-line partnerships (2007)
The Corporate Leadership Council (CLC) concludes that the strategic role is HR's most powerful lever for demonstrating business-level impact. The Council research demonstrates that the people in the role and the design of the job both strongly influence the effectiveness of the HR strategic role.

The person in the role
The CLC research argues that the implication of focusing on the person in the strategic role is critical. Effectiveness in the strategic role requires business analytics, leadership and persuasion skills. Business analytics drives strategic effectiveness, but only if HR can persuasively communicate them (i.e., using data-driven business cases to identify solutions tailored to customer needs has the strongest HR strategic impact). With the problem understood, the person in the HR strategic role must then be able to develop and defend a strong point of view regarding the answer and then take ownership for solution delivery.

The design of the job
The research also indicates that HR must re-examine the design of the job to improve performance. Successful design shifts the role from broad involvement across the HR touch points of numerous projects to deeper ownership on a select few high-impact projects.

Critical HR professional skills identified by the CLC are:

People skills	HR expertise	Implementation skills	Business skills
■ Influencing others ■ Leading people ■ Communicating clearly	■ Recruitment and retention expertise ■ Performance and development expertise ■ Compensation expertise ■ Compliance expertise	■ Driving to results ■ Managing projects ■ Managing change ■ Applying technology ■ Managing vendors	■ Knowing your business ■ Knowing business fundamentals ■ Applying business analytics ■ Taking a global approach

David Ulrich – A new mandate for human resources (1997), from partners to players (2001), masterclass on building sustainable value through your HR value proposition (2007)

Although he did not actually use the expression HR business partner, Ulrich is credited with the emergence of the HR business partner role. In his seminal book in 1997 he describes the new HR role, which can help deliver organisational excellence, in four ways:

1. *Become a partner in strategy execution*
   ■ Define organisational architecture (i.e., five essential organisa-tional components: strategy, structure, rewards, processes and people);
   ■ Guide management through rigorous discussion on fit (e.g., the company culture fit against its strategic goals);
   ■ Lead in proposing, creating and debating best practice in culture change programmes or reward systems;
   ■ Take stock of own work and set clear priorities. HR professionals might have a dozen initiatives in their sights but they must have skills to be able to join forces with managers to systematically assess the impact and importance of each one initiative.
2. *Become an expert in the way work is organised and executed –* delivering efficiency to ensure that costs are reduced whilst quality is maintained.
3. *Become an employee champion –* representing employee concerns to senior management and at the same time working to increase employee contribution. HR also has an important role in holding a mirror up in front of senior executives.
4. *Become a change agent –* building organisation's capacity to embrace and capitalise on change. Using the change model 'who, why, what and how', introduce this to the management team and guide them through it.

Since 1997, Ulrich has used a range of terms to describe the role of HR business partner. In a 2001 book he co-authored with Dick Beatty, he argues that the HR role needs to shift from partner to player to meet strategic challenges. It goes on to explain that there are six ways in which HR players contribute to organisations: coach, architect, builder, facilitator, leader and conscience. Ulrich and Beatty state that by fulfilling these roles HR professionals can make a valued contribution to strategic decision making that builds winning organisations.

Coach

- Coaches executives to change their behaviour.
- Fully grasping and understanding organisation stakeholder scorecard is critical.
- Contracting skills are essential.
- Ability to build relationship of trust with business leader.
- Can give clear, direct, candid and useful feedback.

Organisational architect

- Must have a concept of what constitutes an effective reorganisation in line with the needs of the company, for example, the McKinsey model.

Builder

- Delivers the value proposition to the customer.
- Turns ideas into actions.
- In order to design and deliver he or she must be current in theory and the practice of HR.

Facilitator

- Facilitator role encompasses strategic change leadership.
- Understands importance of getting things done and making change happen.
- Facilitates teamwork. Engages teams to increase team effectiveness and helps teams learn from successes and failures.

Leader

- Exemplar on how to manage.
- Focuses on deliverables.
- Demonstrates capabilities set out in the leadership model.

Conscience

- Ensures organisation plays by the rules.
- HR plays referee role to honestly evaluate business practices.

More recently, a 2007 masterclass referred to the need for HR professionals to build competencies as:

- *Credible activist* – building relationships of trust so that an active stance can be taken to shape culture, drive change, influence direction.

- *Cultural steward, talent manager/organisational designer and strategic change agent* – which are areas HR BPs should know about and do to make a difference.
- *Business ally and day-to-day tactician* – competencies he sees as table stakes. They are necessary but are not sufficient without the above two areas.

Ulrich states that these three roles have a strong correlation with impact on business performance.

B Kenton and J Yarnall – The HR business partner (2005)
In their book on business partnering, the following characteristics were identified:

- *Delivering to the business* – understanding the bigger picture/business environment, systems thinking, being able to apply skills to a wide variety of business needs, providing expertise and support/facilitation, taking a longer term perspective.
- *Working alongside managers in the business* – collaborating, building strong relationships, involving others in finding solutions, building trust, contracting so that work undertaken is transparent, working at both content and process levels.
- *Self-awareness and impact* – focused on learning, questions things, credible, resilient, dynamic, energetic – someone who moves people forward.
- *Creating and leading change* – proactive and inventive, applies knowledge of change theory, influences others to engage them in the change process, creative, works well with ambiguity and complexity, path-finding.
- *Maintaining a business focus* – prioritising, utilises business data, challenges appropriately, seeks feedback for insight and learning, sets measures and defines clear deliverables at the start of any project.

What this means in practice is that excellent business partners will engage with colleagues around strategic themes: sustaining high performance during difficult economic times; integrating new businesses; driving efficiencies and cost management; creating higher levels of employee engagement; identifying new individual and organisational capabilities; shaping and creating a high-performance culture; helping management teams to perform and work together more effectively ... and so on ... that will drive revenue/customer satisfaction, control costs and build reputation. Indeed HR professionals, working as business partners, need to be able to ask and address whatever the key questions are that will help their organisation to deliver high performance.

How we build capability

Over the past decade we have evolved a five-step approach (see Box 10.3) to build HR capability which incorporates an analytical phase as well as a delivery phase. This approach is used to identify and build capability for line managers, shared services and HR professionals (generalists/business partners and specialists/centres of expertise).

Box 10.3 Capability development – A five-step approach

1. *Clarify HR's contribution:* identifying what your organisation needs from HR and the capabilities that will enable HR to make this contribution;
2. *Define performance expectations:* defining what performance looks like for HR professionals with different levels of experience;
3. *Establish a capability baseline*: giving HR professionals a tool to assess their capability and define development goals;
4. *Invest in HR capability development*: designing and running a range of development interventions;
5. *Review learning*: ensuring that lessons learnt are built into ongoing HR professional development.

In Box 10.3 this section, we expand on each of these steps. We also provide examples of how each step has been tackled by different organisations and the tools they have found helpful.

Step 1 – Clarify HR's contribution

It is important that there is a dialogue with business colleagues about the contribution needed from HR and that contribution should be anchored in the critical issues faced by the organisation.

We use a number of techniques to gain clarity on HR's contribution and here we explain two techniques that have proved to be particularly helpful:

1. 'Strawman' discussion document,
2. 'Accountability Workshop'.

Strawman discussion document

For those of you unfamiliar with the term 'strawman' – this is a proposal put up for discussion that is robust enough to stand up to critique (i.e., it has substance), but not so robust that the proposals cannot be taken apart and re-worked. It is therefore different from a draft document where the expectation is that the proposals are well formed.

This document typically sets out the responsibilities and accountabilities for employees, managers, HR generalists, HR specialists, HR shared services (transactional and advisory), outsourcers, etc. as a basis for discussion. An example of how this approach has been used is presented in the case study below.

Case study – Global telecoms business

A four-page discussion document was written setting out the capability shift required in HR professionals and options to address this capability gap. This 'strawman' paper was then discussed one to one with the global HR leadership team and other key stakeholders elsewhere in the business. Feedback enabled a firm proposal to be developed which was then signed off through the HR transformation governance structure without any substantive change. This approach was quick and effective in building a coalition of support for the final proposal and in clarifying the contribution needed from HR professionals.

Accountability workshop

As a precursor to organisational design, we have found it helpful to combine the work on HR delivery channels and the scope of HR services that are delivered through these channels to ascertain where accountability for HR service delivery will lie. (See Chapter 8 for more information on delivery channels.) Our suggested forum to complete this work is through an Accountability Workshop. A 'strawman' scope of HR services document is presented in Appendix 3.

This type of workshop brings together HR and stakeholders from other parts of the business to work through changes in people management accountabilities. Typically statements of the scope of people-related activities are used to stimulate discussion (irrespective of whether these activities are performed by line managers, different members of the HR team or outsourced service delivery channels).

The Accountability Workshop then focuses on identifying, for each activity area, accountabilities for managers, HR and outsourcers, and whether the impact of HR transformation makes these accountabilities stronger, neutral or weaker.

In preparing for the workshop, focus on completing two strawman templates, one template showing the 'as is' and another presenting the known accountabilities in the 'to be' delivery model. Through desk research and interviews, it should be possible to develop a very robust picture of the 'as is' and a good starting point for the 'to be'. What this preparation work is likely to highlight are inconsistencies in accountabilities across the organisation. These templates can be tested in advance with participants and any outstanding issues can be presented for discussion/resolution at the workshop.

The reason for completing both the 'as is and a 'to be' template is to be able to manage implementation more effectively. Knowing how HR transformation will impact different organisational roles will enable communication to be tailored and subsequent interventions to be structured to secure stakeholder buy-in.

We have found that an accountabilities workshop works well when participants are drawn from the HR function and the line and comprise typically around 15–20 people. Participants do not necessarily need to be the most senior people, but should have a grasp between them of the full range of HR services. In the workshop, the aim is to validate the 'as is' template and to finalise a 'to be' template. The balance of time should be spent on considering the 'to be' template.

At the workshop, a process we have found that works well is to:

- Create a large version of the template strawman (sheets of brown paper work well).
- Organise participants into five small groups.
- Introduce the task, setting out the aims of HR transformation, givens, assumptions etc.
- Allocate a heading per group.
- Ask each small group to complete their template, identifying where they believe accountability will lie.
- Rotate groups to comment on the work of their colleagues (a sticky dot can be placed alongside a statement requiring clarification or which needs to be challenged; anything missing can be written on a Post-it™ note).
- Work through each of the templates and reach agreement where issues have been flagged (with dots and Post-it™ notes).

Typically, an Accountability Workshop takes a couple of days to work through all the issues. This is, however, an extremely good investment of time as the output will have been created jointly between HR and other business colleagues and the output also provides a clear statement of role expectations. If there is any ambiguity about what strategic contribution the business needs from HR, this type of workshop helps to bring clarity to this area. The outputs from this workshop will then need to be discussed with key stakeholders.

We have found that the workshop outputs are helpful in framing a number of interventions that need to be undertaken as part of the HR transformation process. For example:

- high-level activity analysis (supporting analysis of future resource needs);
- HR process mapping;
- accountability mapping and role definitions;
- capability identification and development requirements for different roles;
- stakeholder communications;
- structure design.

An extract from the outputs of an Accountability Workshop is shown in Appendix 4.

Step 2 – Define performance expectations

Having clarified the contribution expected from line managers, shared services and HR professionals, the next step is to turn this into a set of performance expectations. We have chosen to use the term 'capability framework' to describe this set of performance expectations.

Our experience in developing HR capability frameworks with a wide range of organisations highlights two general points:

1. All of the capability frameworks we have been involved in developing have over 80% common elements. In this sense, we can claim to have identified a set of capabilities that these organisations believe to be core to the role of business partner and specialist.
2. Each organisation needs to articulate its capability framework in its own way and in language relevant to that organisation. In this sense, there is no one-size-fits-all as each organisation will emphasise different contributions required from HR to deliver its strategic agenda.

Although these statements may appear to be contradictory they are not. What it means is that whilst we have found broad agreement on the capabilities that need to be developed, each organisation will want to express these in a way that is relevant to its circumstances.

Line manager capabilities
Many line manager capabilities will remain those expected of people managers. So, being able to select the right people, set goals, motivate the team, give feedback, deal with under-performance, etc. will remain core to the line manager role. What you will need to work out is where you draw the boundary between the line manager role in people management and HR's. This will include being clear about the extent to which managers must use self-service for reporting, policy and process information; take full or partial responsibility

245

for people processes such as talent acquisition, employee relations and case management, reward and benefits, etc.

Here we give an example of how National Grid has approached this task.

Case study – National grid

As part of implementing a shared services model, National Grid has set out in detail the expectations of managers in delivering their people management responsibilities. These expectations are set out under four headings:

1. Manage ER and Cases
2. Manage Rewards and Benefits
3. Manage Resourcing (recruitment, leavers and contracts of employment)
4. Manage Learning and Development (training, development and talent)

A number of capabilities are then identified under each of these four headings. Some capabilities are common to all areas, for example, ability to access, interpret and act upon policies and processes that relate to that area; understanding of relevant employment legislation for that area. Other capabilities are specific to each area. Some examples for the area of Manage ER and Cases are:

- Compose appropriate correspondence associated with the different stages of a case.
- Effectively manage short- and long-term absence.
- Administer a formal verbal and written warning.
- Conduct a dismissal process.

The National Grid approach emphasises to managers that if they feel out of their depth or if they are dealing with a dismissal or appeal they should phone HR for assistance and advice.

Across all capability areas, some capabilities are essential for all managers and some are not. For example, conducting an appeal is not considered essential for all managers.

Shared services capabilities
Similarly, it is important to define the capabilities required of those people working in shared service centres, if you have these. These also need to reflect the

model adopted by your organisation. So, for some HR shared service centres a 'shallow' model applies where capabilities focus mainly on administration, policy advice and help desk. Other organisations may have a 'deep' model which may also include end-to-end processes including policy development. In this instance your capability requirements are going to overlap with those in specialist roles/ centres of expertise.

We again use an example from National Grid to illustrate the types of capabilities that apply in a 'deep' shared services model.

Case study – National grid

In implementing its shared services centre, National Grid developed a capability framework which differentiated between 'What we do' and 'How we do it'.

- *What We Do* capabilities focused on: Process, Information, Quality.
- *How We Do It* capabilities focused on: Client Relationships, Working Together, Communication and Project Management.

Each of these seven capabilities had a number of capability areas. So, Process, for example, had three capability areas:

1. manages workflows effectively,
2. builds expertise in policies,
3. delivers HR processes.

Four performance levels were then aligned to each of these capability areas. So, for 'Delivers HR Processes', Level 1 performance requirement was 'can follow defined processes' whereas Level 4 performance requirement was 'creates processes and matches them with customers'.

HR partner capabilities

To initiate discussion on HR Partner (generalist and specialist) capabilities, our starting point is typically a 'strawman' capability framework containing the following elements:

1. *Strategy and Change Management* – the ability to both shape and execute the organisation's strategic agenda. Explicit in this capability area is knowledge of the 'business' and of change management tools and techniques that will enable your organisation to deliver its strategic agenda.
2. *Consulting Skills* – the ability to work with clients through a consulting process so that the outcomes are owned by the client. Influencing,

credibility, conflict resolution, facilitation, coaching are all characteristics of effective consulting.

3. *Project Management* – to use the principles of project management (it is not about becoming an expert on Prince 2 or similar Programme Management methodologies) to shape work so that the value proposition is transparent to clients. In this way, work should have clear terms of reference, deliverables, timescales, resource estimates, etc.

4. *Core HR Skills* – we still need to bring our traditional core HR skills (in Talent Acquisition, Employee Engagement, Learning and Development, Recognition and Reward, HR Information) to the table, but our focus needs to be more on their strategic contribution rather than process excellence.

We have found high levels of buy-in to the three new capability areas of strategy and change management, consulting skills and project management. In defining performance criteria, the following considerations are important:

- the number of performance levels you need to put in place to reflect the breadth of capability in your HR team;
- the level of detail you want to go into to describe performance levels;
- how an HR capability framework integrates with other leadership frameworks you may have;
- how the capability framework dovetails with HR career paths.

Organisations we have worked with have tackled these considerations in different ways. Here we present three examples of how largely common content has been developed in different ways.

Example 1: Discovery communications

Discovery Communications have articulated HR capabilities under seven areas:

- Commercial
- Operational
- HR Expert
- Culture and Change Champion
- Organisation Development and Talent
- Credible Activist
- Creative and Innovative

Capability requirements are set out under each of these areas. So, for example,

- *Commercial* includes: knows how the business makes money; understands costs versus value.
- *Culture and Change Champion* includes: effectively manages change programmes; helps leaders share the company's culture and contributes to a positive climate.
- *Operational* includes: helps internal customers navigate through HR processes; customises solutions to achieve the right business results.
- *HR Expert* includes the development of expertise in the areas of ER, L&D, Recruitment, C&B and Project Management.
- *Credible Activist* includes: able to use knowledge and turn it into action; applies a consulting approach to the HR role.
- *Organisational Development and Talent* includes: actively works with the business to design and develop the organisation; supports internal and external talent pipeline growth.
- *Creative and Innovative* includes: customises solutions to achieve the right business results; initiates change and takes proactive suggestions to the leaders.

As Discovery Communications is a leader in creative media it was thought important that HR also mirrored this broader business capability of creativity and innovation. HR needs to be working in that space too!

When Nicky Riding took up the role of HR Director EMEA it was the first time Discovery had an integrated HR function to support its EMEA business. It was also clear that an enthusiastic and able HR team needed to be focused on those capabilities that would help the business perform. A relatively flat structure exists and therefore the approach taken is straightforward with a common list of requirements set out under each heading.

Example 2: AXA UK

AXA uses the visual below to articulate HR capability areas.

For each of the capability areas there are four levels of capability: Entry Level, Foundation Level, Building and Expert.

Performance criteria are set out for each level and capability area. Examples (not an exhaustive list) of those performance criteria used at *Foundation Level* are:

- understands and interprets business strategy,
- understands the KPIs within the business,
- delivers key aspects of organisational change,
- coaches front line supervisors,
- is commercially aware,
- influences, communicates and consults with senior managers, builds relationships with the business.

This approach does not set out the subsets for each capability area but does define performance criteria at levels between Foundation (Entry Point) and Expert (Mastery). In addition, AXA have also defined capabilities in some detail for the new capability areas of organisational design, project management, consulting skills and change management.

AXA have also set out a high-level career path, showing that as people progress hierarchically, their core HR knowledge and expertise become less important and the 'new' capability areas become more important. A visual used by this organisation is given in Figure 10.1.

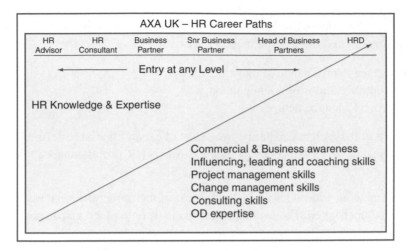

Figure 10.1 AXA HR career paths.

Our third example is again National Grid. In the first edition of this book we presented the National Grid HR capability framework in some detail. This framework has been in place since 2001 and has been updated recently. The initial framework and the outcome of a recent review are shown in Example 3:

Example 3: National grid

HR capabilities were defined around the following framework:

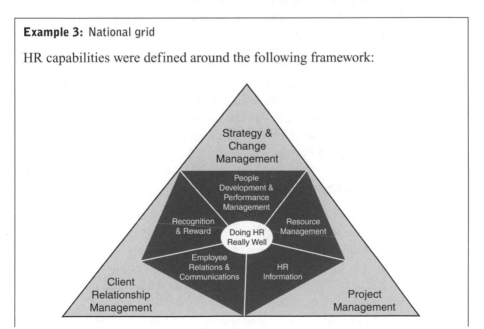

This framework therefore incorporated five core HR capabilities (shown in the pentagon) and three new capability areas:

- Strategy and Change Management,
- Client Relationship Management,
- Project Management.

For each of these eight capability areas a set of capabilities were defined along with relevant performance levels, against which HR professionals could self assess.

This framework was reviewed in 2008. Most of the framework reviewed remained unchanged. The main changes made were to place a stronger emphasis on the following:

- designing and implementing appropriate organisational structures,
- quantifying the value of HR services delivered,
- ensuring projects reflect task (what) and process (how),
- developing resourcing strategies and plans,
- putting in place strategies and plans to build organisational capability.

National Grid is a good example of an organisation that has developed and worked with a framework over time and, through applying the 80/20 rule, has made adjustments to the framework to reflect changing business priorities without losing the robustness of the initial content.

These are not the only ways to express HR Partner capabilities. Other organisations we have worked with have adopted a lighter touch and others have gone into greater detail. What is important is that the capability framework makes sense to your organisation and to your HR professionals and enables you to identify capability gaps and development needs.

Step 3 – Establish a capability baseline

Establishing performance expectations through a capability framework or equivalent will enable you to baseline current capability. This capability assessment can be integrated with the performance review process or stand alone as a developmental discussion. What your capability framework will enable you to do is allow line and HR to self assess against the performance levels and to discuss this assessment with their line managers.

National Grid has adopted a similar approach to baseline capability for line managers, shared services and HR Partners (generalist and specialist). This approach is set out in the following case study.

Case study – National grid

The example below is taken from the line manager self-assessment for
Manage ER and Cases:

Element	Not applicable at this stage	Significant development need	Development need	Adequate	A clear strength
Able to access, interpret and act upon policies and processes that relate to a Case					
Effectively manage short- and long-term sickness absence					
Conduct the dismissal process					

Elements were categorised: essential for all managers, event driven (just in
time development) and not essential for all managers.

For shared services and HR Partners a similar self-assessment, followed by
manager review process, was adopted.

AXA has adopted a different approach to baseline capability and this is reflected
in the following case study.

Case study – AXA UK

Development options are listed for each of the four performance levels to
enable HR professionals to create their development plan. Quite a few of
these options are mandatory. This approach is based on a view that most
HR professionals do not have the required new capabilities. Base lining is
therefore about ensuring people have met mandatory skills acquisition at their
level and that HR develops and uses a common language and toolkit.

An example capability development sheet for business partners and senior
business partners is as follows:

Capabilities	Development needs	Development activity
• Demonstrates the impact of HR interventions on the business KPIs and the strategic plan • Challenges the status quo • Leads specific aspects of organisational change, e.g., organisational design elements • Contributes to the development of business HR strategy • Translates HR interventions into business benefits • Designs and/or supports initiatives and programmes • Coaches middle-senior line managers • Manages key HR projects • Demonstrates a broad understanding of the external influences that impact the business	• Awareness and application of OD best practice • Commercial and business awareness • Consulting skills • Influencing skills • Project management skills • Change management skills • Coaching skills	• Organisation design skills • Consultancy skills • Influencing skills • Facilitation skills • Advanced presentation skills—winning hearts and minds • Project management • Change management • Improving performance through coaching

Step 4 – Invest in HR capability development

Without investment in ongoing capability development many HR professionals will be left knowing what they need to do differently but without the knowledge and skills to contribute differently.

Where possible, we strongly recommend that HR professionals achieve professional qualifications and accreditation through their relevant professional institute or governing body. This is important in building the credibility of HR, in ensuring professional standards and in developing a community of influential HR professionals. However, the acquisition of a formal professional qualification does not always address sufficiently the full range of capabilities that HR professionals need to acquire to operate as effective business partners.

A pre requisite must be to include a cost line for capability development in any business case for HR transformation or in the HR budget. There will be a one-off investment needed (particularly in the new capability areas). There will also be an ongoing need to invest – to keep stretching people and to bring new joiners up to speed.

So, what are the approaches to capability development? In addition to the 'on-the-job' forms for development there are five main strands to consider:

1. Mandatory workshops
2. Optional workshops
3. Action learning groups
4. Coaching
5. Mentoring
6. Self-managed learning/on-the-job development

We have used combinations of each where we have supported capability development. Below we set out things to consider in broad terms for each strand followed by three case studies showing how organisations have blended these strands.

Mandatory workshops
Typically workshops are offered to address the three new capability areas – although one of the case study organisations also made organisational design mandatory. These workshops are intended not just to deliver knowledge and skills, but also to deliver three additional benefits to HR:

- Create a common language
- Deliver a consistent approach and tool kit
- Create a network and community amongst HR professionals

In this way, even if some HR professionals have already acquired the requisite capabilities, there are benefits in their participating in mandatory workshops so that the additional benefits set out above are realised across the HR professional community. Additionally, more experienced members of the HR team should be encouraged to share their knowledge and experience.

Optional workshops
Here, the workshops described above (or slight variations of these) are offered to HR professionals but are not mandatory. In addition, optional workshops have also been offered in areas such as 'Becoming a trusted advisor', 'Influencing skills', 'Facilitation skills' and 'Managing Conflict'.

The main advantage in this approach is that those HR professionals considered to be competent in a capability area need not repeat the training. The benefits of this approach are:

- Training is focused on identified need.
- Overall development costs are reduced (or spent on areas of identified need).
- Individuals considered competent in a particular capability area are motivated to address development gaps rather than attend workshops where they consider themselves skilled.

Action learning groups

Action learning groups typically comprise around 6–8 members, supported by an external facilitator, with the aim over time for the group to become self-managing. The approach is based on the group working on real business issues. Learning is achieved at two levels – applying the knowledge and experience of the group to the issue under discussion. Reflecting on the way the group works together as a learning experience in its own right.

This approach to HR capability development is used in two main ways:

1. Each participant brings his or her own 'live' issue or project to address with the group.
2. The group works on a 'live' business issue together over a period of meetings.

The first of these approaches places the onus on the individual to identify an issue and bring it to the group. In our experience, this approach has not always been successful with the main challenges being that people do not prepare sufficiently and they are not skilled in framing a problem or issue in a way the group can engage with quickly. However, where this approach has succeeded it has enabled participants to apply knowledge in the new capability areas very quickly and there is early pay back to the organisation on the investment made in development.

The second approach is more thematic. Some of the learning groups we have supported have tackled more strategic themes, examples being how to increase levels of engagement; the employee of the future; increasing line manager capability in people skills. With this approach, the learning groups decide how to approach the task and, with the support of the facilitator, take 'time outs' to reflect on how the group is working and to think about how to use tools and techniques related to the new capability areas. This approach builds deep bonds between group members and by the end of the process, groups are also self-managing.

In our experience this is a powerful way of learning as it not only engages theory and practice, but also gives organisations an immediate return on their investment. We anticipate that this approach to learning will gain ground in coming years linked also with virtual learning environments.

Coaching

Coaching has its place in the development repertoire and, in our work with organisations, has been used in two ways:

1. In its more conventional sense of an external coach working on a number of coaching objectives with an individual. Typically, this approach has been used with more senior members of the HR leadership team.
2. As part of the action learning group process – where individual coaching sessions are held between learning group meetings with two objectives: First, to help the individual reflect on the experience of the learning group and their contribution. Second, to address individual development goals that are inappropriate to be tackled at a learning group meeting.

This latter approach has been particularly powerful and has enabled individuals to accelerate the application of new capabilities.

Mentoring
Mentoring has been used in two different ways:

■ Linking HR professionals with other HR professionals. For example, people who are at 'Mastery' in a given capability area with those who are developing that capability;
■ Linking HR professionals with colleagues outside of HR primarily to build their knowledge of the business and to improve the way they influence the organisation.

Where possible, HR mentoring should be integrated into any organisational approach to mentoring.

Self-managed learning/on-the-job development
Individuals clearly need to take ownership for their development too. Most self-managed learning can be linked to general resources available to the wider management population – whether e-learning resources from business schools, library resources or links to external Web sites such as the CIPD.

On-the-job development can include work shadowing, work placements, project roles, temporary assignments, meeting/workshop facilitation, project team leadership.

In terms of HR partner capability, there is also a challenge to HR professionals to read more broadly – including publications like *Financial Times, McKinsey Quarterly, Harvard Business Review, Sloan Management Review* and *The Economist*. Each of these brings interesting insights from the world of Consultancy and Academia which HR professionals should be using with internal clients to change the conversations they hold and bring fresh thinking to the table.

In the following we set out three examples of how different organisations have tackled capability development.

Case study – AXA UK

AXA has combined mandatory workshops, optional workshops and self-managed learning.

Mandatory workshops include (but are not limited to) consulting skills and organisational design. These were chosen because organisational design was considered to be a significant gap across the HR community and a strategic skill set. Consulting skills were also a significant gap and there was a strong need to build a common approach in the way HR professionals engaged with business colleagues.

A suite of optional workshops is available to HR professionals to supplement the mandatory workshops and to address areas such as project management.

E-learning and other learning resources are available through the organisation's Intranet to address specific individual development needs.

Development plans are agreed and monitored as part of the performance review process.

Case study – National grid

National Grid has engaged in HR capability development over some years now and has completed a number of 'waves' of development. Development has focused mainly on mandatory workshops, action learning groups, coaching and mentoring.

The first wave was to put all HR professionals (irrespective of organisational level) through mandatory workshops in the areas of strategy and change management, client relationship management and project management.

The second wave established action learning groups supported by coaching of learning group participants. These learning groups were thematic and coaching reinforced the learning group experience and addressed individual development needs that were inappropriate to address in a learning group context.

A third wave of development is in progress – partly to bring new joiners up to speed on new capabilities and partly to build HR capability in internally developed change management methodology.

As capability development covered all HR professionals, including the HR leadership team, it proved to be very effective:

- HR leaders were able to contribute their experience to more junior members of the team.
- A common language and tool kit were developed which could be reinforced through the line management structure.

Case study – Global telecoms business

This organisation decided to roll out mandatory workshops for the bulk of the HR professional community and run learning groups supported by coaching for the HR leadership group.

The mandatory workshops in all three new capability areas (strategy & change management, consulting skills and project management) were extremely successful and went a long way to creating a common language and toolkit. Although the HR leadership team thought they already had the capability covered by mandatory workshops, this was not the case.

In this instance the approach taken to learning groups was for each person to bring along his or her own 'live' issue. We experienced two problems – first, people did not prepare adequately for the learning group, and second, they did not have the requisite knowledge in the new capability areas and more time was spent in covering ground addressed in workshops than on the 'live' issues.

The main learning here was that adopting a dual approach for the HR leadership team/the rest of HR was ineffective as the HR leadership did not have the foundation tools and techniques they thought they had which meant they played 'catch up' and were unable to provide the coaching and support to team members that would have been beneficial.

Whilst aspects of this capability development approach were successful, the dual approach adopted falls into the 'How not to' category and we do not recommend it.

Step 5 – Review learning and build into on going HR capability development

We have already noted how one of our case study organisations has engaged in HR capability development over some years now and has used the experience of each wave to focus development on new requirements that will help the organisation achieve its strategic goals.

Review can take a number of forms and the following have been beneficial:

- Review after each learning intervention – although this is essentially 'in the moment feedback' it allows you to change design to make the learning experience more appropriate to participants.
- More formal review after a phase of development activity – conducting a short review to identify how participants have used the new knowledge in their work and to gather more considered reflections on the learning experience.
- Use of the capability framework to assess shift in capability – typically as part of a more formal development discussion.
- Customer survey – to assess how colleagues in the organisation have experienced HR and whether they are working with HR professionals in different ways.

We believe that irrespective of how you articulate and build HR capability, the most important thing is that developing HR professionals is not ignored or cut short. HR professionals need to know what is expected of them in their transformed roles and they need to be given support to acquire and apply new capabilities.

HR culture

HR transformation requires HR to change its own culture. In this section, we present a model of culture our clients have found helpful (Figure 10.2) and set out three cultural challenges for HR to address.

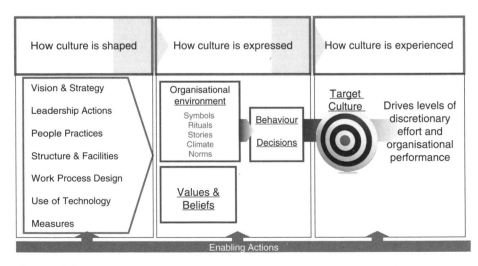

Figure 10.2 Culture model. Copyright 2009 mightywaters consulting limited.

We know that you cannot change culture easily and you cannot change culture by running culture change programmes. You need to be clear about the kind of culture you would like to create and how distant this is from your current culture. You also need to be clear about the values and behaviours that will create the desired culture. But you will not achieve culture change by just focusing on behaviour. Culture is the product of the way the organisational system works and therefore we shape culture by focusing on many different levers.

Figure 10.2 can be broken down into three components.

1. At the right of the model is the experience of culture which ultimately results in performance. A key task here is for HR to define its target culture which should be aligned to the overall business culture; reflect how the HR function will deliver value and which will drive high levels of discretionary effort and engagement from within HR. This task should be addressed at the envisioning phase so that by implementation there are some clarity and commitment to the culture HR is seeking to shape.
2. The middle section sets out how culture is expressed. We hope that this work will build on foundations already laid. For example, we anticipate that HR will be able to work through how organisational values are brought to life through the work of HR. We also expect the HR capability frameworks will reflect the skills and behaviours needed to drive high performance. The areas that may need particular attention are decision-making processes and, what Ed Schein calls, the artefacts – the stories, rules, symbols, climate, etc. that communicate culture. Good examples of work in this area are where:

■ HR teams have communicated the transformation story and the kinds of stories they would like colleagues in the organisation to be telling about HR at work;
■ HR teams have used symbols (like the National Grid capability framework) in order to get the message across;
■ HR teams have changed the rules to make decision making more effective.

These are just some examples but we hope they illustrate the need for you to be very intentional about how culture is communicated verbally and nonverbally.

3. The left of the model lists the shapers of culture. These reflect the different parts of the organisational system (see also Chapter 1 and the organisational levers model) and each of these needs to be aligned with the target culture. So, for example, if the HR leadership does not refer to a new HR capability framework when reviewing performance, identifying development needs or providing coaching, it is unlikely that this capability framework will be embedded.

This is a lot to get right and align and it is unlikely that this will be achieved in one attempt. However, if HR teams are clear about the kind of culture they are seeking to create and take intentional actions to bring this culture to life, the outcome is likely to be a period of fine tuning rather than regular remodelling.

In our discussions with senior practitioners three particular cultural challenges have been highlighted for HR:

■ Challenge 1 – To become more client-focused

Client relationship management is one of the core capability areas for HR – this is about working as a trusted advisor: developing and implementing the strategic agenda whilst securing client buy-in and commitment. But there is a dilemma here. Does client-focused mean giving clients exactly what they want? We do not think so. HR functions must learn lessons from external providers and develop a consulting mindset. As consultants we have yet to come across clients who only want us to agree with them. What they really value is opinion, challenge, research, fresh thinking and an approach that gets to grips with their real problems, not just presenting issues. We do not think HR professionals are any different if they are performing effectively. So, this will mean more HR professionals will need to learn to question and challenge what clients are asking for. Although difficult at times, partnership must be built on a relationship where support and challenge are expressed in equal measure.

■ Challenge 2 – To articulate a clear value proposition

Linked to the need to be more client-focused, HR professionals must be able to articulate how HR adds value. We addressed this at some length in Chapter 3. This means getting better at measuring outcomes and estimating inputs. It means being able to have a sensible discussion about the use of resources and priorities. It also means being able to articulate what will be delivered, by whom, at what cost and when. In this way, the organisation will be able to make better choices and will see the amount of perceived low-value work diminishing.

■ Challenge 3 – To market and sell HR better

This challenge is, of course, linked to the previous two. Lawler and Mohrman (2003), in their survey of trends and directions in HR, point out that perceptions of the contribution made by HR are not changing as fast as the actual change on the ground. This is clearly a cause for concern. Part of the problem is that HR professionals have not traditionally thought about how they market and sell themselves. For example, during our client relationship workshops we spend time thinking about HR's value proposition and about the way HR sells itself to the organisation. Generally speaking, this is often the first time HR professionals have thought about themselves from a selling perspective. They are not very good at thinking about their experiences and packaging them in a way that enables clients to see what they are capable of contributing.

The point we make on all HR transformations is that whatever cultural attributes the function wishes to develop, they need to be hard-wired into the other organisational levers – the way you organise, use technology, manage your work processes, lead, develop people and so on.

In closing this chapter, we want to emphasise the important role that the HR leadership team needs to play throughout the process of HR transformation and have set out below a few of the things that we have found effective HR leadership teams have done well:

- worked collaboratively to create a vision;
- provided strong and visible personal commitment to a transformed HR;
- engaged actively with the implementation process (they have not just delegated and walked away) and put at risk their own personal credibility around delivery;
- seen HR transformation as a process, impacting the whole HR terrain, and been prepared to work through the process with the HR transformation programme team;
- led from the front, taking an active role in influencing and communicating with key business stakeholders and the HR function;
- given time to regular workshops and other interventions throughout the process;
- remained patient – things do not always go to plan – and been prepared to address unexpected challenges;
- used external facilitation and consultancy well – consultants have supported the internal team and have not replaced them;
- acknowledged that members of each team need to work through the implications of change and transition for themselves;
- recognised that they are, themselves, part of the transformation process.

We would like to amplify the last two of the points above. The first point is around the way individuals are supported through transition. We make quite a big deal of this in our capability workshops, and draw heavily on the excellent work of William Bridges (1993) in this area. In providing good change leadership there is a need to help people with endings: to help them to come to terms with the fact that the way things were has gone for good. Some of the things that have been done to help with this include practical actions like changing job titles, working environments and reporting lines. But they also include things like 'end of era' celebrations or the symbolic binning of old material. In helping people with beginnings, things like the capability framework, conferences and symbols (a visual representing the HR capabilities was used very effectively by National Grid) help people to understand the *purpose* of transformation; engage with the *plan* to implement it; see a *picture* of the new world of HR and the *part* they will play in it. Good change leaders make this happen.

The last bullet point above is really important. A huge amount of credibility is gained when the leadership group themselves acknowledge their need to change and then do something about it. Particularly good examples of this have been when the leadership group has participated in the capability development workshop and is seen to be working through the issues of behavioural change as much as the rest of the HR team.

We have also seen some very poor things happening during implementation – and often outside the direct control of HR. We hope that you will not identify with these, but some examples are set out as follows:

- The capability development programme was split so that senior people participated in learning groups and the remainder of the function in capability workshops.
- A travel ban was imposed just after learning groups had been set up on a multinational basis – which prevented non-UK participants from attending.
- Participants were made redundant during a workshop.
- An outsourcing solution for transactional and advisory activities was adopted against the will of the broader leadership group.

The reality is that HR leadership matters. If the HR leadership group does not step out with enthusiasm and keep the drumbeat of change pounding, then your best plans will flounder. It can often be a cliché to talk about the need for senior commitment to a change programme. With respect to HR transformation, we can say with a high degree of confidence that this is true, and we hope that in this section we have set out some of the things for the leadership team to focus on.

Summary

The real value of HR transformation happens when HR professionals work in partnership with the business. Implementation of the HR value model does not just happen. There needs to be a process, and that process needs to be integrated into the overall HR transformation programme. In this chapter, we have presented the main process steps and tools to help you implement quickly and effectively.

The main focus is on what business partners do and how they will know they are performing effectively. At the heart of the HR value model is therefore the development of HR capability. We have shown in this chapter how this may be reflected through capability frameworks and capability development programmes. Finally, we have presented a model of culture to support the re-shaping of HR's culture and underlined the important role the senior HR leadership group has in providing change leadership throughout implementation.

11

Implementation: Process and Technology

We discussed in Chapter 4 how technology can be used to enable both HR and the business to improve the efficiency and performance of key people management processes. We also discussed in Chapter 5 the need to ensure that technology is a key component of the future vision for HR. We turn now to the process and technology side of implementing HR transformation.

When implementing HR processes and technology, it is also important to remember that the impact of the process and technology changes is not just felt in HR but often has a significant impact upon all staff and line management through the implementation of self-service technologies. The key to the successful implementation of HR processes and technology, and the transformation programme itself, depends on line management and staff adopting the new self-service. The buy-in and commitment of the line is, therefore, critical and these staff need to be involved in the design and implementation phases of the transformation programme.

Key themes

■ The implementation of HR process and technology needs to be true to your original vision for HR transformation. The alignment of implementation with your vision and plans needs to be explicitly addressed so that you do not inadvertently diverge and risk the success of your programme.

■ The detailed design and implementation of the processes and technology are important elements of HR transformation. However, it is the adoption of those processes and the supporting technology by HR, employees and line managers that defines whether the change has taken root in the organisation. Therefore, continued involvement of all those impacted by HR transformation in the implementation is critical.

Context

This chapter considers the implementation of HR process and technology; both individually and how they interact, particularly with respect to the impact on the HR function, employees and line managers. Implementation is about realising the vision that you have set out for HR and moves from detailed design, through building and testing, to 'cutover' to the new solution.

Detailed process and technology design

Through envisioning, defining the service-delivery approach and building the business case, the HR transformation solution will have become ever clearer. Careful consideration will have been given to the people, process and technology elements such that the overall solution is one that will deliver the vision and benefits targeted. The first stage of implementation, therefore, is to finalise the design at the detailed level.

Detailed design follows the principles of the systems mindset (see Chapter 3) by considering the multiple linkages between elements of the solution, working from the whole solution to the details of the constituent parts. By utilising this and the target benefits, those charged with developing the detailed process and technology design can begin.

During business case definition (see Chapter 6), the technology solution that best fits your specific needs will have been identified. The task in detailed design is to specify the configuration of this technology solution right down to the level of the system screens on which the transactions are performed. The main decisions that need to be made at this stage are the following:

1. Which elements of the process will be performed by the system and which elements need to be performed outside of the system?
2. Which data fields must be completed in order for the process to work and which are optional?
3. Can the technology solution be configured to support the new processes without needing to modify the underlying code or programming of the system? Often this is termed the 'vanilla' system. Modification over and above the 'vanilla' system means that additional implementation and maintenance costs will be incurred. If the business benefits can be delivered with the 'vanilla' system then clearly this is the ideal route. If this is not the case then the costs (including maintenance costs) of making the modifications need to be weighed against the reduction in benefits if the modifications are not made.

4. In the case of global or multinational implementations, are there local country or regional differences that need to be addressed? Ideally these should only be local statutory differences as these should already be 'pre-configured' in the technology solution. Any additional differences will need to be developed and maintained separately. In a similar way to the 'vanilla' system debate above, modifying the system for local requirements adds to both the initial implementation and the ongoing maintenance costs.

The decisions around detailed design are usually made in workshops with HR and the line, or by the HR and line representatives on the programme team. Involvement of HR and the line is crucial in this process as it provides both a check that what is being designed is pragmatic and workable and that those who will need to operate the new processes and systems are engaged to promote commitment (see Chapter 7 on stakeholders and communication).

As the detailed design proceeds, where resolution on particular design issues cannot be achieved through the workshops or the programme team, it may be necessary to take some of these decisions to the steering board for direction. This 'design authority' role is one that the steering board should play by exception but it can be critical particularly in providing guidance and direction on the degree of customisation or local variation.

From a process design perspective, the main task at this stage is to map the processes onto a diagram that shows what the system will do and what the responsibility of HR, managers, employees or external agencies will be.

Figure 11.1 provides an overview of the key steps in mapping HR processes, summarising key actions and outputs.

A useful tool for mapping and redesigning process is 'brown paper'. In Figure 11.1 after Step 2, where an overview is developed in the 'As Is' processes, these are sketched onto large pieces of brown paper, as demonstrated in Figure 11.2.

A workshop is then convened with HR and, where appropriate, representatives from the line where the process is debated and challenged. This also involves identifying for participants the extent to which the proposed HR technology can automate and change different tasks. Attendees at the workshop then redraw the existing process, identifying strengths that they wish to retain and sketching out improvements to the way that participants interact and the way the information flows through the process. A new brown paper is produced from the workshop as demonstrated in Figure 11.3.

There are a number of issues that need to be taken into account when building a brown paper:

- *Disagreement about how the process is performed is OK.* It is probable that different people perform the same process differently; that is, a significant finding. Try to capture both and get agreement on future processes.

Step	Activity	Tools	Output
1. Define the Target Process	• Define key HR activities as processes • Prioritise key processes • Break processes into manageable chunks • Identify and document key process variations • Involve subject matter experts	Brainstorming, customer focus groups	Prioritise reengineering efforts
2. Develop 'As Is' Models	• Conduct workflow analysis (who does what when, where, how) and identify handoffs • Audit existing constraints in systems (e.g., compatibility, integrity, and consistency of data) • Determine problems in current process from customer's and administrator's perspectives • Identify key measurement related to process (e.g., cost, quality, time, rework, etc)	Workflow analysis, activity analysis, systems audit, focus groups, interviews	Flow map of existing processes and their performance in terms of cost and quality
3. Challenge underlying assumptions	• Challenge each activity in the current process (why is it done, why is it done there, why is it done then, why does that person do it, why is it done this way etc) • Challenge current policies, practices and philosophy • Explore alternative delivery methods • Cut across functional silos • Incorporate and leverage information technology	Visioning, scenario building, brainstorming, critical thinking	Identify opportunities for radical improvement
4. Develop 'To be' Models – Identifying where and how technology will impact the process	• Solicit information from broad base about alternatives • Benchmark other companies • Integrate separate processes • Take detailed design of new information systems • Draft new process flow • Assess potential impact of new process (cost/benefit, risk etc)	Benchmarking, conflict resolution, issues resolution, simulation, consensus building	Design new processes, select best information technology to support process, determine impact of new processes
5. Implement, Roll out, Market	• Implement incremental approach • Conduct pilot testing • Implement systems integration • Market the programme, create curiosity, implement trial use • Offer training to support users • Manage resistance • Anticipate and address morale problems	Marketing, communication, training, coaching, experimentation	Facilitate the smooth migration to new system and user's acceptance of the new processes
6. Measure Business Impact	• Capture business impact of HR processes before and after reengineering • Measure business impact, not just budget and milestones in programmes and activities • Separate short- from long-term impact	Activity analysis, cost analysis, customer service survey, focus groups	Monitor progress and impact

Figure 11.1 Source: Arthur Yeung's teaching materials, based on recognised models from a variety of consulting firms. Cited in Ulrich's *Human Resource Champions: The Next Agenda for Adding Value and Delivering Results* (1997).

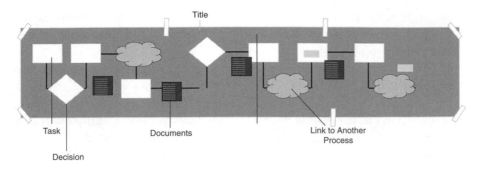

Figure 11.2 Example brown paper.

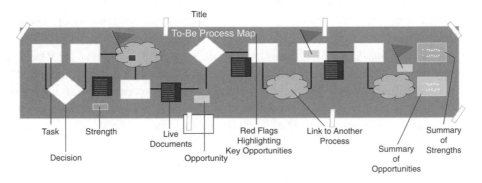

Figure 11.3 Example brown paper.

- *Not knowing the answer to every question is OK.* In the process of asking questions needed to identify the flow, it almost always happens that a question will be asked that no one can answer and people can be tasked to get an answer.
- *Have specialists on hand who can answer questions about what can and cannot be achieved using the HR system.* Participants may come up with solutions that cannot be delivered by technology. It is best that these issues are addressed in the workshop so that participants can design processes that can be delivered and you do not have to ask participants to keep redesigning processes in later workshops. If this is not done, having lots of unanswered questions about what the system can and cannot do, will result in a process that is so high level and has so many questions that it needs more design work after the workshop or further workshops have to be convened.
- *Ask for hard copy and complete examples.* All key documents should be obtained with 'live' information, if possible. Ask for a printed copy of significant computer screens if the function is 'online' or interactive between the user and system.

■ *No value judgements (yet)*. The process of creating the initial brown paper should be a fact-gathering exercise. The evaluation of the information comes later. At this point, all ideas are good ideas.

■ *Identify one stream of activity and do it start to finish: then integrate other streams with it*. Experience has shown that participants may become confused when trying to understand and document several different flows simultaneously. By choosing one and taking it start to finish, similarities and differences can more readily be identified, and the meeting more easily controlled.

■ *Write explanations directly on the brown paper*. The only paper attached to the brown paper should be 'live' documents and their adhesive note critiques.

■ *Be challenging, do not fall into the trap of merely refining existing processes and responsibilities and essentially promoting the status quo*. HR transformation is about shifting from today to tomorrow. Therefore, when reviewing processes, question whether HR should be involved in a task and how that involvement adds value.

■ *Capture the impact on the line and employees*. Where HR is removed from tasks and where the line will use self-service, it is important that this information is captured and detailed. This understanding of how responsibility for process changes is vital for moving to the next stage in the change process, that of determining the impact of the new processes and systems on the organisation and the readiness of the organisation to adopt them.

Impact and readiness assessment

The starting point for assessing impact and readiness is that the stakeholder identification and initial impact and assessment have already been completed (see Chapter 7). The task at this stage is to take the initial analysis down to the next level of detail both in terms of the stakeholder groups themselves, the understanding of the impact on those groups and the levels of resistance-commitment. For example, during initial stakeholder analysis all employees may have been treated as a homogeneous group. This would now be too broad for the differing impacts that they may experience. Therefore, the employee stakeholder group may, in this case, be subdivided into office-based employees and shop floor–based employees in order to take account of the differing impacts of HR self-service technology in their respective areas. The key here is to balance the degree to which stakeholder groups are subdivided. As a rule of thumb, the level of department on a particular site is usually the lowest level of subdivision necessary.

Then for each of the detailed stakeholder groups, the impacts are recorded for each relevant process in terms of change from the 'as is' way of working to the 'to be' way. Clearly, not every process impacts every stakeholder group and the degree of impact differs in each case. From this, a picture of relative impact emerges. Those groups with the greatest impact are often those where most attention must be paid in the change planning that follows.

At this stage, it is also useful to assess the readiness to change for each detailed stakeholder group. This readiness assessment concentrates on the attitude that the detailed stakeholder groups have towards the new processes and systems. There are a number of factors listed here:

1. History of change within the organisation: Has change been managed effectively previously?
2. What is the capacity for change in the organisation? Have major change initiatives been recently completed or are under way?
3. What is the level of awareness of the detailed stakeholder group as to the nature of the change for them?
4. And finally, 'what's in it for me?' On balance, will the detailed stakeholder group view this as a positive or negative change, bearing in mind the nature of the impact on them?

There are a number of approaches to undertaking a readiness assessment, and they are summarised in Figure 11.4.

Tool	What is it?	How & when to use it?
Questionnaires	• A set of questions usually in a tick box format • They can be done as paper exercises, by e-mail or via the intranet	• They can be sent out to a variety of stakeholders • They can be used to gather a lot of information quickly from a large number of people • They are often used as the first vehicle to identify areas that need to be probed in more detail
Focus Groups	• A workshop with a group of people (5-15) to elicit more detail about why particular issues have been raised	• They are usually run either as natural work groups, or as representatives from various stakeholder groups • Format and content are changed to suit group characteristics and issue(s) to be discussed • They allow the 'why' to be explored in more depth
One-to-One Interviews	• A structured interview where individuals are asked a number of questions and answers are recorded and analysed	• These are either used to elicit information around sensitive areas or to ascertain how aligned a particular group is around each stage of the project • They are often used with leadership and managerial groups

Figure 11.4 Approaches to readiness assessment.

When using questionnaires or working with focus groups or conducting one-to-one interviews, examples of questions to assess change readiness can include the following:

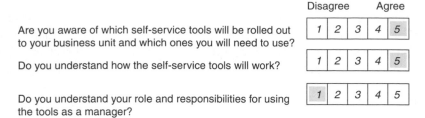

Through this readiness assessment, reports can be produced which detail the likely levels of readiness, as demonstrated in Figure 11.5.

As in the case of the impact analysis, those stakeholder groups who are likely to be least ready are the ones where most attention needs to be paid in change planning.

Often the employees within organisations are more positive to HR transformation than the managers. For employees, the benefits tend to outweigh the negatives as they take control of their transactions. For managers, their perception tends to be the other way round with the perceived disadvantages outweighing the advantages. Their instinct is that they are being asked to do more and that their workload is increasing. On the surface this is the case, with HR self-service transactions needing to be input or approved. The reality is that these transactions

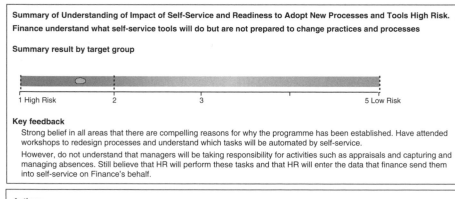

Figure 11.5 Readiness assessment.

were previously completed using phones, faxes, e-mails and paper-based forms and often through a significantly more inefficient, lengthy and circuitous route. However, business change is not only about facts but about perception, behaviour and culture. In some organisations, a rational argument that these transactions were performed by managers previously via different means will prevail and in others it will not. Sometimes the culture of the organisation is such that managers will work online themselves and in others the culture is for managers' assistants and administrators to do this. A contingent approach is of course necessary, focusing on how business benefit can be achieved and ultimately how the organisation's managers can become more effective people managers.

Clearly, it is not only line managers who may feel uncomfortable. The move to managers and employees executing transactions that were previously performed by HR will also take some people within the HR function outside of their comfort zone.

Case study 1

When designing its HR transformation solution, a global IT services organisation considered the different processes and ways of working within the operating units in each country. These processes were very different and it wished to move to a global approach. Through the innovative use of Web-based HR technology and service centres and the processes and information surrounding them, global consistency was achieved through managers and employees using the global Intranet for standard transactions and the regional service centres for the more complex ones.

This was a major change in approach in many of the operating units and considerable time and effort were spent supporting the managers and employees through this change from the early stages of design and consultation through to embedding and sustaining the change post-implementation. Whilst the change from a process perspective was significant, from a cultural standpoint it was commonly accepted and expected that managers use the Intranet to perform transactions.

The change management plan is the means by which the issues identified through impact and readiness assessment are addressed. It is normally developed in a tabular format recording:

- detailed stakeholder group;
- the impact or readiness issues that have been raised for that group;
- a measure of importance or priority for each issue;
- the action that needs to be taken for that issue, by whom and when;
- how feedback on the success of the action is to be gathered.

The types of actions vary depending on where the stakeholder group falls along the resistance to commitment continuum and how far the group needs to move. Actions may be around communications, such as raising awareness, explaining the benefits of the new process or reinforcing 'what's in it for me' for the stakeholder group, or they may be around tangible design elements such as modification of performance management objectives. Typically, the actions are executed through the sponsor and change leader network described in Chapter 6. Sponsors work at the senior levels in the organisation, demonstrating their commitment to HR transformation and the benefits that it will bring to the organisation and cascading this to their teams.

From the detailed design stage onwards, the role of the change leader is particularly important. They deploy their strengths very much at the local level, working on business readiness, the impact of change, making sure activities around communications are working, and representing their areas in the design workshops. Crucially, they will also be trusted to give feedback to the programme team, effectively providing the link between what is needed for their stakeholder groups and what the programme team delivers. This is an excellent opportunity for HR to 'walk the talk' in terms of its prospective business partners enacting their role as leaders of change within the organisation. If those business partners are responsible for change leadership with their group of line managers, this has the dual benefit of HR really demonstrating that its role is changing and begins to cement those relationships between business partners and senior line managers.

As feedback is gathered on the level of success that the actions have achieved then further actions will become necessary. Similarly, as more is known about the detailed design, further impacts may be identified. Clearly, this is an iterative process with the objective of moving the various stakeholder groups to the point where they are ready to move from awareness and understanding of the change into readiness for implementation. The following case study provides a holistic view of the business change approaches discussed.

The theme of iteration during process and technology detailed design applies not only within the process and technology areas themselves but also to the interaction between them. This takes the form of determining what should be performed within and outside the system and what rules should be followed in each case. Therefore, in addition to the process diagrams described in Figure 11.6, it is also useful to record the rules by which each process operates. This is invaluable during the next stage – build and test – as business procedures and training material can be developed from this and the system configuration performed. From an HR transformation programme team perspective, this

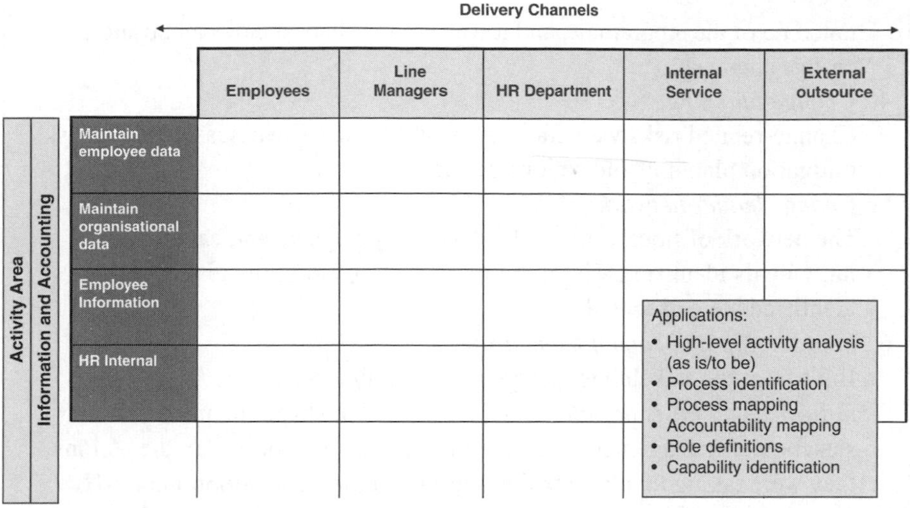

Delivery Channels

		Employees	Line Managers	HR Department	Internal Service	External outsource
Activity Area / **Information and Accounting**	Maintain employee data					
	Maintain organisational data					
	Employee Information					
	HR Internal					

Applications:
- High-level activity analysis (as is/to be)
- Process identification
- Process mapping
- Accountability mapping
- Role definitions
- Capability identification

Figure 11.6 Process diagram.

means that the process and technology work streams clearly need to work together closely and sometimes the individuals within those work streams may fulfil roles on both streams.

Case study 2

A large manufacturer of consumer pharmaceutical products wanted to introduce Web-enabled HR, and quickly realised that it needed to understand where various elements of the organisation stood on the issues. It put together a plan to gather information, which included the following elements:

1. *Stakeholder analysis*
   A 'first-cut' view of the identity of the main stakeholder groups, where they were located, what they stood to gain/lose as a result of the programme, and hence their most likely disposition.
2. *Impact of change assessment*
   A summary of the way in which each of the main changes resulting from the programme would impact each of the stakeholder groups. This enabled some assessment to be made of the depth and breadth of change impacting that stakeholder group, allowing the appropriate involvement to be planned.
3. *Change readiness assessment*
   This examined the organisation's readiness for the overall changes resulting from the programme. It looked at many factors potentially influencing the

---

outcome of the programme, and it was used to shape the overall business change approach.

4. *Change planning*
   Change-related risks were identified, and some early assessment and risk mitigation planning and actions begun.

5. *Change leader network*
   The network of 'local' change leaders was designed, and candidate individuals identified. Through this the actions to mitigate the risks identified were executed.

6. *Sponsorship and commitment strategy*
   Built from the stakeholder analysis to identify *influencers*, *lines of influence* and *basis of influence*. This started to shape the initial stakeholder management plan and the support of sponsors in the actions they were taking to advocate the implementation and adoption of e-HR.

7. *Initial communications planning and delivery*
   Developed in order to ensure clear communications to the organisation concerning the existence of the programme and the design work under way. Whilst its focus was on the future communications, it also summarised the communications that had already taken place and the feedback obtained in order to guide future activity.

One of the key lessons that the team learnt was that whilst e-HR was important to the organisation and had been established as a building block for wider transformation, those impacted by it still had their normal roles and responsibilities and other programmes that they were involved in. This learning was key to the programme team, as whilst the HR transformation programme was their total focus, they recognised that this was not the case with the stakeholder communities and acted accordingly, their target being to move from the programme 'pushing' its messages out, to the business 'pulling' the programme in.

At the end of detailed design, an excellent tool for confirming that the design is effective and for keeping the wider organisation involved in the programme is to perform a series of detailed design walk-throughs. Typically, the diagrams shown in Figure 11.6 are linked together and displayed on a wall to show the detailed, end-to-end process. Programme team members then 'walk-through' these processes with representatives from HR and the line in order to validate and test their feasibility and of course modify processes where necessary. The walk-throughs should try to capture as wide an audience as possible, but as a minimum should include those who have contributed to the design in the design workshops mentioned earlier.

Finally, the overall detailed design needs to be validated to ensure that the benefits targeted at the beginning of this stage are still valid and that the costs are within the cost envelope agreed during the business case. If this is the case, then it is safe to proceed into build and test. However, if not, then it is usual to seek steering board sanction that the change in costs or benefits has not reduced the cost–benefit analysis below the level that is viable for the programme.

Build and test

There are two main alternative approaches to this stage and it is important that you choose the right approach for your circumstances. The first approach is prototyping; that is, the incremental configuration of elements of the systems solution followed by testing with the users followed by further iterations of fine-tuning. This process is repeated for all elements of the systems solution. The second is a full build against a detailed specification or blueprint followed by full system testing.

One advantage with the first approach is that the HR and business users get the opportunity to see and feel HR self-service quite early in the build process. This serves to maintain momentum and enthusiasm and helps to match expectations against system delivery. The main disadvantage with this approach is that it can take longer unless it is tightly managed – the temptation can be to continue with minor refinements rather than to end that element of the solution and move on to the next.

In the case of the second approach, the main advantage is that you have better control of the costs and schedule and at the end of the build you have a more complete solution. But there is less possibility of making changes during the build and after it is delivered any changes will be more expensive. There is a heavy reliance on the quality of the detailed specification that the system configurers are using.

During this stage, there is a greater distinction between the technology- and the process-related activities than during the detailed design stage. Even with the prototyping approach, the system configurers are primarily focused on the technology build and system test activity. The HR and business users, however, should be primarily focused on operating procedure definition, training course preparation, development of user security profiles, test script development and user acceptance testing. The methodology and programme plan provide the means of linking the process and technology (and people) streams here. The interdependencies and 'touch points' are closely aligned through this even though the team members may be working on their own specific tasks.

The change management theme of course continues. The change leaders mobilised during detailed design perform the next iteration of impact and readiness assessments, often at the local functional or site level, and initiate the resulting actions. The change focus should not be restricted to the line areas; HR must be preparing for this change. There is an important link here with the capabilities work (see Chapter 10), as HR needs to get ready to let go of much of the transactional work and begin to focus on what the business partner role really means and how they will equip themselves for this. An excellent way of bringing this to life is the use of 'conference room pilots' where the business and HR users of Web-based HR technology adopt their new roles in a controlled environment, testing how the new roles, process and system fit together in a simulation of the new environment.

Conference room pilots provide a good example of how wider involvement in the programme activities can be achieved and there is greater opportunity during this stage to use involvement in the programme activities as an action to promote awareness and commitment. Typically, involvement from HR and the business in defining operating procedures, preparing training course material and particularly user acceptance testing, make the programme 'come alive' for many. One area that provides excellent opportunity for involvement but is often neglected is that of data cleansing and preparation. This involves checking the validity of existing data, mapping it to the data required in the new system and creating any additional data fields that are not present in the current systems. Involvement in this can be achieved across all employees in the organisation as they are requested to check and validate their own individual employee record data. This is a very powerful approach to moving the perception of the HR transformation programme from concept to reality.

Cutover and the transition to business as usual

With the system and processes now tested and accepted by the HR and business user communities, the attention turns to the planning and execution of the cutover to the new system and processes. Whilst there are distinct technology and process facets to this stage, they are more closely interdependent than those in the build and test stage. Indeed, the interdependency with the capabilities work (see Chapter 10) is also critical as these streams of work need to cut over as a coordinated whole rather than as separate entities. Clearly, the technology and processes need to be in place for the transactional responsibility to shift but the new capabilities within the HR function must also be in place if HR is to vacate its transactional role.

From a technology perspective, the main activities are the following:

- to ensure that the live technical environment (hardware, software and network) is ready for the HR system;
- to ensure that the data are ready to be loaded and the mechanism for performing the load, often a combination of automated and manual approaches, is also ready;

- to ensure all users have the means to access the new system;
- to develop the technical cutover plans.

From a process perspective, the main activities are the following:

- The scheduling and delivery of the system and process training. Often the change leaders take a role in this either as trainers themselves or in a 'train the trainer' role.
- Business cutover planning, including planning data reconciliations, system downtime and any parallel running of the old system and new.

Before the live cutover is performed, many programmes opt for an integrated cutover rehearsal that coordinates the whole technology and process cutover and determines how long and in what precise order each element is addressed.

Throughout this stage and towards the latter part of the build and test stage, the hub of the change shifts from something that the programme is 'pushing out' to the organisation to something that the organisation is embracing and 'pulling in'. The increased involvement of the line areas and HR in the programme is a major catalyst in this. This is then consolidated during this stage, as the transition from the programme team to those responsible for supporting the new system and processes is effected. This is an important symbol in the transition to the new 'business as usual' and begins to draw to a close the 'implement change' phase of the change cycle model. Chapter 12 discusses how to embed the targets and benefits from the transformation programme into business as usual to ensure that these benefits are realised. However, successfully hitting the transformation targets and delivering benefits is not only dependent on getting these targets incorporated into business plans and business as usual but is also dependent on embedding the technology and processes.

The change readiness and impact assessments will have identified where there is resistance to the new technology and processes and the reasons for this resistance. It is important that during the cutover phase, the programme targets this resistance and produces communications, training and briefings that specifically address the reasons why different groups are resistant to change. For example, managers may resist self-service because they regard capturing and managing sickness absence and leave as an additional overhead and 'HR's job'. The communications should emphasise that self-service will make entering this information easier, as it will go straight into a system rather than on a paper form and once it is entered into the system, managers will be able to view reports that provide quick and instant data on staff attendance, thereby enabling the managers to more easily manage and balance staffing across the different working shifts. The advantages of the self-service system will mean that managers are more likely to adopt the new technology and ways of working.

A useful tool to support adoption and embedding of new technology and ways of working can be the 'Day In the Life Of' tool. This tool involves shadowing key managers for a period of time to understand the pressures they face and what they have to deliver on a day-to-day basis. The data collected during this exercise is then analysed and used to identify how self-service and new ways of working will improve managers' jobs. These improvements can be placed into communications, on the Intranet or presented as scenarios in workshops. This enables managers to better understand how the new processes and technology will work and gives them a reason and incentive to adopt and embed the new ways of working. Chapter 12 discusses further how to ensure that managers not only adopt the new technology and processes but also continue to work differently and deliver benefits after the programme has been disbanded.

Summary

This chapter shows that the approach to technology and process implementation moves through a series of clear stages from detailed design to build and test and finally cut over. The linkage between technology and process is such that activities within the stages are often iterative.

Within each stage the focus on change management continues. Work at the detail level to first define the change and then to take actions to effect it is key. Involvement in the programme across the organisation is an important mechanism for promoting commitment.

12

Benefits Realisation

The delivery of business benefits is a key driver for HR transformation. However, the major benefits from HR transformation are not fully realised until implementation has been completed and the transition to business as usual is in place. This chapter will explain how to deliver benefits after the transformation programme is complete.

Key themes

- The successful realisation of benefits depends upon the capability to define measures for the benefits, set challenging targets for these measures and ensure that a system is in place to monitor and track delivery against targets.
- The majority of the benefits of an HR transformation programme will be delivered after the transformation is complete. It is therefore important not only to measure the delivery of benefits during the implementation phase of the programme but also to track benefits after the programme is complete.
- Expectations also need to be managed in terms of the level and timing of benefit delivery. This is done through a benefits plan that explicitly defines when and where benefits will be delivered and who is accountable for their delivery.

Context

The realisation of the envisaged benefits is vital, and benefits that will be delivered 2, 3 or 12 months after implementation can be lost or are often not tracked and measured properly. This can lead to negative perceptions that the transformation programme has failed. This chapter therefore explains how to:

- Ensure that the HR transformation benefits become an integral part of business as usual by embedding the benefits into operational scorecards and making their achievement an integral part of the business plans and objectives.
- Set targets and implement measures that rigorously assess the delivery of benefits and ensure that they are managed and realised.
- Develop plans that detail the timing and delivery of benefits and a process for monitoring progress against this plan.

The key to sustainable benefits delivery is in three key areas, these are:

1. Measuring benefits
2. Managing benefits
3. Sustaining benefits

Measuring benefits

Chapter 6, 'The Business Rationale', discussed briefly the need to link the objectives of the HR transformation programme and its targets and benefits to the organisation's strategy. This chapter presents an approach for defining measures that can be used to track the delivery of the benefits agreed in the business case and ensuring that they are being realised and that the service is performing at the agreed level.

A method of driving out measures that can be used to track benefits is to use the strategic–reputational–transactional–process model that is presented in Chapter 3.

This model is used because it presents an accessible and easy tool for breaking HR into four key common areas, these are:

- Strategic drivers to address the strategic objectives of the organisation for innovation, satisfying 'customers' and achieving value for money;
- Reputational drivers to meet longer term/wider demands to be *different but legitimate;*
- Process value drivers to deliver core processes efficiently and cost effectively, such as recruitment and learning and development;
- Transactional drivers so that key people transactions are cost effective and efficient, such as processing leave, sickness absence, personal information, payroll, etc.

An overview of the model is provided in Figure 12.1. In order to demonstrate how this model can be used to drive out measures, we have used some typical benefits for an HR Transformation Programme. These benefits are summarised in Figure 12.2. Having defined the benefits, the measures can then be driven out in two steps:

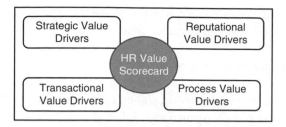

Figure 12.1 The HR value scorecard.

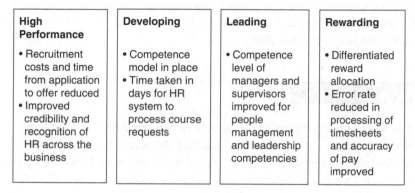

Figure 12.2 Benefits of HR transformation.

Step 1. Place each of the benefits from the HR transformation programme into one or more of the four quadrants in the strategic–reputational–transactional–process model. For example, in Figure 12.3 the high-performance benefit aligns with the process driver in the model because it is concerned with reducing timescales within the recruitment process; however, it also aligns with strategy because it is also concerned with improving credibility and recognition across the business.

Step 2. Using the description of the driver, identify a performance indicator that best measures the benefit. For example, in Figure 12.3, if the high-performance benefit is aligned to the process driver quadrant, then it should be measured through efficiency measures, such as processing times. This means that the high-performance benefit can be measured through such performance indicators as:

- the average length of time to recruit staff in days,
- the percentage of employee appointments offered within 25 working days of receiving the application.

285

If the high-performance benefit is linked to the strategic driver, then it can also be measured through such performance indicators as:

■ percentage improvement in service satisfaction.

Figure 12.3 demonstrates how different benefits can be related to the quadrants in the strategic–operational–reputational–relational model and provides examples of performance measures and targets.

Figure 12.4 presents possible measures and targets for each of the benefits in Figure 12.3 using the criteria in the operational–relational–reputational–strategic model. The targets in this figure can be aggregated into a single scorecard with performance against targets being presented to the HR leadership team. An example scorecard is presented in Figure 12.5.

Managing benefits

The process of managing and realising benefits begins during the implementation phase of the programme. This involves taking the measures that were driven out using the strategic–relational–reputational–operational model, baselining current performance for each of these measures and setting targets that will ensure that benefits and improvements to services are delivered.

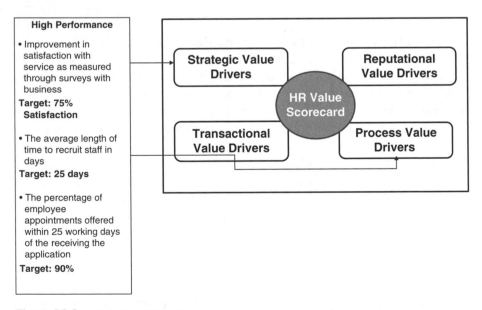

Figure 12.3 Developing measures.

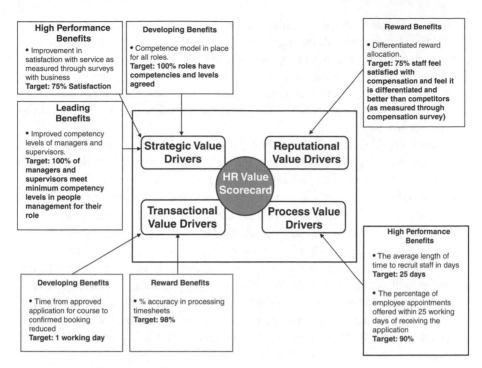

Figure 12.4 Measures and targets against benefits.

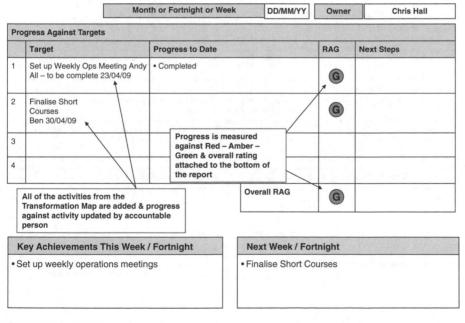

Figure 12.5 HR value scorecard.

Those managers who will realise the benefits and the service improvements should be made responsible during the implementation phase for owning the measures and targets. These managers should be required to set the baseline and take accountability for delivering against the targets. A regular reporting cycle should be instituted during the implementation phase, with benefit owners presenting reports to the transformation board or appropriate governance body, on their progress in meeting targets.

When presenting reports an option for the benefit managers is to present exceptions: that is, rather than working through every measure, just identify those measures where there is considerable variation from the targets and explain the variation and what actions will be taken to address the variation. An example of a report that can be used to monitor performance is presented in Figure 12.6.

In this report the measures and targets are listed on the left and on the right a red–amber–green traffic light system is used to indicate whether the target will be met (green), whether there is minor variance from the target (amber) or whether the target will not be met (red). Where targets are reporting amber or red, then fields will need to be completed, which will state what actions will be taken to address the variance, issues that the benefit owner would like to raise with the governance board for them to action and major risks that will need to be managed and that the governance board needs to be aware of.

During the implementation phase, it is also important to define a benefits realisation plan. This plan forecasts when benefits will be delivered after the programme is complete. An example is provided in Figure 12.7.

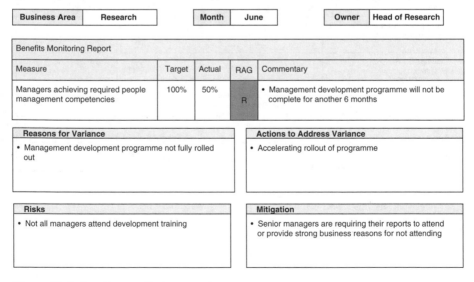

Business Area	Research		Month	June		Owner	Head of Research

Benefits Monitoring Report

Measure	Target	Actual	RAG	Commentary
Managers achieving required people management competencies	100%	50%	R	• Management development programme will not be complete for another 6 months

Reasons for Variance	Actions to Address Variance
• Management development programme not fully rolled out	• Accelerating rollout of programme

Risks	Mitigation
• Not all managers attend development training	• Senior managers are requiring their reports to attend or provide strong business reasons for not attending

Figure 12.6 Benefits-monitoring report.

Expected Benefits	How is it Measured?	Current Level	Breakdown of Benefits Delivery Year by Year			Who is Accountable for Delivery?	Who is Responsible for Delivery?
			Year 1	Year 2	Year 3		
Recruitment Administration							
Media Cost	£	£100K	£30k	£50K	£50k	Manager A	Manager A
Cost of Preparing & Processing Application Packs	£	£30K	£5K	£7K	£10K	Manager B	Manager C
Transition Processing of Hiring Requisitions	Admin Time FTE	25	3	7	10	Manager C	Manager C

Figure 12.7 Benefits-realisation plan.

The benefits realisation plan should not only detail when the benefits will be delivered but should also identify which managers will be responsible for delivering the benefits.

Sustaining benefits

In terms of locking in benefits, the key is what you do immediately post go live to embed and sustain change. We have found the following seven areas to be highly effective in this.

Ensure that benefit targets are incorporated into business plans

It has already been noted that HR transformation will not only deliver important benefits within HR but also across the organisation. The use of HR and self-service technology will make the delivery of core people management processes, such as managing performance, reducing absences and improving skills and development, more efficient and effective and give front line managers greater access to people data for operational management. The use of service centres to provide advice can also deliver greater consistency in the advice and improve access, particularly for staff working outside standard office hours and in different time zones and locations. Whilst the reduction of transactional work and the creation of business partnering roles can provide an opportunity for HR to take a greater strategic role and support the organisation with issues such as how to improve productivity and growth whilst managing costs.

Embedding these changes and benefits, however, requires not only the adoption of new ways of working but also the adoption of new objectives and targets across the business. For example, prior to transformation a key performance measure for learning and development could have been the time taken to book staff into training courses. After transformation, online course booking could reduce the importance of this measure and a more valuable measure could be the number of staff developing the competencies and skills required to meet business performance standards and drive productivity. This measure could also become the responsibility of the operational business, which could use self-service technology to monitor this measure and ensure that staff skills were developed in the areas that were right for their part of the business and the goals in their business plan. When identifying new measures and targets to include in business plans, a good starting point is the benefits-realisation plans that were developed and handed over during go live. The measures and targets within these plans can be transferred across into operational plans, ensuring that they are achieved after the transformation programme has ended.

The HR leadership team can then use the information from the HR systems to identify operational measures which focus on people issues, such as overall absences, competency levels and performance levels and engage with the senior leadership team on how changing these measures can improve performance and productivity and also helping to establish HR in a more strategic role.

Answer the question – 'what's in it for me?'

The introduction of self-service technologies and the move of people management responsibilities, such as managing performance or absence, can be interpreted by some business staff as HR transferring its responsibilities to an already overburdened line area. HR transformation can, however, deliver many advantages to line staff and managers. For example, rather than waiting for HR to book courses, staff can find a course online, get approval from their manager online and instantly book the course and manage course dates themselves. Similarly, when managing sickness absences, self-service places the line manager in control of recording and reporting on information without the need to send data to HR and wait for reports that are invariably out of date. Staff can also make instant updates to their personal information, view holiday balances online and quickly and easily enter timesheets and expense claims, speeding up the process of making payments.

The use of HR service centres also means that when staff have queries they have a single contact point and do not have to look for HR managers and leave answers on voicemail systems if the managers are out of the office and in meetings. Service centres can also be staffed to provide support outside of standard office hours for managers working on shifts or in different countries.

The key is identifying which aspects of transformation will provide a benefit to different groups of staff and managers and then promoting these advantages to each group and demonstrating exactly how the transformation will benefit them in their day-to-day work. Chapter 11 identified that the change readiness assessment, conducted during implementation, will provide a valuable insight into the issues of different staff groups and proposed the use of a 'day in the life of' tool to map out daily activities for different staff groups and clearly state how these activities will be improved by transformation. This should also be reinforced by role-based training.

This involves taking specific roles in the business and working out which aspects of the new HR roles, processes and technology will have the most impact upon them and then constructing training courses which focus on these high-impact areas. For example, for a manager in a call centre, instant and accurate reports on staff leave and absences can be valuable in planning shift patterns. The training for the call centre managers will therefore focus on how to use self-service to capture and report upon staff attendance and absence. This ensures that the training is relevant, benefits day-to-day work and helps to embed the transformation.

Continue training after go live

HR transformation often delivers a combination of new or slightly different roles, new technology tools and new processes and ways of working. It is often only after the transformation is complete and people are in their roles and using new processes and systems that they realise what they needed to learn during the training and implementation phase. Therefore, it is worth planning and budgeting for 'refresher' training after the transformation is complete. This reinforces how staff need to work together, how technology can help them in their work and how they will benefit from adopting the new ways of working, rather than ignoring or resisting them.

Demonstrate leadership from the top

If you can demonstrate leadership from within the highest levels in the organisation, then this will cascade through the organisation, encouraging acceptance of the new ways of working. For instance, the new HR systems will have the capability to produce organisation charts from the information in the system or to report a table of staff attendance or breakdown of staff sickness absence with reasons and performance. Previously, managers would have produced this information using a variety of desk-based and paper-based systems. However, if senior management uses this system to access this data themselves and insist that only this data is used in presentations, then the new ways of working will have clear and strong sponsorship. Similarly, if leaders use different HR services, such as a call centre, and promote and advocate the use of these services, it will encourage staff to use these services.

Performance management

HR transformation can introduce change in both HR and line management. For example, line managers may become responsible for ensuring that appraisals are all completed in accordance with the performance management timetable or that they monitor and manage sickness absences or that they check staff qualifications against Continuing Development, professional or statutory standards. These may have been responsibilities that HR held for a long period and line managers will therefore regard them as 'HR' activities and be slow or unwilling to adopt them. It will therefore be important to make the delivery of these responsibilities part of the criteria against which staff and managers are evaluated. Targets can be incorporated into performance criteria, such as 100% completion of staff appraisals on time, all sickness absences logged within 1 day of notification and any return to work interviews completed within 1 day of a staff member returning from sickness absence. This will drive compliance and the process of embedding transformed processes and activities into business as usual.

Staff can also be required to demonstrate that they have adopted new competencies as part of their performance management. This can be achieved by defining the competency levels that each role or group of roles needs to achieve and then checking that staff have achieved these levels through such criteria as achievement on training and/or 360° feedback.

The incorporation of targets and competencies into performance criteria can be a highly effective tool for embedding change.

Remove the old ways of doing things

If old systems and ways of working remain, there is always a risk that people will revert to using them. For example, if you require line managers to call a service centre for HR advice and guidance, this will be undermined if they continue to contact their old HR managers and these managers continue to provide advice and guidance. Both managers and HR staff need to be required to use new ways of working and systems. Similarly, if you are using an online approach to recording sickness absence where managers input the data through self-service, this will be undermined by allowing managers to send this information via e-mail or fax to the service centre and getting HR staff to input the data.

Using an incremental approach, you can remove the old processes in a systematic and planned way, which is a powerful demonstration that something has changed permanently.

Make measurement an ongoing activity

Having taken these actions and others post go live, you should continue to measure benefits and changes post-implementation, so that doing so becomes part of how the 'new' HR function evaluates itself and demonstrates value going forward. As you will be assessing actual delivery against benefits, you will need to be ready to take action when there is any shortfall, not only up to implementation but also beyond.

Summary

The focus on benefits realisation begins at the business case stage and continues post-implementation. The measures, scorecard and benefits realisation plan are the mechanisms by which you can monitor and drive through benefit delivery at the detail level. The need to focus on benefit delivery will continue after go live and through to 'business as usual'. Paying attention to benefits and ensuring that they are delivered or adapted to suit changing circumstances will demonstrate the value of the transformation and prove its success.

Part 4

Realising the Promise of HR Transformation

Part 4 looks to the future and identifies key themes for a transformed HR function.

Chapter 13: The Business of HR identifies six themes HR functions will need to address in coming years and the challenges that remain if HR is to support the creation of high-performing organisations.

13

The Business of HR

If HR is transformed, how will it help create high-performing organisations? In the United Kingdom, the Chartered Institute for Personnel and Development has recently embarked on a 3-year investigation – under the banner 'Shaping the Future' – into the foundations of high-performance working. We fully support this initiative and hope our thinking will contribute to this critical theme both in the United Kingdom and beyond.

The aim of this chapter is, therefore, to set out what some may regard as a visionary agenda and to identify key themes we believe will help create high-performance working. We hope it will provide you with a basis for discussion with colleagues as you try and make sense of the current economic situation and identify where the focus on people should lie with your organisation. We have naturally taken a 'people' slant and our intention is to identify those themes where HR professionals should be leading and shaping thinking and delivery in their organisations. This chapter will also remind us that the point of HR transformation is that by transforming itself, HR professionals are able to make contributions that help their organisation deliver sustainable high performance.

Key themes

- Unprecedented economic situations will require an even stronger contribution from HR.
- HR professionals need to focus on what their organisations *need* and not on what HR departments have traditionally done.
- Six themes are likely to dominate the business of HR in the coming years.
- HR needs to continue to transform itself.

Context

At the time of writing the world economy is in its worst shape since the end of the Second World War. Robert Peston, the BBC's Business Editor, has written that 'Economic conditions in 2009 will be treacherous. There will be formal recession in most developed economies and the economic contraction is highly likely to be more severe in the UK than almost anywhere else ... there will be a sharp rise in unemployment and many businesses, especially big ones, will become unviable and will present the Government with an appalling dilemma of which ones to put on life support'. Peston goes on to write that across the developed world, 'taxpayers' financial support for the banking system alone is now equivalent to more than 25% of global GDP, or more than £9,000bn'. And that is just the banking sector!

Phrases such as 'the end of capitalism' and 'restructuring of the economic order' are being used more frequently in the business press to describe the severity of the current crisis. Whether these phrases are understatement, reality or hype remains to be seen. While no one can say how long this current crisis will last, what is certain is that we will do business differently.

Historically, downturns have driven change in the ways we do business. For example, in the 1980s the recession changed people's views on 'job for life' and, certainly in the United Kingdom, fundamentally changed the relationship between employers and trade unions. In parallel with these changes grew experiments in flexible working, an expanded 'temporary' workforce, more project-based work and an opening up of opportunity for women in workplaces. For those of us involved in industrial/employee relations at the time, we were re-writing collective agreements, partly to reflect new labour laws enacted by the then Conservative government, but also to embrace the new reality.

The recession in the early 1990s accelerated these trends and the growth in information technology/personal computing made the notion of home working possible. As organisations sought to cut costs 'globalisation' became the watchword for economic survival. What started as a shift of low-cost work to emerging economies became a much more fundamental shift as talent markets also globalised. Examples of this are best seen in the areas of information technology and research. Eastern European countries and India have particularly benefited from this shift.

A KPMG/CIPD Labour Market Outlook (Winter 2008/09) reported the following:

- 80% of organisations surveyed believe the United Kingdom economic situation will get worse over the next 3 months.
- 46% do not expect a change in the financial performance of their organisation.
- 64% have either experienced an organisational budget cut or are expecting one.
- Average pay increases are expected to fall.

- There is a marked increase in the number of employers who will not be awarding a pay increase this year.
- There is a significant decline in the number of employers intending to recruit.
- 34% of employers expect to make some redundancies in the next 3 months.

These statistics are only a snapshot in time, but reflect well the economic situation HR professionals need to address.

As we peer through the fog of this current economic crisis, we can identify some of the characteristics of the emerging order:

- *Government will play a bigger role.* In the United Kingdom, the government now owns majority shareholdings in significant retail banks, public sector debt is set to spiral and a significant regulatory restructuring will come. Regulation in particular is likely to be more widespread and deeper. From a people perspective, we can anticipate greater scrutiny of executive compensation and reporting of the people 'profit and loss' account.
- *Money will be tighter.* This will mean that those companies that previously grew through high financial leverage will suffer reduced returns. It also means that growth will need to come through a rather more traditional route – productivity. From a people perspective, this offers exceptional opportunities for HR professionals to identify ways for their organisations to drive productivity improvements through people.
- *A new realism concerning growth targets.* The US and UK economies in particular have been fuelled by high personal debt since the late 1990s. This dependence on debt as a driver of consumption and growth will not be sustained. High income and consumption growth will most likely be found in Asia, providing there is no fundamental backlash against capitalism. From a people perspective, there will be a continued shift in focus eastwards and those organisations working globally will need to adjust to a more eastern influence.
- *Adoption of technological advances will continue.* We have featured Web 2.0 in this book and this technological advance is still largely unexploited by organisations. Web 2.0, alongside other technologies, will emerge from the world of pure social networking and will start to be used to share knowledge, creation and innovation.

There are bound to be other characteristics of the emerging order which are not yet known. We may hope, for example, that a greater focus on business ethics may emerge from this current crisis – but this is perhaps more hope than reality. What is clear is that there is a golden opportunity for HR professionals to embrace the current uncertainties and bring fresh thinking into their organisations. In the following section, we set out our thoughts on what this fresh thinking may need to address.

The business of HR – Six themes

Although we live in a period of disruptive change, this does not mean that the proverbial baby should be thrown out with the bath water. As with all change there is also continuity and what we expect to continue is:

- a focus on value;
- improved organisational performance through ongoing efficiency improvements;
- alignment of people practices to specific organisational needs;
- cost reduction and service improvements;
- HR's ongoing 'control and regulation' function.

These are contributions we expect HR will continue to make. But there are also things that need to change. One important change is about the language we use. HR needs to stop talking about 'HR' as being separate from 'the business'. There are no HR agendas, only business agendas and HR is much a part of the business as any other function. This also challenges HR to abandon some of its obsessions with fads and fashions and to work with business colleagues on those issues that really make a difference to organisational performance. As Ian Muir (Cable & Wireless) put it, 'strip down the agenda to the things that really matter; simplify, then simplify again'.

As we strive to add value through people, we have identified six themes (Figure 13.1) where HR can really add value in coming years. We are not saying that these themes have equal weighting for all organisations – but they are all relevant. We also recognise that some HR functions are already contributing strongly in one or more of these areas. Even so, we encourage you to address the relevance of each to your organisation, review how well you are responding to each theme and identify strengths and shortfalls.

Theme 1: Being at the heart of organisational development

We refer back to our discussion on HR and OD in Chapter 1 and use the term 'organisational development' in its broadest definition – the development of the whole system to create a healthy and effective organisation. In this sense, HR needs to be closely involved in:

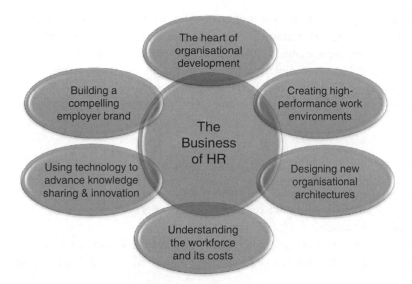

Figure 13.1 The business of HR – Six themes.

- defining and shaping organisational strategy and plans;
- delivering the strategy – using change management tools and techniques to help organisations realise the target benefits for change;
- enhancing organisational health;
- building organisational capability.

This theme has a strong future orientation: it is about creating future organisational capability. This means being able to change what we do now, without a dip in performance and embed new ways of working and behaving so that they make a difference to future performance.

No serious commentator will argue that the speed of change will slow in coming years. The trend is in the opposite direction. Change management is not something you do from time to time, it is a core capability. How we manage the people and organisational aspects of change are usually the deciding factor in whether the change succeeds or not.

Given the current economic climate a future orientation may be about surviving the next 12 months – or it could be about laying the foundations for success in the next 3–5 years. Whichever place your organisation finds itself in, there will be a change agenda.

Organisations need people who can get under the skin of what drives performance, identify what needs to change (with the necessary data to back this up) and then make this change happen. This is practical stuff. It is important stuff as well.

We have argued in this book that HR professionals need to develop new capabilities in the areas of strategy (which includes commercial/financial skills) and change management, consulting skills and project management skills. We reiterate this point. HR professionals will be heard if they have something interesting to say. We strongly believe that HR should make a major contribution in this area, bringing its knowledge of organisational development to bear on critical business issues.

Theme 2: Creating high performance work environments

Creating environments where individuals and teams can perform remains an aim for organisations, but how we reward people for performance is a debate heightened in recent months.

A Corporate Leadership Council paper 'Improving Employee Performance in the Economic Downturn' (December 2008) identified four additional challenges:

Challenge 1: employee performance is declining;
Challenge 2: the disengaged are staying;
Challenge 3: high potentials are more likely to quit;
Challenge 4: senior leaders' effort has dropped.

We accept that these are conclusions drawn from more general research, but it is important you understand what is going on in your organisation and how productivity and performance are holding up. Loss of talent and a decline in performance can quickly hit the bottom line, potentially counteracting the impact of efficiency programmes and undermining their ability to hit set objectives.

Linked to other themes, HR has an opportunity to work with colleagues to:

■ use restructuring projects as an opportunity to redesign roles and review levels of accountability so that key people are given increased opportunity;
■ make a case for critical development expenditure which will grow strategic capabilities;
■ develop clear career paths for talent and maintain career discussions;
■ ensure internal resourcing processes are in place to support proactive redeployment and career movement around the organisation;
■ identify the development needs of leaders so that they are given support to help them run the business through turbulent times;
■ keep developing people's skills;
■ understand which roles add the most value.

There is also an opportunity to strengthen teamworking and collaboration. We build on this regarding the use of technology below. But whether as line teams or project teams, physically proximate or virtual teams, HR needs to help organisations create the environments where people can collaborate effectively. This may be to share knowledge as a means to innovate and drive creativity, learn or to bring expertise together to work on a business project. Research still underlines that it is generally failure to get the people side of collaborate working right that leads to failure in teams to deliver. HR should bring knowledge about group facilitation, the creation of effective learning environments and high-performance teams to help the organisation drive performance through individuals and teams.

How we reward performance will require a fundamental examination in the coming years. For too long, performance-related pay has failed to motivate with excess amounts of managerial time spent in haggling over minuscule bonus pots. The principle of rewarding performance is sound. That these bonus pots may not exist in their current form in the future may be a blessing in disguise, providing organisations take this opportunity to find better ways of rewarding people across the organisation. We expect HR to be shaping the thinking in this area.

In the following case study, we present an example from National Express East Anglia (as the business is now called) which demonstrates well how HR can contribute powerfully in both the organisational development and high-performance environment spaces.

Case study—National express

In 2006, the rail franchise 'ONE' was underperforming. It needed to deliver fundamental change in four business areas in order to raise performance and put itself in a strong position for a franchise extension. These four areas were operational performance, customer at the heart, right people, right culture and external partnerships.

The HR team led by Andy Meadows, HR Director, and supported by Steph Oerton, then Head of L&D and now Director of Leadership and Talent for National Express UK, already had strong credibility in the organisation and were given the task of leading the right people, right culture work. The business had never really embarked on a change programme of this magnitude before, so a number of actions were taken initially to enable the senior team to demonstrate effective change leadership:

■ The executive team met every 8–10 weeks for a day specifically to focus on the change programme and how they led the change.

- An extended leadership group of the top 40 managers started to meet every quarter—partly to cover similar ground to the executive team and build a broader change leadership capability and also to engage this group of leaders in working collaboratively on key change issues.
- A number of ways were used to engage the wider management population of around 250 managers in the change challenges from large conferences through to more local events.

This focus on teams and getting the environment right for performance was really important as it involved a broad leadership base in identifying and then delivering iconic leadership actions (such as out of hours visibility of leaders at stations), communications and other engagement actions.

One of these was the identification of a group of around 40 internal change agents who were drawn from all organisational levels. These people were given tools and skills to support a number of specific initiatives which were then rolled out to support change. Some of these initiatives included:

- promise, purpose and values workshops linked to the adoption of the National Express brand and which engaged people with the aims of the business change and how the National Express values could be brought to life in day-to-day work;
- delivering action plans linked to the employee engagement survey;
- improvement of local communications.

Other HR facilitated work included the development of a target culture which framed actions to be taken to shape culture. This work was linked strongly to the work on customer at the heart.

Since 2006 performance improvements have been achieved against all indicators—but particularly employee engagement which has increased by 50%.

Theme 3: Designing new organisational architectures

Linked to the above two themes is the application of organisation design tools. There are tools and techniques that will help managers restructure more effectively and HR professionals should be able to bring these to the table. The application of these organisational design tools will enable HR to make contributions that will:

- underpin sustainable cost reduction initiatives;
- align organisation with strategy;
- take a whole systems view of restructuring;

- evaluate different structural approaches so that the organisation is better placed to identify where organisational boundaries should lie – particularly with regard to the core organisation and the flexible organisation – whether this flexible organisation comes in the form of contractors, temps, agencies acting on the organisation's behalf, outsourcers, consultants, interims, third parties, alliances and partnerships;
- engage in informed debate about issues such as flexible working hours and home working;
- bring the customer perspective into re-organisation so that we create organisation around the customer experience.

As organisations respond to the current economic situation, being able to explore alternative organisational models becomes critical. We need to know why it is preferable to take someone on as a full-time employee rather than use a contractor, consultant or interim rather than assume that just because the organisation has more control over that person it is the right solution. Organisations need to explore how to scale without necessarily building high fixed costs and maybe how to scale down without having to go through demoralising redundancy programmes. We need to ensure we never lose sight of the customer and build organisations that deliver exceptional customer experiences.

The bottom line is that more creative approaches to organisation are needed and HR needs to understand the economics of organisations to help senior teams work their way through to the right decisions.

Theme 4: Understanding the workforce and its costs

HR has a great opportunity not only to help the business cut costs but also, and more importantly, to optimise the cost base – do more with less. Optimising the cost base requires the ability to evaluate and change cost structures in such a way as to create sustainable and long-term value, as well as deliver immediate cost reduction.

Some of the ways this is achieved relates to other themes such as new organisational architectures and high-performance environments and we have addressed linkages in the relevant section.

With regard to workforce modelling there is an urgent need to focus on four areas:

1. *Workforce planning* – understanding the breakdown of the current workforce from a multi-level perspective (demographics, grading, core/temporary, part time/full time, etc.).
2. *Workforce cost management* – understanding the workforce costs associated with different types of workers and how you align rewards more closely with desired behaviours. We need to understand better which roles drive the most value in the organisation.

3. *Organisational capability* – understanding the capability profile of the organisation, the talent pipeline and where key capability shifts need to be made or where capability gaps exist.
4. *Human capital reporting* – being able to produce a people profit and loss/ human capital account.

HR needs to be able to interrogate workforce data to address strategic questions so that the organisation has better information about why particular mixes of employee work better than others, how spending money to develop capability will drive value and where value is actually added so that people are rewarded for the right things.

The point of workforce modelling is not just to inform resourcing or development agendas – it is to engage more effectively in predictive forecasting, to provide clearer and more insightful data to senior management and engage more purposefully with colleagues in finance concerning budgets and investment decisions.

The following case study shows how AXA UK is starting to tackle this theme. As we state in the case study, this is not a finished product but very much a work in progress and we hope it will stimulate thinking in how you can get started.

Case study—AXA UK

AXA UK is an excellent example of an organisation taking steps to address the area of workforce planning. Although AXA were recruiting to over 4000 posts per annum there was little workforce planning, forecasting or modelling. Given the volume of recruitment, the organisation recognised the potential to drive greater value through effective workforce planning.

A role of Senior Resourcing Partner was therefore introduced into each of the four UK Business Units to focus on workforce planning. Working with both operational recruitment and HR Business Partners this role provided dedicated resources to an area that was struggling to get organisational attention.

Samantha Rich, Head of Group Resourcing Practice, has led the work to improve workforce planning, focusing on three areas:

1. Identifying critical data inputs: drawn from the recruitment candidate tracking system, payroll, training and development and budget systems and Business Unit plans.
2. Investing in and developing a predictive planning tool (called a8i horizons and developed in partnership with activ8 Intelligence) which uses predictive technology/artificial intelligence to support scenario modelling and 'what if' analysis.

---

3. Identifying a number of business issues to focus on initially (rather than a whole organisation roll out) so that this approach to workforce management gains credibility with line and HR alike and early successes are delivered.

An example of a business issue being addressed is the placement of graduates coming off the AXA graduate programme. A significant investment has been made in this population of young talent, so there is a business imperative of retention and then placement in roles where they can make strong contributions. In the current economic conditions, fewer vacancies are opening up so work has been undertaken to identify patterns of attrition amongst managers and to forecast where vacancies are likely to emerge (roles, organisational level and location). This is enabling proactive action to be taken to match graduates with vacancies and, perhaps more importantly, is providing people with information to hold discussions with and manage the expectations of graduates.

Examples of questions being addressed through workforce planning and which get under the skin of business issues include: If we change the skill set of a group what will be the cost/business implications? Does the volume of learning and development received by someone affect his or her performance and retention?

Although these changes are by no means the finished article yet, the approach taken illustrates the importance of being relevant to the context of your organisation (even if you have looked at what other organisations are doing in this area—which AXA did—you have to find out what works for you) and ensuring that actions are focused on issues that matter to the business. This approach is expected to demonstrate a tangible Return on Investment (ROI) and has already identified savings through coordinating more effectively around recruitment campaigns, working with 'at risk' pools to maximise placements and thereby reducing recruitment and redundancy costs and improving the retention of key people.

Theme 5: Using technology to advance knowledge sharing and innovation

Think about the following – Facebook, blogs, Twitter, wikis, podcasts, virtual worlds, YouTube, RSS feeds, interactive media – just for starters. Some of us may have had to learn to use these Web 2.0 technologies. The generation already entering the workplace are already fluent in these technologies. They promote a democratic, user-led and content-rich experience. Everyone can have an opinion and everyone does. They encourage the personal and the shared experience. People keep in touch and collaborate in ways that makes even the telephone seem a little slow.

In Chapter 4, we looked at people and technology across a broad landscape. Technology is an inherent part of the HR delivery model. In the coming years, we can expect the use of technology to support the people agenda to escalate in importance. Marketing has already and typically been early adopters of emerging technologies. For HR progress has been much slower.

HR professionals must become more technologically literate – early adopters and experimenters. The areas of graduate recruitment and internal communications are perhaps the best examples of how Web 2.0 is being used in the people space and some of this activity is led outside of HR.

A critical challenge for many organisations remains collaboration – how do we get people sharing knowledge, working together effectively, learning so that we drive creativity and innovation to address business issues?

Whilst not a panacea, technology is going to play an increasing role in promoting more effective collaboration. The technology is there and much of it is free. What is missing is attention to the human side – how do we create effective virtual learning environments, how do we create trust and build commitment when people aren't in the same place, how do we make it as culturally acceptable for people to engage virtually as it is for them to meet physically?

There are other issues for sure, but they aren't going to be solved by information systems. These emerging technologies are not fads; they aren't going to go away. There are significant productivity gains to be made if businesses use technology well to foster greater collaboration. This means HR has an opportunity to contribute.

Theme 6: Building a compelling employer brand

More money is being dedicated by organisations to employer branding to create a positive or distinctive association with actual and potential employees. The place of a strong employee value proposition in attracting talent and in shaping their expectations has been accepted for some time. What is less well developed is the link between a strong employer brand and existing employees – creating a strong psychological contract which drives high levels of employee engagement and commitment leading to greater discretionary effort, productivity and performance.

The extent to which the traditional roles of a brand (e.g., differentiation, loyalty, satisfaction and affinity) drive higher levels of internal engagement is still in the early days of research. Gary Davies (Manchester Business School) has recently published research which seeks to test this relationship and has found encouraging results and states that 'employers concerned about their image with their managers can use the results presented here to improve satisfaction, affinity and perceived differentiation and, to some extent, how long employees might wish to stay in post'. He also states that by comparison with the literature on the influences on customers the literature on the impact of brand on employees is very much in an emergent phase – which in many ways leaves the barn door open for HR to step into.

Another observation made by Davies and also made by Martin Edwards (Kings College) and Graeme Martin (Glasgow University) is that internal marketing of the employer brand is still largely top-down with two main goals – to align employee views of the corporate brand and their behaviour to what is being promoted externally to customers and to treat employees as customers who need to be communicated with so that they have a favourable view of their employer.

As such, questions need to be asked concerning the employee voice and how this plays out in terms of the employer brand development and engagement. There is clearly a link between the employer brand and the psychological contract, but how this is forged and how we bring the employee voice (or voices) into our thinking so that the brand is co-created needs to be grasped by HR, as does the playing out of the employer brand in terms of an employee value proposition. This may be seen as too risky for some organisations. Bringing the employee voice into our thinking means the organisation loses control and people may say things we don't want to hear. In our opinion this is a risk well worth taking. As the next generation enters the workforce with very clear expectations about being heard – generation V (virtual) – there is an even stronger case for pursuing an approach based on involvement and co-creation. This willingness to take risks is well illustrated in the AXA case study.

The importance of developing a coherent employer brand is more than just internal marketing or slick recruitment. It plays strongly into the delivery of reputational value addressed in Chapter 3.

Is employee engagement relevant in a downturn when the overriding focus is on cutting costs and preserving cash? You bet! How we deal with our people now defines our employer brand. The brand is not flashy imagery, it is the substance. It is what people actually experience. As with a consumer brand it is when things go wrong that we discover the true brand identity. Does the brand deliver its promise? The same is true for organisations. Our organisations are currently facing their defining moments for employees. How we respond now will lay the foundations for future performance.

The following case study shows how AXA UK has used Web 2.0 technology to support more effective employee engagement. Again, this is a relatively recent development but highlights how organisations are making a start and, if there is clarity of purpose, how a very simple approach can be quickly embraced and developed by people in the business.

Case study—AXA UK

The UK business faced a challenge. Having made a significant investment in putting every employee through a high-energy and extremely successful 1-day workshop to engage them with the AXA values (called ICE), there was no outlet for people to express themselves, discuss issues and generate ideas after the event. This situation was not satisfactory and the business knew that something needed to happen quickly if all the positive energy generated by the ICE programme was to have a business impact.

Sonia Carter, Head of Internal Online Communications, was handed this challenge. With hardly any budget and a tight deadline to put something in place, she was asked to come up with ideas. She and a small team came up with 'Our Space'.

'Our Space' is built on Web 2.0 technology and has two main functions: discussion forums and ideas generation. The philosophy behind Our Space was to create a strong identity different from other on-line applications—not corporate, informal, user owned and moderated. This approach meant taking a risk with employees as people were encouraged to say what they wanted—but *trust* is an AXA value and it was decided that this would be a good way to bring the value of trust to life.

So what has happened?

The Forum provides different zones where people can generate or join discussions: by business area, IT, working life, etc. There are also guest forums which are often linked to big organisational changes and announcements. These forums are kicked off with a Board member hosting an interactive session for between 1 and 2 hours allowing people to pose questions and get real-time answers. Other one-off forums have included:

■ using AXA's in-house experts to host a session on pensions advice;
■ a diversity forum where employees have been introduced to three diverse characters and have been asked to engage with dilemmas faced by these people as a way of engaging people with diversity issues.

The ideas generation part of Our Space gives people a chance to identify barriers to delivery. Someone can post an idea and others then have an opportunity to build on the idea or challenge it. Ideas are voted on and the top ideas each month are investigated. Within its first year, over 70 ideas were implemented.

Our Space has already won a 'Computers in Business' award for excellence and there are now plans to extend the functionality of Our Space to enable people to ask any questions (AXA answers), a video channel (based on the YouTube concept) and blogs.

The immediate success of Our Space has already brought benefits. It has given employees a voice and, with only a brief 'acceptable use' statement, has been used extremely constructively and it has established itself as a key platform for engagement. Its success has also been partly down to the dynamics of Web 2.0 and social networking. It is user led and can start small. People will gravitate to and generate content they are interested in and therefore do not depend on a grand strategy at the outset (or much money!) to add value quickly.

As we try to shift HR's contribution, it is important to think through at a practical level how this might be achieved. As we have said many times in this book and as Maggie Hurt (Renold) puts it: 'Nothing we do in HR is governed by the laws of physics, there is no one right answer. It is all a social construct and therefore there is no 'have to' other than working within the law. Our job in HR is primarily about providing business solutions'. So we need to think through these themes in relation to our own organisation, and in the following we give you some pointers we hope will help to move thinking forward on these themes in your business:

- Identify one action related to each of the six themes that would really help your organisation to perform better.
- What is your organisation currently doing about each of these actions?
- What would different look like?
- What practical next steps might you take to take action? What support might you need (either political or knowledge) either from within HR, from other functions or outside the organisation?
- How might you dip your toe in the water – find an area where you might start experimenting?

You may also want to think about these themes from a more personal perspective. As you read the above, how did you feel – excited, intimidated, challenged, afraid, competent, or incompetent? Our own reactions are important. We need to think about how comfortable we feel with this vision for HR. It is people in HR who decide how HR contributes and what effort they will make to change what is done. If you are excited by these six themes, think about the following:

- How does my current skill set and experience match with these six themes?
- Where can I best make a contribution?
- What new capabilities might I need to develop to make this contribution?
- What help do I need and where can I get this help at a personal level?
- Whom do I need to talk to?

The ongoing transformation of HR

If HR is to deliver on the themes set out above, we suggest that whatever progress you have made to date in shifting HR's contribution in your organisation still has some way to travel. The implications for the HR delivery model are given in the following subsections.

Structure

Changing job titles will not transform HR. So there is a need to ensure new roles are embedded and in particular that the new set of organisational boundaries – within HR and between HR and internal functions and external providers – are clear and accountabilities agreed. As HR careers start to coalesce around shared services, centres of expertise or partnering-type roles, new career paths need to be developed so that depth of expertise is recognised and valued and genuine partner roles draw in people with the right skill sets – either from within HR or other functions.

Technology

The greatest challenges here are less with core ERP/Information databases but with:

1. distributed use – fully implementing self-service and adopting the potential of Web 2.0;
2. the application of more powerful software to support predictive forecasting/ scenario modelling/data interrogation;
3. information quality, relevance and insights.

Processes

Much progress has been made on process efficiency and effectiveness but opportunity remains to drive out process value. This was explored at some length in Chapter 3.

Capability and culture

This is by far the greatest gap that still needs to be bridged. Capabilities identified some years ago – especially for those seeking to operate in the change/strategic space – have not been adequately developed (see Chapters 1 and 10) and additional capability gaps are also emerging. Analytical skills, skills drawn from marketing (e.g., research, segmentation, branding, communications and engagement), technology awareness, commercial/financial skills, data modelling are all increasing in relevance for some if not the many in HR professional roles.

Culturally, the need to be relevant, credible and client focused remains, along with a need to be proactive, intellectually curious and challenging. The increasing emphasis on analytical capability and numeracy underlines the need for HR to develop a more evidence-based culture too. To deliver all this HR needs credible leaders who are comfortable with the business and who can create the confidence for people to want to step out into largely unchartered waters.

Performance

Understanding how HR delivers value through people is still largely underdeveloped and we hope Chapter 3 has helped to stimulate thinking on how this might be addressed. HR functions must stop measuring what is easily measured and work hard understanding how people practices drive and sustain high performance.

The difficult people issues we face in our organisations won't go away. The need to create value through people won't diminish. The issue is whether the HR function as we know it will exist to tackle these issues.

There is no guarantee that HR will exist. A number of scenarios could materialise. HR could become just shared services – process, advisory and transactional in focus. Or these functions could be absorbed into a large shared services function covering a number of back office roles.

Other aspects of the people agenda could plausibly be picked up by other functions:

- organisational development, organisational design, high-performance environments by the Strategy team;
- the application of technology to the people agenda by the Information Systems team;
- the employer brand and employee engagement by the Marketing and/or Communications team;
- workforce modelling by Finance.

Alternatively, HR functions may secure good people from marketing, finance, IS and even consultancies to work with the HR team for a while – sourcing talent from outside of HR – to help develop skills HR teams don't possess in abundance currently.

Another approach may be to use cross-organisational solutions – so that HR works collaboratively with other functions on, for example, employer branding, workforce planning, etc.

In many ways all these scenarios are possible and your organisation will need to make the right choice for its situation. Our hope is that HR professionals will rise to these complex but fascinating people and organisational challenges and will take their place alongside business colleagues in figuring out how the organisation is going to perform well. That is the underlying aim of this book – to give HR the tools to transform itself so that it can make contributions in organisations that will drive value through people.

Conclusion

We face an unprecedented and unpredictable economic situation. The people challenges that need to be faced by organisations are growing in complexity. We have identified a visionary agenda for HR focused on six themes which, if addressed, will help organisations deliver value through people. These themes are not the exclusive domain of HR but are all areas where HR can make a significant contribution in delivering high organisational performance.

HR transformation does not stop. The next phase must focus decisively on the contribution HR makes. HR must look outwards, focus on business needs and make these the catalyst for action.

Summary of Key Points and Actions

We thought that it would be helpful to hold in one place a summary of key actions associated with each chapter. So here it is ...

Chapter 1 A Transformational Mindset

- Effective business change benefits from the application of tried and tested Organisational Development (OD) tools and approaches.
- HR professionals often fail to influence effectively because they are unfamiliar with OD tools and approaches.
- To be more effective in shaping transformational change, HR professionals need to focus on the development of a 'system mindset', 'process consulting mindset' and 'project mindset'.
- Systems thinking places HR transformation within the context of the wider organisational (and extra-organisational) system and challenges us to integrate the different facets of HR transformation.
- Process consulting is about being client-centred and focuses on the steps needed to effect change in ways that brings key stakeholders with you step by step. It also ensures that at each stage of the transformation journey there is learning and engagement with what is really happening in the organisation.
- A project mindset uses programme and project management principles to ensure HR transformation is delivered in a coherent and timely way.

Chapter 2 HR Transformation – How Are We Doing?

- Recent research presents a fixed view on the progress of HR transformation.
- HR's proximity to, and interaction with, other business functions is a key

indicator of the success of transformation. The ubiquitous 'seat at the table'; HR as change leaders; what HR generalists and specialists actually do and the reputation of HR within the organisation are all relevant indicators of progress.

■ The seven issues we identified and key questions we posed in our earlier edition remain valid.

Chapter 3 What Is HR's Value Proposition?

■ There is little academic consensus on what value creation is and how it can be achieved.
■ Value creation needs to be understood from a contingency perspective – value is in the eye of the beholder.
■ HR value-add is delivered through four key sources: transactional value, process value, strategic value and reputational value.
■ HR professionals need to get much better at analysing data and understanding financial management.
■ Challenges remain for HR functions to deliver value in organisations.

Chapter 4 People and Technology

■ The range of technologies that are available are many and varied. Packages which run payroll, deliver an HR database, deliver self-service and integrate HR with other back-office services such as finance and procurement exist. Packages are also available which exploit Web technology to support online recruitment, online learning and development and to create virtual environments in which it is possible to engage in a two-way communication process with staff. Technology, including Web 2.0, is opening up new ways to deliver key people processes and engage with staff.
■ The key to choosing the right technology is to understand how you currently use technology, what you wish to change within HR and people management and to be clear on what you want from technology. This provides a clear scope and criteria against which to select a package or different packages.
■ Web 2.0 creates opportunities to add business value by improving employee engagement and collaborative knowledge sharing. A multiplicity of options is available and HR practitioners need to be aware of their uses and not left behind in the groundswell of interest which is driving these new social media technologies.

Chapter 5 Envisioning the New World of HR

- Whilst there are many common factors influencing the direction of HR, there is no 'one size fits all' solution to HR transformation; that is, each organisation will need to develop its own unique vision for HR transformation.
- HR transformation needs to be aligned with the goals and needs of your business and the vision for HR needs to be one that encapsulates technological, process, structural, cultural and capability.
- A shared vision for HR needs to be developed quickly amongst critical stakeholders.
- A range of envisioning tools can be employed effectively to stimulate discussion and conversation, and ensure the speedy development of a shared vision.
- Envisioning is the springboard to build an effective and robust business case for HR transformation.

Chapter 6 The Business Rationale

- A business case serves three purposes. It makes the case in terms of the return on investment (ROI) for the transformation; it is a tool by which HR can engage with business colleagues in shaping the future services and value that HR delivers and it is the key control document by which the transformation and change programme guides action throughout the life of the programme.
- The proposed model for delivering HR services in the future is an important input into the business case because it will identify what will need to change in terms of organisation and technology. The service delivery model will be used in the business case to identify the costs and benefits of the transformation. The most significant areas of cost will be people and technology.
- The business case needs to address the hard ROI elements of the proposed transformation. Spending time and effort on both the costs and benefits of this will pay dividends both in terms of the credibility that this gives to your case and the baseline that this gives you for measuring possible benefit delivery.
- The business case is fundamental in making the case for change and as such is not only about numbers but also about understanding and articulating what the nature of the change is and why it is important to the organisation. This needs to be made real for your business colleagues. Developing a roadmap of what will change, and when, provides a very tangible way of describing this change in practical terms.

Chapter 7 Stakeholder Communication and Engagement

- Perspectives on human change can help to map out the stakeholder topography.
- The stakeholder mapping process can inform the change sponsors and agents about the most effective ways to manage resistance and reduce negative impact on the programme.
- A variety of methods, including Web 2.0, can be used to secure receptive and positive stakeholder outcomes.

Chapter 8 Service Delivery Approaches

- The elements of Web-based HR, shared services and outsourcing can all play a part. Good overall design and addressing the question 'who does what?' are essential.
- The emergence of boundary issues associated with different structural approaches creates tensions which, if not unchecked, can impair the HR transformation effort.
- There are a range of key considerations involved in finding the best outsourcing arrangements and these need to be properly considered before you commit to a deal.
- Web-based HR impacts the HR/line manager relationships. Understanding these impacts can enhance the design of the solution.

Chapter 9 Programme Management

- Good governance is a prerequisite of successful HR transformation programmes.
- All programmes give rise to conflicts with attendant risks and issues. Knowing how to manage through these is vital.
- Understand the relationship between people, process and technology work streams and maintain a connected view of these aspects throughout.
- Don't be afraid to admit to problems and maintain close attention to programme health.

Chapter 10 Implementation: Capability and Culture

- Investment in capability development is essential if we are to change significantly HR's contribution in organisations.

- The impact of HR transformation on HR, line managers and others involved in HR service delivery needs to be assessed to identify and agree on role expectations.
- HR professionals will need to develop stronger capabilities in strategy and organisational development, client relationship/consulting and project management.
- Capability development needs to be sustained and cannot be seen as a once-off exercise.
- We need to be intentional about the way we shape the culture of HR, becoming more customer focused and with a stronger emphasis on internal consultancy and marketing.

Chapter 11 Implementation: Process and Technology

- The implementation of HR process and technology needs to be true to your original vision for HR transformation. The alignment of implementation with your vision and plans needs to be explicitly addressed so that you do not inadvertently diverge and risk the success of your programme.
- The detailed design and implementation of the processes and technology are important elements of HR transformation. However, it is the adoption of those processes and the supporting technology by HR, employees and line managers that defines whether the change has taken root in the organisation. Therefore continued involvement of all those impacted by HR transformation in the implementation is critical.

Chapter 12 Benefits Realisation

- The successful realisation of benefits depends upon the capability to define measures for the benefits, set challenging targets for these measures and ensure that a system is in place to monitor and track delivery against targets.
- The majority of the benefits of an HR transformation programme will be delivered after the transformation is complete. It is, therefore, important to not only measure the delivery of benefits during the implementation phase of the programme but also to track benefits after the programme is complete.
- Expectations also need to be managed in terms of the level and timing of benefit delivery. This is done through a benefits plan that explicitly defines when and where benefits will be delivered and who is accountable for their delivery.

Chapter 13 The Business of HR

- Unprecedented economic situations will require an even stronger contribution from HR.
- HR professionals need to focus on what their organisations need and not on what HR departments have traditionally done.
- Six themes are likely to dominate the business of HR in the coming years.
- HR still needs to continue to transform itself.

Appendix 1: Organisational Levers Output

In this appendix, we show an example of how a client has used the organisational levers model to develop a set of 'as is' and 'to be' statements. We show just two of the levers, 'Technology' and 'People and culture', to illustrate its use.

As you will see, the descriptors are succinct but specific enough to enable the next steps in the process to take place: gap analysis and project planning.

The example shown was actually produced 1 year after the initial envisioning exercise. By this stage, the HR transformation process was well under way, and this review point enabled the HR leadership group to take stock of where they were and to energise for the next 12 months.

'As is'/'To be' descriptors for technology

As is	To be
■ SAP chosen as the global HR back office system; blueprint for development still being defined/outsourcing options still being considered	■ Global HR back office system fully implemented, whether in-house or outsourced
■ Areas for workflow have been identified, for example, recruitment and learning, but not yet implemented	■ e-Tools implemented for all areas in e-HR business case
■ e-HR implementation route map defined, limited functionality available and speed of implementation now critical for HR to realise greater efficiencies	■ e-Learning is embedded throughout the organisation
	■ HR systems integrated with non-HR systems
	■ Common data standards and definitions
	■ Common HR reporting and enhanced HR decision support capability
	■ HR knowledge databases implemented
	■ HR has a high level of Web enablement

- Integration with non-HR systems planned but not yet implemented
- Good progress has been made in defining common data standards and definitions
- There is still some way to go before HR reporting is robust; ownership and accountability for business headcount is still an issue
- High levels of IT literacy in the use of HR and office systems
- Acquisitions and disposals cause no systems problems to HR or to the business
- HR has stopped doing lots of transactional work following technology and culture/capability change

'As is'/'To be' descriptors for people and culture

As is	To be
- A smaller HR function is now mainly comprised of HR business partners and specialists	- HR delivers to a high standard on the basics, mainly through e-HR and outsourcing
- HR performance levels have been agreed and capability has been assessed at a high level, although much more communication is needed	- The use of capability workshops, learning groups and knowledge management online will be the primary ways used to share knowledge, build capability and shape culture
- A programme to build HR capability has been agreed but not yet implemented	- The programme to build HR capabilities will have been delivered successfully
- The function still has a way to go in changing the way it works with the line	- Business partners and specialists will be influencing at a strategic level
- The vision for manager and employee self-service has still to be fully communicated to the business	- A high proportion of work will be delivered as a project with clear deliverables and scope
- The HR conference touched on HR transformation, but there is still work to be done to engage the HR community with the HR transformation challenge and to develop the skills needed to deliver the task	- Business partners are aligned with key business stakeholders
	- HR professionals are valued by line managers as much for their business skills as their technical capability in HR matters
	- Knowledge and capability are valued within the HR team more than seniority and length of service
	- HR is considered by the line to be a valued consulting resource

Glossary of terms

Aggregation Collecting information from various sources and displaying it together in customisable formats, such as on a Web site (e.g. pulling news data in from a source and displaying it on your own Web site), or a desktop or a browser-based aggregator that can manage several 'social networking' or 'social book-marking' sites, blogs, RSS fees, various types of media and other content from one location and allow these various types of data to be easily accessed, used or shared.

Avatar Three-dimensional characters created to represent themselves and/or reflect an identity they want to portray, in video-games and virtual worlds, such as Second Life.

Blog A blog (a *Web log*) is a Web site, usually maintained by an individual, with regular entries that are commonly displayed in reverse chronological order. Many blogs provide commentary or news related to a particular subject; others function as more personal online diaries. A typical blog provides text, images, and links to other blogs, Web pages, and media related to its topic, as well as the facility for readers to leave comments. http://en.wikipedia.org/wiki/Blog

Browser A browser is an application that allows users to display Web pages and files on the Web through an Internet connection. There are a number of widely used browsers, such as Internet Explorer, Firefox, Opera, Safari, Chrome.

del.icio.us A *social bookmarking* Web site that is designed to allow users to store and share bookmarks on the Web instead of inside their browser. Bookmarks are organised by 'tags', which are searchable keywords assigned by users. http://del.icio.us/about/. *See also 'tagging', 'social bookmarking'*

Digital native A person raised in a technological environment, who accepts that environment as the norm. This person has often grown up surrounded by digital devices, such as MP3 players and cell phones, and regularly uses them to interact with his people and the outside world. http://www.digitalnative.org/wiki/Glossary#Digital_Native

Discussion forum An application that allows users to post original messages and replies on a Web site. Forums are often divided into topics and conversational 'threads' which allow users to follow conversations on certain topics.

Disruptive technologies Disruptive technology is a term coined by Harvard Business School professor Clayton M. Christensen to describe a new technology that unexpectedly displaces an established technology. This is contrasted with 'sustaining technology' which relies on incremental improvements to an already established technology. http://whatis.techtarget.com/definition/0,,sid9_gci945822,00.html

Enterprise 2.0 Enterprise social software, also known as Enterprise 2.0, is a term describing social software used in 'enterprise' (business) contexts. It includes social and networked modifications to company intranets and other classic software platforms used by large companies to organise their communication. http://en.wikipedia.org/wiki/Enterprise_social_software

Facebook   Facebook is a free-access social networking Web site. Users can post messages for their friends to see, and update their personal profile to notify friends about themselves. http://en.wikipedia.org/wiki/Facebook and http://www.facebook.com. *See also 'social networking'*

Firewall   A system designed to prevent unauthorised access to or from a private network, using either hardware or software, or a combination of both. Firewalls are frequently used to prevent unauthorised Internet users from accessing private networks connected to the Internet, especially intranets. All messages entering or leaving the intranet pass through the firewall, which examines each message and blocks those that do not meet the specified security criteria. http://www.webopedia.com/TERM/f/firewall.html

Flickr   Flickr is an online photo management and sharing Web site. Users can add comments, notes and 'tags' to photos to create their own ways of viewing, searching for and sharing them. http://www.flikr.com/. *See also 'tagging'*

Hit   The retrieval of any item, like a page or a graphic, from a Web server, also called a page hit. Alternatively, any time a piece of data matches criteria you set, e.g. each of the matches from a Yahoo or any other search engine search is called a hit, http://www.webopedia.com/TERM/H/hit.html

Information aggregation   Information aggregation is a service that collects relevant information from multiple sources for easy access and to help users to effectively access the growing amount of information on the Web. http://digital.mit.edu/research/papers/106%20SMadnick,%20Siegel%20Information%20Aggregation.pdf. *See also 'mashups'*

Instant messaging   Instant messaging (IM) and chat are technologies that facilitate near real-time text-based communication between two or more participants over a network. Some IM systems allow users to use webcams and microphones so that users can have a real-time conversation. http://en.wikipedia.org/wiki/Instant_messaging

Internet architecture   The Internet is a meta-network, a constantly changing collection of thousands of individual networks intercommunicating with a common protocol, TCP/IP, which is designed to connect any two networks despite any differences in internal hardware, software, and technical design. http://www.livinginternet.com/i/iw_arch.htm

Mashups   Mashups are Web applications that combine data from more than one source into a single integrated tool, thereby creating a new and distinct Web service that was not originally provided by either source. These Web applications are always composed of three parts:

- the content provider or source of the data.
- the Mashup site itself – the Web application which provides the new service using different data sources that are not owned by it.
- the client Web browser which is the user interface of the Mashup.

http://en.wikipedia.org/wiki/Mashup_(web_application_hybrid)

Massively multiplayer online game (MMOG or MMO) MMOGs are video games which are capable of supporting hundreds or thousands of players simultaneously. By necessity, they are played on the Internet, and feature at least one persistent virtual world. http://en.wikipedia.org/wiki/Massively_multiplayer_online_game

Media sharing Media sharing occurs in online social networks and digital communities where users can aggregate, upload, compress, host and distribute images, text, applications, videos, audio, games and new media. It is the process of sending, posting or linking to media on a Web site or blog. As media is shared it takes on a variety of different contexts and meanings as it is uploaded to different online 'places', tagged and/or commented upon and shared and possibly changed in various ways. http://en.wikipedia.org/wiki/Media_sharing

Metadata Metadata is 'data about data'. http://en.wikipedia.org/wiki/Metadata Metadata is structured data which describes the characteristics of a resource. It shares many similar characteristics to the cataloguing that takes place in libraries, museums and archives. A metadata record consists of a number of pre-defined elements representing specific attributes of a resource, and each element can have one or more values. http://www.library.uq.edu.au/iad/ctmeta4.html

My Space MySpace is an online social networking community that lets you meet your friends' friends and in which you can share photos, journals and interests with your growing network of mutual friends' www.myspace.com. *See also 'social networking'*

Net or V(irtual) generation The Net or Virtual generation is made up of people from multiple demographic age groups who make social connections online – through virtual worlds, in video games, as bloggers, in social networks or through posting and reading user-generated content at e-commerce sites like Amazon.com. http://www.pcworld.com/article/id,139748-c,researchreports/article.html

Don Tapscott describes the Net Generation as having the following characteristics:

- they are able to multitask
- they have little tolerance for delays, expecting Web pages to load quickly, responses to e-mail immediately, etc.
- they prefer to be interactive – they want to be users, not just viewers or listeners

http://academictech.doit.wisc.edu/resources/products/netgen/index.htm

Network effects The core description of a network effect is when a good or service has more value the more that other people have it too. Examples include e-mail, Instant Messaging, the blogosphere, and even the Web itself. Various authors have tried to describe the raw potential of network effects in computer networks, including Robert Metcalf, David Reed and Odlyzko and Tilly. Whichever formulation you believe is right, the result is clear: At even an early point, the cumulative value of a large number of connected users goes exponentially off the charts. http://web2.socialcomputingmagazine.com/web_20s_real_secret_sauce_network_effects.htm

Open source   Open source is a development methodology for software that harnesses the power of distributed peer review and transparency of process. Programming code for open source software is freely available and this code can be redistributed and modified and must adhere to open source principles regarding licensing. http://www.opensource.org/

Podcasting   Podcasting is delivering audio content to iPods and other portable media players on demand, so that it can be listened to at the user's convenience. The main benefit of podcasting is that listeners can sync content to their media player and take it with them to listen whenever they want to. http://www.podcastingnews.com/articles/What_is_Podcasting.html

Remixing   Remixing describes the customisation of Web pages created by others and/or data provided by others for re-use on another Web page. Extracting and combining samples of content to create a new output. The term was originally used in music but is now also applied to video and other content.   http://www.rossdawsonblog.com/weblog/archives/2007/05/launching_the_w.html. *See also 'information aggregation' and 'mashup'*

Reputation management software   Reputation management software gathers ratings for people, companies, and information sources. Reputation management software can create a track record for each user that acts as an incentive for them to exhibit good behaviour and make them accountable for their actions. This is important because it adds elements of expectation and possible repercussions that can effect future interactions. http://www.moyak.com/researcher/resume/papers/reputation.html

RSS feeds   Really Simple Syndication (RSS) is a lightweight XML format designed for sharing headlines and other Web content. It provides a wimple way to quickly view rapidly changing content such as news headlines, blog entries or podcasts. http://www.webreference.com/authoring/languages/xml/rss/intro/. *See also 'Web feed'*

Second life   Second Life is an Internet-based 3D virtual world created by its residents. In the online world, residents can explore, socialise and communicate as well as create and trade items in a virtual martketingplace using a virtual unit of currency, the Linden Dollar. http://secondlife.com/. *See virtual worlds*

SlideShare   SlideShare is an online community for sharing presentations. Users upload presentations to share their ideas, connect with others, and generate leads for their businesses. Presentations can be tagged, downloaded, or embeded in other Web sites or blogs. Slides can also be shared privately to facilitate collaboration.

Social bookmarking   Social bookmarking is a method for Internet users to store, organise, search, and manage bookmarks of Web pages on the Internet with the help of metadata. Most social bookmark services encourage users to organise their bookmarks with informal tags instead of the traditional browser-based system of folders. http://en.wikipedia.org/wiki/Social_bookmarking

Social networking   Social networking is a phenomena defined by linking people to each other in some way, in this case using the Internet to form communities and build networks. These communities or networks may be based around anything, geographical location, shared schools or employers, shared interests or hobbies, etc. or may be designed to allow 'new' networks for develop for making new online 'friends' or creating new professional connections. http://www.topicguru.net/?c1=webmaster&c2=glossary

Social software   Social software is used to build online social networks. Most services are primarily Web-based and provide a collection of various ways for users to interact, such as chat, messaging, email, video, voice chat, file sharing, blogging, discussion groups, and so on. http://en.wikipedia.org/wiki/Social_network_service

Streaming media or video streaming   Streaming media is streaming video with sound. With streaming video or streaming media, a Web user does not have to wait to download a large file before seeing the video or hearing the sound. Instead, the media is sent in a continuous stream and is played as it arrives. http://searchunifiedcommunications.techtarget.com/sDefinition/0,,sid186_gci213055,00.html

Tagging   A tag is a (relevant) keyword or term associated with or assigned to a piece of information (e.g. a picture, a blog entry, a bookmark etc.), describing the item and enabling keyword-based classification and search of information. Tags are usually chosen by item author/creator or by its consumer/viewers/community. http://en.wikipedia.org/wiki/Tag_(metadata)

Viral marketing   Viral marketing describes any strategy that encourages individuals to pass on a marketing message to others, creating the potential for exponential growth in the message's exposure and influence. Like viruses, such strategies take advantage of rapid multiplication to explode the message to thousands, to millions. Off the Internet, viral marketing has been referred to as 'word-of-mouth' or 'creating a buzz' but on the Internet it is called 'viral marketing'. Viral marketing is often characterised by giving away some sort of product or service, allowing for effortless transfer to others, exploiting common motivations and behaviours, utilising existing communication networks and others' resources. http://www.wilsonweb.com/wmt5/viral-principles.htm

Virtual learning environment A virtual learning environment (VLE) is a software system designed to support teaching and learning in an educational setting. A VLE will normally work over the Internet and provide a connection of tools such as those for assessment, communication, uploading of content, return of students' work, peer assessment, administration of student groups, collecting and organising student grades, questionnaires, tracking tools, wikis, blogs, RSS and 3D virtual learning spaces, etc. While originally created for distance education, VLEs are now often used to supplement the face-to-face classroom as well to add more flexibility to learning. http://en.wikipedia.org/wiki/Virtual_learning_environment

Virtual worlds A virtual world is a computer-based simulated environment intended for its users to inhabit and interact via avatars which are usually depicted as textual, two-dimensional, or three-dimensional graphical representations. The computer accesses a computer-simulated world and presents perceptual stimuli to the user, who in turn can manipulate elements of the modelled world. Communication between users has ranged from text, graphical icons, visual gesture, sound, and rarely, forms using touch and balance senses. http://en.wikipedia.org/wiki/Virtual_world. *See second life*

Web services Web services are pieces of a software program or Web site that are exposed for third party systems to interact with, often providing a question/answer dialogue. For example, Web services allow any Web site to ask an airline if a flight is delayed and receive an answer back that can be displayed in any format. http://www.tocquigny.com/knowledge/the_semantic_web/

Web feed A Web feed (or news feed) is a data format used for providing users with frequently updated content. Content distributors *syndicate* a Web feed, thereby allowing users to *subscribe* to it. http://en.wikipedia.org/wiki/Web_feed

Widgets A generic term for the part of a GUI (graphical user interface) that allows the user to interface with the application and operating system. Widgets display information and invite the user to act in a number of ways. Typical widgets include buttons, dialog boxes, pop-up windows, pull-down menus, icons, scroll bars, forms, etc. http://www.webopedia.com/TERM/w/widget.htm

Wiki A Wiki is a piece of server software that allows users to freely create and edit Web page content using any Web browser. Wiki supports hyperlinks and has simple text syntax for creating new pages and crosslinks between internal pages on the fly. Wiki is unusual among group communication mechanisms in that it allows the organisation of contributions to be edited in addition to the content itself. http://www.wiki.org/wiki.cgi?WhatIsWiki

Wikipedia Wikipedia is a free, multilingual, open content encyclopaedia project operated by the non-profit Wikimedia Foundation. Its name is a blend of the words *wiki* (a technology for creating collaborative Web sites) and *encyclopaedia*. Launched in 2001 by Jimmy Wales and Larry Sanger, it is the largest, fastest-growing and most popular general reference work currently available on the Internet. http://en.wikipedia.org/wiki/Wikipedia

XML   Extensible Markup Language (XML) is a markup language like HTML. It was designed to transport and store data, with a focus on what data is. HTML was designed to display data, with a focus on how data looks. http://www.w3schools.com/XML/xml_whatis.asp

YouTube   YouTube is the online video sharing Web site. YouTube allows people to easily upload and share video clips on http://www.YouTube.com and across the Internet through Web sites, mobile devices, blogs, and email. Videos in YouTube can be commented upon, shared, tagged and turned into playlists. http://youtube.com/

Appendix 2: Illustrative Survey Statements

Statement	Dimension
For each of the statements below, please select the one option that most closely reflects your own view and agreement or disagreement with each statement.	
e-HR provides me with the personal information I need as an employee	D1
e-HR provides me with the personnel management information I need as a manager	D1
e-HR is easy to navigate	D1
I can easily find the personnel management information I need through e-HR	
For each of the statements listed below, please choose the one option that most accurately reflects your own view of their usefulness to you.	
e-HR offers significant benefits to me, as an employee	D1
e-HR offers significant benefits to me, as a manager	D1
e-HR saves me time, when seeking personnel data I need in my manager role	D1
For each of the statements below, please select the one option that most closely reflects your own view and agreement or disagreement with each statement.	
Communications I receive regarding e-HR are useful to me	D3
Online help provided through e-HR is useful to me	D3
I received sufficient initial training on e-HR to give me a head start in using the tools	D3
The training I have received on e-HR makes me comfortable in using the tools	D3

Additional training would be helpful in enabling me to get the most out of e-HR	D3
The tools are so easy to use that I do not need training	D3
For each data category listed below, please choose the one option that most accurately reflects your own views of data quality.	
Personal employee data (e.g., dates of birth and joining, family data and home address information)	D2
HR policy information	D2
Individual performance data	D2
For each of the statements below, please select the one option that most closely reflects your own view and agreement or disagreement with each statement.	
HR should monitor and audit personal data to assure that it is being properly maintained by employees	D2
Individual employees should be held accountable for maintaining their own personal data	D2

Categories: Dimensions: D1 = e-HR Tools, Perceived Usefulness and Ease of Use; D2 = Data Quality and Maintenance; D3 = Change Communications, HR Support and Training for e-HR.

Appendix 3: Scope of HR

This appendix shows a scope of HR services template that we have found useful. It should be remembered that this template should be used in conjunction with the delivery channels, as many services will be delivered through multiple channels. HR will also be engaged in core management processes such as business/people strategy development and planning, budgeting and policy development.

Service area	Scope
■ People and organisational development	■ Organisational values and culture ■ Organisational and role design ■ Change management ■ Organisational learning ■ Leadership development ■ Team development ■ Individual development (including coaching) ■ Technical/product training ■ Skills training (including e-learning) ■ Talent management ■ Succession planning ■ Employee opinion surveys ■ Performance management ■ Board governance ■ Corporate social responsibility
■ Resource management	■ Workforce planning (including people cost base) ■ Sourcing approaches ■ Interviewing/assessment

	■ Induction/on-boarding
	■ Staff development
	■ Employee release
	■ Non-core and temporary employee management
	■ International placements
■ Employee relations and communication	■ Employer brand/employee value proposition
	■ Internal communication
	■ Internal publications
	■ Counselling/welfare
	■ Employment law
	■ Grievance/disciplinary
	■ Employee consultation and negotiation (including national/local TU relations)
	■ Inclusion and diversity
	■ Health and safety
	■ Employment policies
■ Retention and reward	■ Reward strategy
	■ Retention strategies
	■ Role/job evaluation
	■ Performance-related pay
	■ Commission schemes
	■ Incentive plans
	■ Share schemes
	■ Pensions
■ HR information	■ HR information strategy
	■ Maintain employee data
	■ Maintain organisational data
	■ Reporting and information
	■ Payroll
	■ Pensions
	■ Help desk
	■ Case work
	■ HRIS administration
	■ Definition of transactional processes
	■ Contract management
	■ HR Intranet
	■ Benefits and other payment administration

Appendix 4: Extract from an Accountabilities Workshop

This appendix shows an example output from an accountabilities workshop, in particular, the use of the scope of services document and delivery channels to record the changes in the role of line manager.

We also show the impact on the employee, another outcome of an accountabilities workshop.

The role of the line manager in people management

Activity	Expectations
Strategy and organisation ■ Business planning and budgeting ■ HR strategy, planning and budgeting ■ HR structure and work processes ■ External benchmarking	*Stronger* ■ Engages with the HR business partner early to ensure that the people issues are captured into the thinking ■ Works with the HR business partner to influence budget decisions, particularly in presenting the case for investments in building human capital ■ Signs off and executes the people (HR) strategy ■ Defines acceptable HR performance standards and ensures they are met ■ Involves the HR business partner in mergers and acquisitions due diligence *Neutral* ■ Responsible for driving the business strategy and operational plans in their area ■ Responsible for setting the budgets in their area, and for working within the constraints placed upon them

- Reviews regularly the effectiveness of the strategy and employees' understanding
- Communicates the strategy to direct reports and to peers
- Works with other people's strategies

e-HR impacted
- Availability of management information to development of strategy and plans

People development and performance management
- Organisational values and culture
- Organisational and role design
- Business change management
- Organisational learning
- Team development
- Individual development
- Technical/product training
- Talent management and succession planning
- Reward and retention strategy
- Skills training

Stronger

- Plays a leading role in making effective change happen in their area and is expected to use appropriate change management, tools and techniques
- Works in ways to shape the target culture and sets an example
- Responsible for writing role definitions
- Coaches individuals to help them raise their performance
- Selects and builds high performing teams
- Identifies and nurtures talent in their area, and acts as an advocate for the team
- Employs appropriate retention strategies
- Evaluates the effectiveness of learning and formalises feedback with HR

Neutral
- Responsible for the design of their department/area
- Helps employees to shape their personal development plans
- Supports employees to keep their knowledge and skills up-to-date
- Ensures that direct reports are developed to perform effectively in their current role and for the future
- Supports people through change

■ Sets and reviews performance against objectives
■ Acts as a mentor, for example, graduates and new joiners

e-HR impacted

■ E-authorises development/learning opportunities
■ Participates in the design and implementation of e-learning solutions
■ Performance management

Resource management	*Stronger*
■ Workforce planning ■ Recruitment and selection ■ Induction ■ Staff development ■ Assessment of potential ■ Employee release ■ Temporary employee management ■ Global assignees	■ Prepares the job/person specification and role requirements ■ Operates the recruitment process – which means picking up most (workflow generated) recruitment administration ■ Involved in pre-selection, interviewing and other assessment activities ■ Involved in attracting candidates via chat rooms, fairs, networking, etc. ■ For direct reports, holds first induction meeting and determines local induction requirements ■ Works with approved external suppliers ■ Handles most candidate queries *Neutral* ■ Initiates the recruitment need ■ Takes the recruitment decision ■ Defines the contract offer ■ Recruits internal staff in ways consistent with policy ■ Provides feedback on external suppliers *e-HR impacted* ■ Uses e-HR to capture learning around recruitment ■ E-recruitment process ■ Internal vacancy to employee profile matching ■ Automated employment contracts

Employee relations and communication

- Employer brand
- Internal publications
- Counselling/welfare
- Compliance
- Grievance/disciplinary
- Consultation and negotiation
- Diversity/equal opportunities
- Communication of reward levels
- Role evaluation

Stronger

- Works in ways to promote a positive employee relations climate
- When required, handles grievance, disciplinary and poor performance issues in a timely and compliant manner
- Ensures compliance with policy and procedures
- Consults team on proposed changes to working practices (especially important in EU countries in the light of Works Council Directive)
- Understands and uses market data on rewards to inform decisions
- Culturally sensitive, and promotes this sensitivity in the team
- Able to work in different employment/legal environments
- Involved in company consultative bodies (wherever appropriate)
- Responsible for communicating with their teams
- Manages in a fair way, without reference to race, gender, disability, etc.

Neutral

- Provides first instance counselling and welfare support
- Responsible for health and safety in their area
- Sets expectations on reward levels and recommends individual compensation awards
- Recommends people for promotion

e-HR impacted

- Pay review process

HR information	*Stronger*
■ Maintain employee data ■ Maintain organisational data ■ Employee reporting and ■ Payroll ■ Pensions ■ Benefits and payment admin	■ Maintains organisational data (e-HR related) ■ Gives feedback on the information effectiveness of e-HR/participates in systems improvements *e-HR impacted* ■ Maintains organisational data – information on their staff ■ Authorises a whole range of amendments via e-HR, where financial changes are involved; contractual changes; absence; awards; health tests; learning; company equipment; carry-over of leave ■ Self-service reports

The workshop considered the likely tension between line pull (e.g., wanting more flexible compensation arrangements) and HR push (e.g., making time to run assessment centres will lead to more effective recruitment decisions). People thought that this tension was inevitable and desirable. They did not believe that this tension detracted from the aim of making the line more accountable for people management and HR more accountable for providing a unique contribution to improve performance.

Line manager: Priority knowledge and skills

If the line manager is to meet the HR management requirements of their role as defined in the section above, the largest capability gaps that need to be closed are the following.

Teams

■ Selecting excellent people, who will not only perform well individually but also as part of a team (real or virtual);
■ Building high-performing teams, which includes the skills and activities that underpin this, such as coaching.

There was an issue raised under the label of delegation that relates to 'team'. The underlying issue was that too much manager time is spent on technical problem solving and not on managing. The need is to redress this imbalance, for managers to develop capability in their team to deliver on the technical side while they focus on the task of management. Part of the reason for this imbalance is that people are promoted to the position of manager usually because of their excellent technical skills.

Operating as a global manager

- Working across geographies;
- Working across different national cultures;
- Understanding different legal employment frameworks;
- Working in virtual teams.

Change management and change readiness

- Using appropriate tools and techniques to prepare for change;
- Using appropriate tools and techniques to bring about effective change in their area.

Communication

- Specific communication skills such as using video conferencing, speaking in other national cultures, and public speaking;
- Broader communication skills such as identifying stakeholders, and communicating in a matrix organisation.

Other skills identified that were not considered quite so high a priority were:

- IT literacy;
- Managing conflict;
- Diversity;
- Decision making;
- How the line can use different elements of the reward tool kit;
- Leadership, the ability to motivate the organisation;
- Commercial awareness, where they fit into the overall strategy.

The role of employees in delivering HR management

Activity	Expectations
Strategy and organisation	*Neutral* ■ Should be engaged in the business planning process for their area ■ Provides feedback to inform business and HR planning through surveys, such as employee opinion surveys ■ Should be able to articulate the basic principles of the strategy
People development and performance	*Stronger* ■ Provides feedback on manager (and management peer) performance ■ Shares knowledge with colleagues ■ Recommends improvements in work ■ Demonstrates the values and culture *Neutral* ■ Works with their line manager to shape their personal development plan ■ Works with their line manager to keep their skills and knowledge up-to-date ■ Attends booked training/learning ■ Implements agreed change *e-HR impacted* ■ Self-service e-learning opportunities ■ Places learning bookings online ■ Registers/enrols in learning events ■ Provides feedback on training received ■ Maintains training records
Resource management	*Stronger* ■ Refers vacancies to friends *Neutral* ■ Provides personal information for records and payroll in time specified

	e-HR impacted ■ Candidate application online ■ Candidate accept/decline online ■ Makes use of available e-induction ■ Uses e-recruitment for internal applications ■ Candidate chat rooms ■ Provides personal information for records and payroll in time specified
Employee relations and communication	*Stronger* ■ Represents company and promotes the employment brand ■ Demonstrates cultural awareness and sensitivity *Neutral* ■ Understands and follows grievance procedure ■ Participation in communication/consultation activities ■ Provides feedback on employee satisfaction surveys ■ Maintains high safety standards *e-HR impacted* ■ Intranet-delivered communication ■ e-delivered employee surveys ■ HR policies delivered through e-HR
HR information	*Stronger* ■ Self-service update of personal details as defined by the system (e-HR impacted) *Neutral* ■ Initiates changes in personal details, whether manually or electronically ■ Initiates recording of absence, vacation, sickness, etc. *e-HR impacted* ■ Self-service update of personal details as defined by the system ■ Makes changes to benefits

Appendix 5: Return on Investment and Internal Rate of Return (IRR)

Internal rate of return

The internal rate of return refers to the return which can be earned on the capital invested in the project. If the IRR is greater than capital costs then an investment in the business case should be made; however, if the IRR is less than the capital costs then the investment should not be made as it will not cover capital costs.

Return on investment

Return on investment is a profitability ratio, which measures the overall return on an investment expressed as a percentage of the amount invested. It is calculated by taking the overall financial benefit of the transformation (after all costs have been deducted) and dividing this by the total sum of money that is required for the transformation. The result is divided by 100 to obtain a percentage figure.

References

Anderson, C. (2008). *The longer, long tail* (2nd ed.). New York: Hyperion Publishing.

Becker, B. E., & Huselid, M. A. (1998). High performance work systems and firm performance: A synthesis of research and managerial implications. *Research in Personnel and Human Resources Management, 16,* 53–101.

Beckhard, R., & Harris, R. T. (1987). *Organizational transitions.* New York: Addison-Wesley.

Bell, B. S., Lee, S., & Yeung, S. K. (2006). The impact of e-HR on professional competence in HRM: Implications for the development of HR professionals. *Human Resource Management, 45*(3), 295–308.

Birkinshaw, J., & Pass, S. (2008, September). *Innovations in the workplace: How are organisations responding to generation Y employees and Web 2.0 technologies?* London: CIPD.

Castells, M. (1996). *The rise of the network society. The information age: Economy, society and culture* (Vol. 1). Oxford: Blackwell.

Chartered Institute of Personnel and Development. (2008, March). *Smart working: The impact of work organisation and job design.* Research Insight Report.

CIPD. (2002). *Sustaining success in difficult times.* London.

Coyle, D., & Quah, D. (2004). *Getting the measure of the new economy.* London: The Work Foundation. Available online at: http://www.theworkfoundation.com/research/isociety/new_economy.jsp

Economist Intelligence Unit/Deloitte. (2007). Aligned at the top.

Field, A. (2008). Building a road map for e-HR at the London Stock Exchange. In Martin, G., Reddington, M., & Alexander, H. (Eds.), *Technology, outsourcing and transforming HR.* Oxford: Elsevier.

Guetal, H. G., & Stone, D. L. (Eds.). (2005). *The brave new world of e-HR: Human resources in a digital age.* San Francisco: Jossey.

Holbeche, L., & Cheung-Judge, M.-Y. (2009, February). Organisational development—What's in a name. *CIPD Impact,* (26), 6–9.

Lawler, E. E., Boudreau, J., & Mohrman, S. A. (2006). *Achieving strategic excellence.* Stanford: Stanford University Press.

Lawler, E. E., & Mohrman, S. A. (2003). *Creating a strategic human resources organisation.* Stanford: Stanford University Press.

Lawson, E., Mueller-Oerlinghausen, J., & Shearn, J. A. (2005). *A dearth of HR talent.* McKinsey Research.

Lepak, D., Smith, K. G., & Taylor, M. S. (2007). Value creation and value capture: A multi-level perspective. *Academy of Management Review, 32*(No. 1), 180–194.

Lev, B. (2001). *Intangibles.* Washington, DC: The Brookings Institution.

Li, C., & Bernoff, J. (2008). *Groundswell: Winning in a world transformed by social technologies.* Boston, MA: Harvard Business Press.

Madden, M., & Jones, S. (2008). *Networked workers. Pew Internet and American Life Project.* Available online at: http://pewinternet.org/pdfs/PIP_Networked_Workers_FINAL.pdf (accessed December 4, 2008).

Malone, T. W. (2004). *The future of work: How the new order of business will shape your organization, your management style and your life.* Boston, MA: Harvard Business School Press.

Martin, G. (2005). *Technology and people management: The opportunities and challenges.* London: Chartered Institute of Personnel and Development.

Martin, G., & Hetrick, S. (2006). *Corporate reputations and people management.* Oxford: Butterworth Heinemann.

Martin, G., Reddington, M., & Alexander, H. (Eds.). (2008). *Technology, outsourcing and transforming HR.* Oxford: Butterworth Heinemann.

Martin, G., Reddington, M., & Alexander, H. (2008). *Technology, outsourcing and transforming HR.* Elsevier.

Martin, G., Reddington, M., & Kneafsey, M. (2009). *Web 2.0 and human resource management: 'Groundswell' or hype?* London: CIPD.

McQueen, B. (2006). *Scottish executive e-HR and HR transformation: Enquiry report to Paul Pagliari.* This report can be viewed at: http://www.scotland.gov.uk/Resource/Doc/923/0041338.doc

Nathan, M., Carpenter, G., Roberts, S., Ferguson, L., & Know, H. (2003, November). *Getting by, not getting on technology in UK workplaces.* London: The Work Foundation.

Parry, E., Tyson, S., Selbie, D., & Leighton, R. K. (2007). *HR and technology: Impact and advantages.* CIPD: London.

Pfeffer, J., & Sutton, R. I. (2006). *Hard facts, dangerous half-truths and total nonsense: Profiting from evidence-based management.* Boston: Harvard Business School Press.

Porter, M. (1985). *Competitive advantage: Creating and sustaining superior performance.* New York: Free Press.

Presnky, M. (2001). Digital natives, digital immigrants. *On the Horizon, 9*(5), 1–6.

Reilly, P., Tamkin, P., & Broughton, A. (2007). *The changing face of the HR function: Transforming HR?* London: CIPD.

Richards, J. (2007). *Unmediated workplace images from the internet: An investigation of work blogging.* Paper presented to the 29th Annual Labour Process Conference, University of Amsterdam, April 2–4.

Sarner. (2008, September). *The business impact of social computing and 'generation virtual'.* Special Report, Gartner Consulting, ID Number: G00161081.

Schuen, A. (2008). *Web 2.0: A strategy guide.* Sebastopol, CA: O'Reilly Publishing.

Shrivastava, S., & Shaw, J. B. (2004). Liberating HR through technology. *Human Resource Management, 42,* 201–222.

Slevin, J. M. (2000). *The Internet and society.* Cambridge, UK: Polity Press.

Sparrow, P. R., Brewster, C., & Harris, H. (2004). *Globalizing human resource management.* London: Routledge.

Tapscott, D., & Williams, A. (2008). *Wikinomics: How mass collaboration changes everything* (2nd ed.). London: Atlantic Books.

Taylor, R. (2004). *Skills and innovation in modern Britain.* ESRC Future of Work Programme Seminar Series. Available at: http://www.leeds.ac.uk/esrcfutureofwork/downloads/fow_publication_6.pdf

Ulrich, D. (1997). *Human resource champions.* Boston: Harvard Business School.

Ulrich, D. (1998). A new mandate for human resources. *Harvard Business Review, 76*(1), 124–134.

Ulrich, D., & Brockbank, W. (2005). *The HR value proposition*. Boston, MA: Harvard Business School Press.

Whittaker, S., & Marchington, M. (2003). Devolving HR responsibility to the line: Threat, opportunity or partnership? *Employee Relations*, *25*(3), 245–261.

Willman, P., Bryson, A., & Gomez, R. (2006). The sound of silence: Which employers choose no employee voice and why? *Socio-Economic Review*, *4*, 283–299.

Yin, R. K. (2003). *Case study research: Design and methods* (3rd ed.). Thousand Oaks, CA: Sage Publications.

Further Reading

Becker, B. E., & Huselid, M. A. (1999). *Overview: Strategic human resource management in five leading firms*. Human Resource Management.

Becker, B. E., Huselid, M. A., & Ulrich, D. (2001). *The HR scorecard: Linking people, strategy and performance*. Boston: Harvard Business School.

Bridges, W. (1993). *Managing transitions: Making the most of change*. Cambridge, MA: Perseus Books.

Coetsee, L. (1999). From resistance to commitment. *Public Administration Quarterly*, *23*.

Connor, D. L. (1998). *Managing at the speed of change*. New York: Wiley.

Hirsh, W., Carter, A., Gifford, J., & Baldwin, S. (2008, September). What customers want from HR. In *Report 453*. London: Institute of Employment Studies.

Holbeche, L. Building high performance—The key role for HR. *CIPD Impact*, (20).

Kettley, P., & Reilly, P. (2003). e-HR: An introduction. In *IES Report 398*.

O'Farrell, B., & Furnham, A. (2002, October). *2002 European e-HR survey*. London: University of London and IHRIM Europe.

Reddington, M., & Martin, G. (2006). *Theorizing the links between e-HR and strategic HRM: A framework, case illustration and some reflections*. In First European Academic Conference on e-HR, October 2006, Twente University, Netherlands.Oxford: Elsevier.

Reddington, M., Williamson, M., & Withers, M. (2003). *Delivering value from HR transformation*. Oxford: Roffey Park Institute.

Reddington, M., Williamson, M., & Withers, M. (2004a, March 23). Shared vision. *Personnel Today*, *26*.

Reddington, M., Williamson, M., & Withers, M. (2004b, March 30). Secure the stakeholder's commitment. *Personnel Today*, *24*.

Reddington, M., Williamson, M., & Withers, M. (2004c, April 06). Realising the benefits. *Personnel Today*, *22*.

Reddington, M., Williamson, M., & Withers, M. (2005). *Transforming HR: Creating value through people* (1st ed.). Elsevier.

Reilly, P. (2007, September 20). Facing up to the facts. *People Management*.

Reilly, P., & Williams, T. (2003). *How to get best value from HR—The shared services option*. Gower.

Richardson, R., & Thompson, M. (1999). *Issues in people management: The impact of people management practices on business performance*. The Chartered Institute of Personnel and Development.

Rozenweig, P. (2007). *The halo effect and the eight other business delusions that deceive managers*. New York: Free Press.

Schein, E. (1998). *Process consulting revisited*. Boston, MA: Addison-Wesley.

Thew, B. (2004, April). *Dramatic changes in store for HR in outsourced future*. Paper published by Ceridian.

Towers Perrin. (2004). *HR BPO comes of age: From expectation to reality*.

Watson Wyatt. (2002). *eHR™: Getting results along the journey—2002 survey report*.

Contributing Senior Practitioners

We have been grateful for the time, thoughtfulness and insights of all who helped us with this book, in particular, the following senior HR practitioners:

Frances Allcock	Director of OD and Change – BBC
Jerry Arnott	Director, Organisation and People Development – Department of Work and Pensions
Sonia Carter	Head of Internal Online Communications – AXA UK
Janice Cook	HR Director – NCH
Yvette Dorman	Change Enablement Workstream Lead, HR Transformation Programme – Metropolitan Police Service
Claire Elwin	HR Manager Strategic Projects – AXA UK
Andrew Field	HR Operations Manager – London Stock Exchange
Alison Grace	HR Director – National Express Group
John Hallett	HR Director – HBOS
Pam Hasson	Senior Resourcing Partner – AXA UK
Claire Hunt	Programme Director, HR Transformation Programme, Metropolitan Police Service
Maggie Hurt	Group HR Director – Renold Engineering
Karan Hutchinson	HR Director – AXA UK
Sheila Hyde	Managing Director, Spirita Limited
Ruth Lovering	Vice President Human Resources, Talent and Development Downstream – Shell
Kath Lowey	Managing Director, HR Services, Xchanging
Martin Moore	Head of HR and OD – Royal Mail Group

Stephen Moir	President, Public Sector Personnel Managers Association (PPMA) and Director of People and Policy – Cambridgeshire County Council
Ian Muir	HR Director – Cable & Wireless International
Martin Rayson	Lead Officer, HR Transformation Network (PPMA) and Director of Resources – Boston Borough Council
Peter Reilly	Director HR Research and Consulting – Institute for Employment Studies
Samantha Rich	Head of Group Resourcing Practice – AXA UK
Nicky Riding	VP HR Europe – Discovery Communications
Anne Shiels	HR Director – HBOS
Martin Tiplady	Director of Human Resources – Metropolitan Police Service
Nick Tooley	Former Head of HR TaskForce – HR Strategy and Policy Team, HMRC
Martin Warlow	Former Head of HR TaskForce – HR Strategy and Policy Team, HMRC
Nick Worrall	HR Director Global Operations – National Grid

All company and job details are those current at the time of interview.

Index